PENGUIN

AN ORGANIZER'S TALE

CESAR CHAVEZ was a civil rights and labor leader, a farmworker, a crusader for nonviolent social change, and an environmentalist and consumer advocate. He was born on March 31, 1927, near his family's farm in Yuma, Arizona. His family lost their farm in the Great Depression and became migrant farm workers when Chavez was ten. Throughout his youth and into his adulthood, he migrated across the Southwest, laboring in the fields and vineyards, where he was exposed to the hardships and injustices of farmworker life. After achieving only an eighth-grade education, Chavez left school to work in the fields full-time to support his family. He joined the U.S. Navy in 1946 and served in the western Pacific in the aftermath of World War II. Chavez's life as a community organizer began in 1952 when he joined the Community Service Organization (CSO), a prominent Latino civil rights group. While with the CSO, he coordinated voter registration drives and conducted campaigns against racial and economic discrimination primarily in urban areas. In the late 1950s and early 1960s, Chavez served as CSO's national director.

In 1962, he resigned from the CSO to found the National Farm Workers Association, which later became the United Farm Workers of America. For more than three decades Chavez led the first successful farmworkers union in American history, achieving dignity, respect, fair wages, medical coverage, pension benefits, and humane living conditions for hundreds of thousands of farmworkers. Chavez led successful strikes and boycotts that resulted in the first industry-wide labor contracts in the history of American agriculture. His union's efforts brought about the passage of the groundbreaking 1975 California Agricultural Labor Relations Act to protect farmworkers. Today it remains the only law in the nation that protects the farmworkers' right to unionize.

A strong believer in the principles of nonviolence practiced by Mahatma Gandhi and Dr. Martin Luther King Jr., Chavez effectively employed peaceful tactics such as fasts, boycotts, strikes, and pilgrimages. In 1968 he fasted for twenty-five days to affirm his personal commitment and that of the farm labor movement to nonviolence. He fasted again for twenty-five days in 1972, and in 1988, at the age of sixty-one, he endured a thirty-six-day "Fast for Life" to highlight the harmful impact of pesticides on farmworkers and their children. Chavez died on April 23, 1993, in San Luis, Arizona.

ILAN STAVANS is the Lewis-Sebring Professor in Latin American and Latino Culture and Five-College 40th Anniversary Professor at Amherst College. His books include *The Hispanic Condition* (1995), *The Riddle of Cantinflas* (1998), *The Essential Ilan Stavans* (2000), *On Borrowed Words* (2001), *Spanglish* (2003), *Dictionary Days* (2005), *The Disappearance* (2006), and *Love and Language* (2007). He is the editor of, among other works, *Growing Up Latino* (1994), *The Oxford Book of Latin American Essays* (1998), and *The Poetry of Pablo Neruda* (2003). He is the recipient of numerous awards and honors, including a Guggenheim Fellowship, the Latino Hall of Fame Award, Chile's Presidential Medal, the Rubén Darío Medal, and the National Jewish Book Award. Stavans writes a newspaper column syndicated throughout the Spanish-speaking world.

CESAR CHAVEZ

An Organizer's Tale

SPEECHES

Edited with an Introduction by
ILAN STAVANS

PENGUIN BOOKS

PENGUIN BOOKS

Published by the Penguin Group
Penguin Group (USA) Inc., 375 Hudson Street, New York, New York 10014, U.S.A.
Penguin Group (Canada), 90 Eglinton Avenue East, Suite 700, Toronto,
Ontario, Canada M4P 2Y3 (a division of Pearson Penguin Canada Inc.)
Penguin Books Ltd, 80 Strand, London WC2R 0RL, England
Penguin Ireland, 25 St Stephen's Green, Dublin 2, Ireland (a division of Penguin Books Ltd)
Penguin Group (Australia), 250 Camberwell Road, Camberwell,
Victoria 3124, Australia (a division of Pearson Australia Group Pty Ltd)
Penguin Books India Pvt Ltd, 11 Community Centre, Panchsheel Park, New Delhi – 110 017, India
Penguin Group (NZ), 67 Apollo Drive, Rosedale, North Shore 0632,
New Zealand (a division of Pearson New Zealand Ltd)
Penguin Books (South Africa) (Pty) Ltd, 24 Sturdee Avenue,
Rosebank, Johannesburg 2196, South Africa

Penguin Books Ltd, Registered Offices:
80 Strand, London WC2R 0RL, England

First published in Penguin Books 2008

1 3 5 7 9 10 8 6 4 2

Copyright © Cesar E. Chavez Foundation, 2008
Introduction copyright © Ilan Stavans, 2008
All rights reserved

Grateful acknowledgment is made for permission to reprint the following copyrighted works:
"Marcher," an interview with Cesar Chavez, by Daniel Chasan, The New Yorker, May 27, 1967.
By permission of Daniel Jack Chasan.
"Sharing the Wealth," by Cesar Chavez, Playboy Magazine, January 1970.
By permission of Playboy Enterprises, Inc.
Introduction by Cesar Chavez to Forty Acres: Cesar Chavez and the Farm Workers
by Mark Day. Copyright © 1971 by Praeger Publishers, Inc. Reprinted with permission of
Greenwood Publishing Group, Inc., Westport, Conn.

LIBRARY OF CONGRESS CATALOGING IN PUBLICATION DATA
Chavez, Cesar, 1927–1993.
An organizer's tale : speeches / Cesar Chavez ; edited with an introduction by Ilan Stavans.
p. cm.
ISBN 978-0-14-310526-8
1. Chavez, Cesar, 1927–1993. 2. Labor leaders—United States—History—20th century. 3. United Farm
Workers—History—20th century. 4. Migrant agricultural laborers—Labor unions—United States—History—
20th century. 5. Mexican American migrant agricultural laborers—History—20th century. I. Stavans, Ilan.
II. Title.
HD6509.C48A24   2008
331.88'13092—dc22   2008006934
[B]

Printed in the United States of America
Set in Sabon

Contents

AN ORGANIZER'S TALE

Introduction

"The end of all knowledge should be service to others," Cesar Chavez once said. He ought to know. A man of deep faith, he spent his life organizing people, in particular *mexicanos*, hoping to better their lot. From his humble beginning in Arizona as a migrant worker to his rise in status of national idol, his mantra was familiar: justice, equality, and the pursuit of happiness. Poverty was his prime target. Farmworkers, he often argued, are involved in the planting, cultivating, and harvesting of an abundance of food. Isn't it ironic, then, and even tragic, that they don't have enough food to feed themselves? To be aware of the miserable labor conditions of migrants and not do anything was to become an accomplice. Nobody should be forgotten in America.

Chavez belongs to a time, the latter half of the twentieth century, when the United States underwent a profound demographic makeover, which itself opened up a reevaluation of the nation's collective identity. For centuries, the United States had accepted immigrants from the Old World (Ireland, Germany, Scandinavia, Italy, France . . .), but after World War II the waves of newcomers from the so-called Third World intensified. This trend started with the Spanish-American War of 1898, but only in the 1950s did it become apparent that a different type of ethnic ingredient was now present. Mexicans, Puerto Ricans, and Cubans, to name only three Spanish-speaking groups, dramatically increased their numbers from midcentury onward, as did Filipinos, Chinese, Nigerians, Senegalese, and Francophone Caribbean peoples. Their arrival announced a redrawing of the political map and a reconfiguration of the culture as a whole. A different type of leader was needed, one capable of drawing attention to the plight of a heterogeneous underclass.

Chavez's maturity as a speaker representing the undocumented indigents in the fields coincided with the civil rights ferment. Time and again, he emphasized that the anxiety of the era wasn't exclusively about the deteriorated relations between whites and blacks, as it's still being perceived today. It was about another type of American, an invisible, silent one who performed menial jobs for a pittance. His quest, then, was two-pronged: improve working conditions and recognize the protean quality of the nation's ethnic mosaic. He wanted people to concede that the United States now lived in Technicolor.

Named after his grandfather, Cesario Estrada Chavez was born to Librado and Juana Chavez on March 31, 1927, on a small farm near Yuma, Arizona. On August 29, 1937, when Chavez was ten years old, the state took possession of the family ranch, which they had owned since the 1880s. A year later, Librado Chavez left home with several relatives to look for work in California, where he found a job threshing beans in Oxnard, a small town near the coast an hour north of Los Angeles. Librado wrote home to Juana telling her to come with the children. Thus, the Chavezes became a family of migrant workers.

The physical conditions of itinerant labor were awful—and, to a large extent, they still are today. Workers, adults and children alike, labored fifteen-hour shifts under the inclement sun. They moved seasonally from one state to another, from field to field, depending on need. Payment per hour was notoriously low, way under the minimum wage. No benefits were granted. Housing, too, was sparse. Families of six to eight members lived in a single room without a toilet. Worse even was the degrading attitude of the employers, for whom the Mexicans were simply subhuman, one individual indistinguishable from another.

Interest in the farmworkers' plight as a national issue began in the late thirties and early forties. Fred Ross and some other followers of Saul Alinsky (the author of *Reveille for Radicals* and considered the father of community organizing, responsible for the organizing of the Back of the Yards neighborhood in Chicago, which appears in Upton Sinclair's *The Jungle*) looked away from major metropolitan areas to the countryside as their theater of action. There was also concern among intellectuals and in the media.

Carey McWilliams, an editor of *The Nation*, was captivated by the changes under way in the state of California. He was also gripped by the atrocious circumstances in which migrant labor lived. McWilliams published a couple of seminal works connecting the two topics: *Factories in the Field* and *Ill Fares the Land*. Likewise, Edward R. Morrow, the radio and TV anchorman known as the face of CBS News, who later went after Wisconsin senator Joseph McCarthy, made migrant workers a focus of his coverage.

As was the case with all migrant children, Chavez's schooling was a series of interruptions. Overall, he attended some thirty elementary and middle schools. The experience left him scarred. In an interview with Jacques E. Levy, part of *Autobiography of La Causa*, he said that getting to school was a chore. "I never liked it," he maintained:

> They made me go, so I went, but they always had to push me to go. It wasn't the learning I hated, but the conflicts. The teachers were very mean. I also didn't like sitting in the class-room. I was bored to death. I'd just go to sleep. Once the teacher even sent a note home saying I was ill, that I had to be taken to the doctor because I was always falling asleep.

Chavez was part of a generation of Mexican Americans (the term "Chicano," in circulation since 1937, became fashionable in the sixties) for which Mexico was the country of their past, where their heritage lay. But, having crossed the border, his parents became an integral part of the fabric of the United States. He spoke unschooled Spanish, but, as he later recalled, teachers insisted migrant children learn English. "They said that if we were American, then we should speak the language, and if we wanted to speak Spanish, we should go back to Mexico."

Throughout his life, he remained loyal to *el español*. Of the scores of transcriptions of his speeches collected in the Farm Workers Archive at Walter P. Reuther Library, at Detroit's Wayne State University, a handful are in Spanish. Some, like "*Peregrinación, penitencia, revolución,*" a rendition of the legendary piece "The Plan of Delano," have been published. Associates lent him a hand in the endeavor. The extent to which Chavez was able to write freely in Cervantes's tongue is debatable. In any case, by then he already recognized the value of articulating one's thoughts coherently. "A language," he said, "is an exact reflection of the character and growth of its speakers."

In a way, the tension between his two languages, Spanish and English, was a symptom of Chavez's dual status, which troubled him deeply. Was he an American, like all the white kids in the different schools he attended? It seemed to him that his Mexicanness—*la mexicanidad,* in Spanish—conferred a second-class status. That status, in his mind, was intricately linked to work. As John Steinbeck's novel *The Grapes of Wrath*, about a fictional family of Dust Bowl refugees, eloquently portrays, the crash of 1929 turned a vast number of people in the Southwest into drifters.

Life for migrant workers meant no home, no secure job, not even the promise of food after a day in the fields. It was a nerve-wracking existence. Families felt uprooted; the Chavezes, and hundreds of others like them, didn't belong anywhere. He looked back on his early years as a period of anxiety and was appalled by how widespread the sense of deprivation was. In "An Organizer's Tale," one of Chavez's most introspective pieces, he stated: "There are vivid memories from my childhood—what we had to go through because of low wages and the conditions, basically because there was no union." He added: "I went through a lot of hell, and a lot of people did." Actually, the lack of a union (*el sindicato*) was, in retrospect, a feature of his ordeal. Chavez recognized that lack when, in 1941, at the age of fourteen, he first encountered a union. Members of the CIO (Congress of Industrial Organizations) came to his house to talk to Librado and his brother about organizing with other workers.

After the eighth grade, he quit school and worked in the fields to help support the family. World War II was under way and Chavez, like thousands of other *mexicanos*, was ready to serve his country. He wanted to flee from the harsh working conditions that beat him down day after day—heat, exhaustion, boredom, and underpayment. In 1946, once the war was over, he joined the navy as a deck hand. He served in the western Pacific.

In the forties, when the Chavez family was living in Delano, signs that read "No dogs or Mexicans allowed!" weren't uncommon.

The Zoot Suit Riots and the Sleepy Lagoon Murder are representative of the ethnic volatility in California at that time. In a cauldron of racial hostility, the movie theaters were segregated. The left-hand side was reserved for Anglos and Japanese customers. Just before departing for his service in the Pacific, in a move foreshadowing Rosa Parks's courage a decade later in Alabama, Chavez defied the ban. When the authorities asked him to give up his seat, he refused. He didn't put up a fight. It would be his first stay in prison.

Two years later, Chavez married Helen Fabela, whom he had met while working the vineyard fields in San Jose, California. Together they had eight children. The family moved to San Jose and lived in a neighborhood nicknamed Sal Si Puedes (in Spanish, "escape if you can"), where they joined the congregation of Father Donald McDonnell. It was through Father McDonnell that Chavez began to read voraciously and became mesmerized by St. Francis, who preached absolute humility, and Mahatma Gandhi's philosophy of nonviolence captured Chavez's imagination. He became familiar with the Encyclicals and discovered the transcripts of the so-called La Follette Civil Liberties Committee on Education and Labor, chaired by Wisconsin senator Robert M. La Follette Jr., which investigated free-speech and labor-rights violations between 1936 and 1941.

Among the countless findings of the committee was evidence of the disruption of union activities, the disruption of strikes, and the formation of spy networks and secret police systems to monitor workers. Such systems, it concluded, place "the employer in the very heart of the union council from the outset of any organizing effort. News of organizers coming into a town, contacts the organizers make among his employees, the names of employees who join the union, all organization plans, all activities of the union—these are as readily available to the employer as though he himself were running the union." Chavez was shocked by what he found. Simply put, the freedom of the average American worker was in question.

Was there shame in being poor? Not in Chavez's eyes. But there wasn't any pride either. The country didn't seem to recognize the rights of the underclass. It preferred to look elsewhere. The

American Dream worked insofar as it utterly rejected poverty. The objective was to leave it behind, to become successful. But the logic of the dream was false, for in a society constantly infused by immigrants, there would always be someone at the bottom. Furthermore, capitalism isn't about equality. It's a system designed for individuals to flourish. The poor, and Chavez himself was among them, need to find their reservoir of dignity and self-confidence. These ruminations led Chavez to expound an argument in favor of social justice. In an essay he published in *Playboy* in 1970, he wrote:

> Nothing is going to happen until we, the poor, can generate our own political and economic power. Such a statement sounds radical to many middle-class Americans, but it should not. Though many of the poor have come to see the affluent middle class as its enemy, that class actually stands between the poor and the real powers in this society—the administrative octopus with its head in Washington, the conglomerates, the military complex. It's like a camel train: The herder, way up in front, leads one camel and all the other camels follow. We happen to be the last camel, trudging along through the leavings of the whole train. We see only the camel in front of us and make him the target of our anger, but that solves nothing. The lower reaches of the middle class, in turn, are convinced that blacks, Mexican Americans, Puerto Ricans, Indians and poor whites want to steal their jobs—a conviction that the power class cheerfully perpetuates. The truth of the matter is that, even with automation, there can still be enough good-paying jobs for *everyone* in this country. If all of us were working for decent wages, there would be a greater demand for goods and services, thus creating even more jobs and increasing the gross national product. Full and fair employment would also mean that taxes traceable to welfare and all the other hidden costs of poverty—presently borne most heavily by middle-income whites—would inevitably go down.

In June 1952, while working in an apricot orchard outside San Jose, Chavez met Fred Ross. It was a fateful moment. Ross, the founder of the Community Service Organization (CSO), was an outsider whose calling was improving labor conditions, and he was very much aware of the substantial number of *mexicanos* working in the fields in California, Texas, Colorado, and Arizona.

He was looking to recruit an insider not only able to speak Spanish but to communicate with Mexican workers on their own terms.

In *Conquering Goliath,* Ross wrote about Chavez's beginnings. He details their first encounters, the conversations they had, and the early struggles before Chavez became a national figure. The book is a humble memoir focusing on the confrontation, in 1958, between a small number of farmworkers pitted against some two hundred growers supported by the government. In a poignant section, Ross describes Chavez's reluctance to get involved in organizing people, mainly because the approach came from outside the community:

> Cesar found out, years before, that whenever a Gringo wanted to meet you, look out! In those days, Sal Si Puedes was right in the path of a stream of college people coming down from Berkeley and Stanford to write their theses about the barrio. They would ask insulting questions like "How come the Mexican-Americans have so many kids? And how come they all eat beans and chile?" Then they would all go back and become professors and teach their students how to go down to the barrio and write their theses.
>
> So Cesar thought I was one of them, he told me later. Except he wasn't completely sure about it because I had this old beat-up car and wore wrinkled clothes.

Ross sums up Chavez's adventures thus:

> . . . he just walked into history. But before the Grape Strike and Boycott, before the highly publicized marches and fasts, before the Kennedys, before the millions of people from all over the world who rallied behind his cause—before all of that, there was just Cesar, with a single-minded doggedness that kept him trying no matter what the odds or how long it would take.

The friendship between the two is an example of an invigorating cross-ethnic encounter. It's told in an accessible tone by a *gringo* advocate about a *mexicano* who at first is reluctant to get involved in activism and then, without noticing, redefines activism altogether. At the time of Ross's own death, in San Francisco, Chavez offered a eulogy, dated October 17, 1992, in which he chronicled their lasting relationship. He stated:

> Fred used to say that "you can't take shortcuts, because you'll pay for it later." He believed society would be transformed from within by mobilizing individuals and communities. But you have to convert one person at a time, time after time. Progress only comes when people just plow ahead and do it. It takes lots of patience. The concept is so simple that most people miss it.

Fred enlisted Chavez, and between 1952 and 1962, the two organized twenty-two CSO chapters across California. With the help of Chavez's leadership, CSO became the most effective Latino civil rights group of its day. It helped Latinos become citizens and gain the right to vote.

That decade was formative for Chavez. By 1962, at the age of thirty-five, he had learned his lesson. He realized migrant workers were a largely underrepresented class about which nobody in the power circles, whether in California or Washington, gave a damn. Workers needed a leader with an authentic style, ready to air their claims. Furthermore, he understood that, with the proper orchestration, the power of this constituency was enormous. What they needed was to join forces, to work as a unit.

On March 31 of that year, he resigned from the Community Service Organization to dedicate himself full-time to organizing *mexicanos*. The family moved back to Delano, where he believed he could start building his organization. Focusing on the farmworkers posed unique challenges. In a speech he delivered at Harvard in March 1970, four years into the Grape Strike in Delano, a struggle undermined by the Department of Defense's purchase of grapes, Chavez announced:

> Organizing farm workers is very different from organizing any other workers in the country today. Here we don't have any rules, any regulations. We don't have any prescribed methods, no precedents. There is no law for farm labor organizing, save the law of the jungle. The citizens and their rights for seven years have been ignored and the employers have seen to it that they don't survive. Agriculture in this country is not a family with a small plot of land.

That is not agriculture. That is not where the fruits and the vegetables, the nuts and the grapes are produced. They are produced in large factory farms, huge corporate farms. They themselves have adopted a new name: they call themselves "agro-business."

Chavez's strategy was first to establish a farmworker's organization and, in quick succession, to arrange a national convention in which its mission would be established. Indeed, on September 20, 1962, such gathering of the National Farm Workers Association (NFWA) convened in Fresno, in an abandoned theater. By underlining the national, not the regional, Chavez sought to build a structure with far-reaching influence. About one hundred and fifty delegates and their families attended the convention. Members voted to organize the farmworkers and elect temporary officers. They agreed to lobby for a minimum wage law covering farmworkers. The term *la causa*, the cause, was embraced. The motto of the convention became *"¡Viva La Causa!"*

Finally, a union representing poor Mexican labor in the fields had been born. For the next three years, Chavez worked tirelessly to expand the membership base. In the spring of 1965, NFWA organized its first strike against the rose industry. And then, on September 16, which commemorates Mexico's independence, the NFWA joined a strike against the grape growers in the Delano area. On the first day alone twelve hundred workers joined in. It would become one of the most publicized periods of Chavez's career.

The media provided extensive coverage of the five-year strike. Arguably the most lucid, incisive narrative account appeared in serialized form in the *Saturday Evening Post*, penned by John Gregory Dunne, the author of *Dutch Shea, Jr.* and *Playland*. It would culminate in a book entitled *Delano: The Story of the California Grape Strike*. By nature, Dunne wasn't prone to look favorably upon labor unrest. As his career would prove, he was attracted, as he told George Plimpton in a *Paris Review* interview in 1996, to "extraordinary grotesqueries—nutty nuns, midgets, whores of the most breathtaking abilities and appetites." But as a Californian, he was puzzled by the collision between the haves and have-nots, the Anglos and the *mexicanos*.

In his account, he is initially rather cold, maybe even unsympathetic toward Chavez. He grapples with the journalistic need to remain impartial to the events unfolding before him. But as he plows along through piles of documents and firsthand accounts, Dunne warms up to Chavez and the NFWA members. "The curious thing about Cesar Chavez," Dunne declared, "is that he is as little understood by those who would canonize him as by those who would condemn him." He perceives him through an edgy lens as a rural folk hero.

> To the saint-makers, Chavez seemed the perfect candidate. His crusade was devoid of the ambiguities of urban conflict. With the farm workers there were no nagging worries about the mugging down the block, the rape across the street, the car busted in front of the house. It was a cause populated by simple Mexican peasants with noble agrarian ideas, not by surly unemployables with low IQs and Molotov cocktails. . . . The saintly virtues he had aplenty; it is doubtful that the media would have been attracted to him were it not for those virtues, and without the attention of the media the strike would not have survived. But Chavez had the virtues of the labor leader, less applauded publicly perhaps, but no less admirable in the rough going—a will of iron, a certain deviousness, an ability to hang tough in the clinches.

The concept of *la huelga*, the strike, is an integral part of labor history. During the Industrial Revolution, it was strictly prohibited. The rise of social democracy as a philosophy of labor relations at the end of the nineteenth century and the beginning of the twentieth established it as a right of workers. Chavez studied a number of strikes, including the 1906 Cananea strike, in the Mexican state of Sonora, against the Cananea Consolidated Copper Company owned by the U.S. colonel William C. Greene, which, as portrayed by historians, made the decades-long dictatorship of Porfirio Díaz all the more unpopular and triggered the Mexican Revolution four years later. By organizing migrant workers, Chavez took *la huelga* to unforeseen heights. He scheduled marches that, at a time when the American news media was consolidating its status as an independent tool in the democratic dialogue, became spectacular events.

Overall, the Delano Grape Strike lasted five years. As a leader, he had identified a genuine feeling of solidarity among his constituents. In "An Organizer's Tale," Chavez affirmed:

The people who took part in the strike and the march have something more than their material interest going for them. If it were only
material, they wouldn't have stayed on the strike long enough to win.
It is difficult to explain. But it flows out in the ordinary things they
say. For instance, some of the younger guys are saying, "Where do
you think's going to be the next strike?"

I say, "Well, we have to win in Delano."

They say, "We'll win, but where do we go next?"

I say, "Maybe most of us will be working in the fields." They say,
"No, I don't want to go and work in the fields. I want to organize.
There are a lot of people that need our help."

So I say, "You're going to be pretty poor then, because when you
strike you don't have much money." They say they don't care much
about that.

And others are saying, "I have friends who are working in Texas.
If we could only help them."

It is bigger, certainly, than just a strike.

In fact, it was. The union and the strike were Chavez's devices, to
which he soon added another one: the boycott. The NFWA started
a grape boycott in November and December 1965. Members followed grape trucks and set up picket lines wherever grapes were
sold in the country. In a speech at Riverside Church in New York
City in 1970, he argued for boycotts as a potent weapon to bring
about dignity and justice. "It is very difficult to get people involved
unless what we ask people to do is very simple, very concrete and
very painless."

The largest, most renowned marches Chavez orchestrated took
place in 1966. Between March and April, to make the case for the
farmworkers' cause in the court of public opinion, he and strikers
from the NFWA, joined by the AWOC (Agricultural Workers Organizing Committee), engaged in a 340-mile pilgrimage from Delano to the steps of the capitol in Sacramento. Organizers of the
NFWA devised the so-called "El Plan de Delano" (The Plan of Delano), in which they outlined the rights of farmworkers.

We the undersigned, gathered in Pilgrimage to the capital of the State
in Sacramento in penance for all the failings of Farm Workers, as free
and sovereign men, do solemnly declare before the civilized world

which judges our actions, and before the nation to which we belong, the propositions we have formulated to end the injustice that oppresses us.

The statement included the following inventory:

[1] This is the beginning of a social movement in fact and not in pronouncements. We seek our basic, God-given rights as human beings.

[2] We seek the support of all political groups and protection of the government, which is also our government, in our struggle.

[3] We seek, and have, the support of the Church in what we do. At the head of the Pilgrimage we carry La Virgen de la Guadalupe because she is ours, all ours, Patroness of the Mexican people.

[4] We are suffering.

[5] We shall unite.

[6] We will strike.

The imagery used was drawn from the quest for Mexican independence, in 1810, by Father Miguel Hidalgo y Costilla, against the Spanish rulers, where a partnership between church and state was established. Chavez inserted in the plan much of the rhetorical motifs he ended up using throughout his life: pilgrimage, penitence, revolution.

The growers were distraught and bitterly complained of bias against them. Oftentimes, they brought in braceros to substitute for the striking field workers or cut deals with immigration officials to hire illegal workers without risk of penalties or worker deportation. These practices made Chavez a fierce opponent of the Bracero Program and of undocumented aliens. As a result of the growers' tactics, sporadic violence erupted. Rumors of Chavez's Communist sympathies circulated widely. But such was the public pressure that during the march itself, and four months into the grape boycott, Schenley Vineyards capitulated and signed a contract with the NFWA. It was the first genuine union contact between a grower and a farmworker's union in the nation's history.

Subsequently, the NFWA organized a strike and boycott against

DiGiorgio Fruit Corporation that lasted from the spring to the summer, forcing the grower to hold an election among its workers. In response, the company called in the Teamsters to oppose Chavez's NFWA. The NFWA and AWOC decided to merge, thus creating the United Farm Workers Association (UFWA), and DiGiorgio workers voted for the UFWA. And in 1967, Chavez's UFWA went after Giumarra, the largest grower of table grapes, against which farmworkers had endless grievances. Nearly all of Giumarra's workers joined in the strike, although, to Chavez's dismay, days later many returned to the fields. Consequently, UFWA began a boycott of Giumarra products, but it lost effectiveness when Giumarra changed its labels. Chavez's response was categorical: he instructed the UFWA to boycott all California table grapes, without distinction.

It is of paramount importance to place Chavez's mobilization of migrant workers in the proper context. His push for improvement was staged at a time when anticolonial fever was palpable worldwide. The word *revolución* was in the air. From Cuba to Algiers, guerrilla movements attempting to overthrow repressive dictatorial regimes captured people's imagination. Sacrifice for a cause was a slogan, a catchword. To redistribute wealth, to seek less hierarchical forms of government, to expand the horizons of education, those were the issues worth dying for. Figures like Ernesto "Che" Guevara were universally adored. The beatniks in San Francisco and New York City, and the antiestablishment philosophy endorsed by their followers, the hippies, were the order of the day.

Soon Chavez's efforts were not exclusively about *mexicanos*. He represented Filipinos, Puerto Ricans, blacks, and other underserved minorities. He organized them to resist, in nonviolent ways, the oppressive labor conditions they were subjected to and to have a collective bargaining voice. Nonviolence was his trademark. Of course, it was in the zeitgeist of the sixties, with Dr. Martin Luther King Jr. advocating a pacifist attitude toward change. Chavez's relationship with the black civil rights leader was based on a shared sense of commitment, and also on the endorsement of nonviolent means to achieve a political objective. In the archives at Wayne State University, there are telegrams from Dr. King expressing sympathy at various turning points in Chavez's career, as in the strike against the DiGiorgio Fruit Corporation. But the closeness between them didn't run deep. Chavez's primary inspirations for his nonviolent views were divorced from traumas like slavery, defined by the implicit hatred accrued over centuries. His crusade, although based on ethnic difference, was mainly about labor relations. In a three-paragraph comment for *The Catholic Worker* published in June 1969, he described his belief that violence is for the weak.

Many people feel that an organization that uses nonviolent methods to reach its objectives must continue winning victories one after another in order to remain nonviolent. If that be the case then a lot of efforts have been miserable failures. There is a great deal more involved than victories. My experience has been that the poor know violence more intimately than most people because it has been a part of their lives, whether the violence of the gun or the violence of want and need.

I don't subscribe to the belief that nonviolence is cowardice, as some militant groups are saying. In some instances nonviolence requires more militancy than violence. Nonviolence forces you to abandon the shortcut, in trying to make a change in the social order. Violence, the shortcut, is the trap people fall into when they begin to feel that it is the only way to attain their goal. When these people turn to violence it is a very savage kind.

When people are involved in something constructive, trying to bring about change, they tend to be less violent than those who are not engaged in rebuilding or in anything creative. Nonviolence forces one to be creative; it forces any leader to go to the people and get them involved so that they can come forth with new ideas. I think that once people understand the strength of nonviolence—the force it generates, the love it creates, the response that it brings from the total community—they will not be willing to abandon it easily.

In the landscape of the civil rights era, Chavez's pursuit became part of *El Movimiento*, as the Chicano Movement came to be known. Other *mexicanos* became active, under the leadership of figures like Reies López Tijerina and Rodolfo "Corky" González. Within the NFWA, Chavez collaborated with an array of people who brought other needs to the table, such as Arturo Rodríguez,

David Martínez, and Dolores Huerta, the latter representing the voices of women.

The intention was to alter, once and for all, the marginalized status of Mexican Americans in the United States, and to put an end to segregation practices that, over time, they claimed resulted in an alienated mentality. The movement included intellectuals (Luis Valdez), newsmen and radio broadcasters (Rubén Salazar), muralists (Yolanda López, Rupert García), as well as students, teachers, housewives, and others. In particular, Luis Valdez's theater troupe, El Teatro Campesino, made up of farm laborers, assisted Chavez by staging short plays called *actos* at rallies to promote political awareness, and shifted to *mitos*, pieces about symbols in Mexican history. The concept of *La Raza*, the race, served as glue. It was intimately linked to *mestizaje*, the miscegenation of the European colonizers in the New World with the aboriginal population.

In 1925, the Mexican philosopher José Vasconcelos, formerly his country's minister of education, who helped secure public space for the art of muralists Diego Rivera and José Clemente Orozco, published a controversial, sensationalist book, *The Cosmic Race*, which argued that *La Raza*, the *mestizo* race, would ultimately take over the globe. The Chicano Movement, whose models included the Virgin of Guadalupe, Emiliano Zapata, and Frida Kahlo, loosely built its foundation on Vasconcelos's claim. For the movement, a Chicano was a Mexican American with an attitude.

In short, the quest for pride and self-esteem as an authentic sense of self was embraced by Chicanos. Chavez often went out of his way to distinguish between *El Movimiento* and *La Causa*. He wasn't a symbol of all Chicanos, he declared. His central drive was to better workers' lives, and not the radical makeover of an entire ethnic minority. Of course, insofar as his cause helped create change for Mexican Americans, he was delighted. What was essential, in his view, was that change took place sooner rather than later. He affirmed: "We want to be recognized, yes, but not with a glowing epitaph on our tombstone."

Undoubtedly, Chavez's weltanschauung was defined by his devout Catholic faith. "God writes in exceedingly crooked lines," Chavez believed. As a nation, Mexico has a *mestizo* identity shaped by a religious sentiment brought along by the Spanish conquistadors. He identified with Christ's teachings. "I've read what Christ said," he told Jacques Levy. "He was very clear in what he meant and knew exactly what he was after. He was extremely radical, and he was for social change." But Chavez was wary of the Catholic Church as an institution. "It's common knowledge that the Catholic Church is a block of power in society and that the property and purchase of the Church rate second only to the government," he wrote in 1968.

He challenged bishops, priests, and the clergy in general to take action. "To build power among Mexican Americans presents a threat to the Church; to demand reform of Anglo-controlled institutions stirs up dissension. . . . However, if representatives of the Church are immobilized and compromised into silence, the Church will not only remain irrelevant to the real needs and efforts of La Raza in the barrios; but our young leaders of today will continue to scorn the Church and view it as an obstacle to their struggle for social, political and economic independence."

Perhaps the single most provocative facet of Chavez's career was self-immolation. He used religious imagery (the term "pilgrimage," to begin with) to emphasize his message. The centerpieces of that message were suffering and sacrifice. "We're suffering," he contended about his fellow UFWA members. "And we're not afraid to suffer more in order to win our cause." And: "It takes a lot of punishment to achieve change. . . ."

Chavez's supreme sacrifice came in the form of a series of fasts he embarked on over a period of almost two decades. In February 1968, for instance, after several discouraged strikers began to contemplate the use of violence against growers, he fasted to encourage his members to adhere to nonviolence. The response was overwhelming: eight thousand farmworkers, as well as California senator Robert F. Kennedy, attended a Mass to break Chavez's twenty-five-day fast. Clearly, by now he had become an emblem. In a famous scene filled with religious meaning, Kennedy gave Chavez a piece of bread and called him "one of the heroic figures of our time." (Only six days after the fast ended, Bobby Kennedy announced his candidacy for the presidency. Before long, he would be assassinated.)

The rationale behind Chavez's fasts was entangled with his understanding of Christ's legacy. He lived to say it openly: "when any

person suffers for someone in greater need, that person is human."
In his view, the poor had a "tremendous capacity to suffer." It was
a matter of suffering with some kind of hope, rather than with
no hope at all. Clearly he had internalized the pathos of his constituency, establishing a bridge between his own physical being
and the farmworking community at large. The agony of one was
the distress of the other. He recognized his own value by suffering
in public, which isn't an essential ingredient of the Hispanic character, more prone to experiencing pain in private.

This is an appropriate place to reflect on the topic of Chavez
and the media. For the researcher exploring his career, it seems as
if, from 1966, with the Plan of Delano, onward, he was constantly
in the spotlight, with cameras and microphones pointed at him.
News organizations and freelance photojournalists regularly visited the UFWA's headquarters. Aside from a minuscule number of
Hollywood stars (Rita Moreno, Anthony Quinn, Chita Rivera),
and of international figures like Fidel Castro, this type of fascina-
tion over a Hispanic activist was unheard of. Obviously, Chavez
thrived in it. But to what extent did he also manipulate it? The fast
is a perfect example. In humbly seeking remorse, contrition, and
atonement, did he also turn into a pop icon, a mirror of sorts in
which people projected their own existential pursuits? A pictorial
history of Chavez's transformations waits to be done.

By 1970, the grape boycott put Chavez and the UFWA in the international spotlight. Grape strikers spread across North America
in an effort to start an international grape boycott. The nation
tuned in. Supporters outside supermarkets and grocery stores from
New York to Illinois, from Ohio to Arizona, displayed their em-
brace of Chavez and the marchers. That spring and summer, most
California table grape growers signed UFWA contracts. Chavez
then called for a national boycott of lettuce after Salinas Valley
growers signed contracts with the Teamsters Union to help keep
the UFWA out of the fields. On December 10, the UFWA singled
out Lester Victor "Bud" Antle on the lettuce boycott. It was an in-
cendiary move: Chavez was arrested and thrown in jail for ignoring
the injunction prohibiting the UFWA from boycotting him. In a
gesture of empathy, Coretta Scott King, widow of Martin Luther
King Jr., as well as Ethel Kennedy, widow of Robert F. Kennedy,
paid him a visit in jail.

The UFWA membership had grown to eighty thousand by 1971. The FBI had been investigating Chavez and the UFWA for alleged Communist activities since 1965. The bureau, under the Freedom of Information Act, ended up releasing 2,021 pages of the Chavez files, where accounts of disturbances, meetings, marches, and boycotts were recorded. It was also around then that several plots to assassinate Chavez came to light. The animosity against him had grown exponentially in antilabor quarters. No-nonsense, vigorous leaders such as Chavez represented a threat to the establishment. It was better to eliminate them. Indeed, political assassination was a recurrent practice in the period.

In 1971, the union's headquarters were moved to La Paz, in Keene, California. A year later, the UFWA became an independent affiliate of the AFL-CIO, converting itself into the United Farm Workers of America. The American Farm Bureau Federation, along with other grower organizations and extreme right-wing groups, pushed legislation in California and other states outlawing boycotting and strikes at harvest time, and setting up election procedures geared to allow only a few people to decide whether a union would be welcome. Bills passed in Kansas, Idaho, and Arizona. Between May 11 and June 4, 1972, Chavez again fasted, this time in Phoenix, to protest the recent legislation.

Rather than renew their three-year contract with the UFWA, table grape growers signed contracts in the spring and summer of 1973 with the Teamsters without going through an election. In response, thousands of grape workers began a three-month strike in the Coachella and San Joaquin valleys. Some were arrested, beaten, and shot for violating antipicketing injunctions. Chavez's nonviolence tactics were called into question. To prevent further agitations and the spilling of blood, he called off the strike and began a second grape boycott.

A Louis Harris poll showed that between 1973 and 1975, millions of Americans were boycotting grapes, Gallo wine, and lettuce. Approximately 17 million Americans were boycotting grapes alone. Chavez went on a European tour in 1974 to spread his gospel. In quick succession, he visited England, Norway, Italy, Switzerland, Denmark, Belgium, France, and other places. In Rome he had a twenty-minute audience with Pope Paul VI.

"To see the Pope is a big thing in Europe," he commented to a colleague in his rough-and-tumble travelogue, "not just religiously but politically." Overall, the trip served Chavez as an opportunity to internationalize his struggle. With his revered status in the United States, he was eager to make contacts with European politicians and labor leaders. Among others, he spoke to agricultural, construction, and carpentry workers. He talked about organizing and about the boycott as a weapon to reach people through the media. He also met exiled Americans, such as Porfirio Gutiérrez, " 'the only Chicano in Norway,' from Denver," stated Chavez's travelogue. "He was happy to host us—walked on clouds for days, made all kinds of Mexican food for us. He has a grocery store and a wine-making store (because he's Latin, the Norwegians think he's an authority on wine)." In Sweden he found himself defending his Americanness. From the trip's report:

> I didn't let them take pot-shots at the United States. What's true is true, but not clear shots. At one point I said, "It's my country. It's not all good, but it's not all bad either." For example, they said after the way the documentary *Why We Boycott* was made that "we were taught that America is the home of democracy, but now we must reexamine that." I said, "Democracy is expensive." They said, "Can the rich afford democracy?" I said, "They own it." I wouldn't let them take pot-shots, but I could. After the film they were very pissed off with the police—they can't stand oppression. Also, they just couldn't understand why people cannot vote.

Europe might have been a respite—and an education—but upon his return Chavez was again in a quagmire. Growers agreed to a state law in June 1975 known as the Agricultural Labor Relations Act, guaranteeing California farmworkers the right to organize and bargain with their employers. Chavez was able to get the Agricultural Labor Relations Act through the state legislation once the liberal-minded Jerry Brown became governor of California. In the mid-to-late seventies, the UFWA won the majority of the elections it participated in and signed contacts with a large number of growers. The Teamsters Union signed a "jurisdictional" agreement with the UFWA and agreed to leave the fields.

Finally, in 1978 the UFWA called off its boycotts of grapes, Gallo wine, and lettuce. The following year, from January to October, the UFWA continued to strike growers to negotiate better wages and benefits.

It was at a time of introspection that striker Rufino Contreras was shot dead in an Imperial Valley lettuce field by a foreman on February 10, 1979. Four days later, Chavez, in a eulogy, turned him into a martyr for *El Movimiento*. "The day of Contreras's death," Chavez said, was a day that should live in infamy, "a day without joy. The sun didn't shine. The birds didn't sing. The rain didn't fall." He added:

> What is the worth of a man? What is the worth of a farm worker? Rufino, his father and brother together gave the company twenty years of their labor. They were faithful workers who helped build up the wealth of their boss, helped build up the wealth of his ranch.
>
> What was their reward for their service and their sacrifice? When they petitioned for a more just share of what they themselves produced, when they spoke out against the injustice they endured, the company answered them with bullets; the company sent hired guns to quiet Rufino Contreras.

In the early eighties, with the aid of one million dollars in growers' contributions, Republican Courken George Deukmejian Jr. defeated Los Angeles Mayor Tom Bradley and was elected governor of California. A native of New York and an Armenian American by background, he portrayed himself as a probusiness, law-and-order politician. He wanted his followers to know he was particularly tough on crime. The state was in economic depression. He went against consumer and environment protections and went against justices who were openly opposed to the death penalty. Clearly, Chavez didn't have a friend in the state's highest person in command. In general, the atmosphere was antilabor. Ronald Reagan was in the White House and individualism was the philosophy of the day. Governor Deukmejian, who held office from 1983 to 1991, made it clear that he didn't appreciate the NFWU's activities. And his views were heard nationwide. The governor was a potential running mate for George H. W. Bush. Furthermore, he

quickly stopped enforcing California's farm labor law, and, as a result, thousands of farmworkers lost their UFWA contracts and, in
quick succession, their jobs.

Martyrdom again came to the forefront. In his distress, Chavez was
ready to become a rallying symbol leading his disciples in the form of
labor organizing. In 1983 worker René López was shot after voting
in a union election. As in the case of Contreras, Chavez humanized
his ordeal and immortalized his odyssey. He touched upon the theme
of sacrifice in the eulogy he delivered in Fresno. "We who live must
now walk an extra mile because René has lived and died for *his* and
our dreams," he announced. "We who keep on struggling for justice
for farm workers must carry in our hearts *his* sacrifice. We must try
to live as he lived, we must keep alive his hopes, and fulfill, with our
own sacrifices, his dreams." On occasions like this one, Chavez, in
the public eye, was obviously not only a leader but a preacher. His
speeches were infused with sorrow as well as optimism.

In his most private moments, though, he was overwhelmed by
despair. He realized the nation had shifted gears and it was much
harder now to get people's attention. In 1984, he launched a third
grape boycott, but by then his momentum was lost. To increase
awareness of pesticide poisoning of grape workers and their children, Chavez, in a speech in 1986, began what he called the "Wrath
of Grapes" campaign, an obvious reversal of the title of John Steinbeck's legendary novel and, indirectly, a flashback to his own
childhood experience during the Depression.

Chavez fought Governor Deukmejian's probusiness policy,
arguing that the "powerful self-serving alliance between the California governor and the four-billion-dollar agricultural industry
has resulted in a systematic and reckless poisoning of not only
California farm workers but of grape consumers throughout our
nation and Canada." He appealed to what he called "the greatest
court, the court of last resort," the American people, to boycott
grapes. His efforts were prescient. The environmental movement
was still in diapers, yet Chavez was already laying the foundation
stone.

The response to his appeal was halfhearted. It was between July
and August 1988 when Chavez began his last and longest fast. At
the age of sixty-one, he fasted for thirty-six days to raise awareness

about the poisoning of grape workers and their children. In the late eighties and early nineties, Chavez continued the third grape boycott. And then, in 1992, Chavez and his son-in-law, UFWA's vice president, Arturo Rodriguez, lead vineyard walkouts from the spring to the summer in the Coachella and San Joaquin valleys. With the help of the walkout, grape workers won their first industry-wide pay hike in eight years. His model had also become an impetus for younger labor leaders beyond California. In the Midwest, the Farm Labor Organizing Committee negotiated contracts with tomato and cucumber growers and with corporations such as Campbell Soup and H. J. Heinz. Other young leaders organized workers in Hawaii, Oregon, Pennsylvania, New Jersey, and New York. Cesar Chavez died in his sleep on April 23, 1993, in the town of San Luis, in the house of a retired Arizona farmworker. On April 29, forty thousand mourners marched behind Chavez's pine casket in Delano. Peter Matthiessen, a frequent contributor to *The New Yorker* and the author of *At Play in the Fields of the Lord* and *In the Spirit of Crazy Horse*, knew him well. They had become friends decades earlier, when Matthiessen wrote his book *Sal Si Puedes: Cesar Chavez and the New American Revolution* in 1969, mostly about the Delano strike. Upon Chavez's death, Matthiessen wrote an obituary in which he contended:

> With the former scourge of California safely in his coffin, state flags were lowered to half-mast by order of the Governor and messages poured forth from the heads of Church and State, including the Pope and the President of the United States. This last of the UFWA marches was greater, even, than the 1975 march against the Gallo winery, which helped destroy the growers' cynical alliance with the Teamsters. "We have lost perhaps the greatest Californian of the twentieth century," the president of the California State Senate said, in public demotion of Cesar Chavez's sworn enemies Nixon and Reagan.

And:

> Anger was a part of Chavez, but so was a transparent love of humankind. The gentle mystic that his disciples wished to see inhabited the same small body as the relentless labor leader who concerned himself with the most minute operation of his union. Astonishingly—this

seems to me his genius—the two Cesars were so complementary that
without either, La Causa could not have survived.

Chavez was buried in La Paz, the UFWA's California headquarters, in front of his office. In 1994, on the anniversary of Chavez's
passing, UFWA president Arturo Rodriguez led a march retracing
Chavez's pilgrimage from Delano to Sacramento. Seventeen thousand farmworkers joined Rodriguez on the steps of the state capitol to kick off another UFWA contract negotiating campaign.
President Bill Clinton presented the Medal of Freedom, America's
highest civilian honor, to Chavez posthumously. His wife, Helen
Chavez, received the medal at a White House ceremony.

I Iowever, his legacy is in question. By the time of Chavez's death,
the word "Chicano" had been rejected by a young generation of
Mexican Americans disconnected from the activism of the sixties and
seventies. The country as a whole was going through a period of
economic expansion and Latinos were beginning to move into the
middle class, looking for a share of the pie. Chavez's message of organizing and speaking out seemed remote to them. Meanwhile, his image was turned into a national commodity. Streets, schools, libraries,
and parks are named after him today. The United States Postal Service
issued a stamp with his likeness. There's even a motion to declare
his birthday a national holiday commemorating immigration. Yet
Chavez's legacy was one of a prophet manqué. A poll conducted in
2005 suggested that the vast majority of young people in the country
don't know who he was, what he stood for, what his legacy is. Even
though his mission is part of the elementary school curriculum in
most states, his words are easily reduced to sound bites.

Oratory was Chavez's strength. Not having received a formal
education but realizing the power of a Sunday sermon at church,
he concentrated on improvising in public speeches. His talent as
speaker was, first and foremost, finding the right tone for the listeners he had before him. Aside from migrant workers, he spoke
to students, politicians, clergymen, lawyers, antiwar protesters, the
automobile and construction industries, and Vietnam veterans. He
testified at the House of Representatives. He even delivered a nomi-
nation address to the Democratic National Convention in New
York's Madison Square Garden on July 14, 1976, where Jimmy
Carter and Walter Mondale were endorsed as the party's presidential

and vice-presidential candidates, respectively. Given Chavez's extraordinary activism, the material I've gathered is but a small representative selection of the man's life and work.

My purpose is straightforward: to give readers unadulterated access to Chavez's own words and thoughts. Clearly, he didn't have Martin Luther King Jr.'s rhetorical talents, offering polished, inspiring sentences. The transcription of his speeches is evidence of his accessible, down-to-earth, unconventional style. He didn't develop arguments as much as he compiled a sequence of forceful thoughts. And he offered them to his audience with passion, pointing to injustices people easily recognized. If, in fact, Chavez's material is rather flat, it's because he refused to hide his background or emulate someone else's elegant delivery. On the contrary, he humbly exhibited his philosophy at every turn, proving that poor people might lack the sophistication to build fanciful sentences but not conviction and clarity of mind.

Isocrates suggested that "the argument which is made by a man's life is of more weight than that which is furnished by words." What, in the end, did Cesar Chavez teach us? That the American experiment, to remain viable, needs to constantly make room for all kinds of people. That the principles on which the Founding Fathers established the Republic—justice, equality, and the pursuit of happiness—apply to everyone, without exception. That poverty isn't a type of shame. That work is where a person finds pride and that the workplace ought to be a healthy, balanced, dignified environment. That no matter how one looks at it, the exploitation of others is an aberration. That to sacrifice one's life for a cause is to know its true worth. That letting people go hungry is a sin. And that no matter how religious an individual might be, faith in one's mission is the first step toward achieving one's goals.

More than anything else, Chavez showed that hope is never for sale and that progress is only achieved by moving forward together and not by encouraging some to move forward while leaving others behind. He claimed: "When the man who feeds the world by toiling in the fields is himself deprived of the basic rights of feeding and caring for his own family, the whole community of man is sick."

The forty-eight selections in this anthology include an assortment of speeches delivered in front of live audiences and later transcribed, and currently housed at the Walter P. Reuther Library. His method as a speaker underwent various changes; while most often he used notes from which he improvised, on other occasions he read prepared texts. This volume includes correspondence, such as the "Good Friday Letter," written in Delano to E. L. Barr Jr., president of the California Grape and Tree Fruit League, a growers' organization (it appeared in *Christian Century* on April 23, 1969), as well as a handful of replies to queries and fan mail. Chavez was an assiduous interviewee. I've counted more than a hundred interviews for radio, newspapers, and TV, and that is by no means an exhaustive list. I've showcased some interviews for publications like *El Malcriado* and *The New Yorker*. As a coda, there's a collection of aphorisms, for which Chavez has become famous. They come from the almost inexhaustible well of material he left behind. The majority of the section titles are my own.

I've done as much as possible to find out when entries were composed. The material is ordered chronologically by date of composition or, when unavailable, by date of publication, although for a couple of pieces I'm only able to offer approximations. Since Chavez lived a hectic life and didn't arrange his archives meticulously, minor editorial changes have been made for the sake of accuracy and consistency. Every entry is accompanied by a headnote that places it in context.

A word about authenticity. Throughout his career, associates collaborated with him in drafting his texts, from eulogies to op-ed pieces. A subaltern component is hence injected into his legacy. What was his alone and what came from others? Even though they were signed by him, some entries, such as "Sharing the Wealth," show quite a bit of tinkering, and not only at the editorial level. Were they perhaps written by someone else? The same applies to his typed correspondence, which Chavez probably dictated. Does this amount to illegitimacy? Not in my view. Luminaries like him have an entourage whose purpose it is to maintain the public persona, to offer a signature style.

Suggestions for Further Reading

The literature on Cesar Chavez is substantial, but far less so was his own writing output, which remains largely dispersed in anthologies and periodicals. The brief bibliography below lists only essential books and movies. I've left out references in periodicals and the plethora of poems, songs, appearances in fiction, and young-adult literature on him. For readers interested in further research, Beverly Fodell's *Cesar Chavez and the United Farm Workers: A Selective Bibliography* (Detroit, Mich.: Wayne State University Press, 1974) is a useful tool, although it doesn't cover Chavez's last eighteen years and the notices published after his death.

The first section lists volumes that include Chavez's speeches, correspondence, and other material written by him. The second is an inventory of biographical disquisitions on his odyssey and the UFWA. The third contains studies about him: his ordeal, ideology, rhetorical style, and connection with the Catholic Church. And the last section lists documentary movies.

WORKS BY CESAR CHAVEZ

Day, Mark. *Forty Acres: Cesar Chavez and the Farm Workers*. Introduction by Cesar Chavez. New York: Praeger, 1971.

Jensen, Richard J., with John C. Hammerback, eds. *The Words of César Chávez*. College Station: Texas A&M University Press, 2002.

López y Rivas, Gilberto, ed. *The Chicanos*. New York: Monthly Review Press, 1974.

Simmen, Edward, ed. *Pain and Promise: The Chicano Today*. New York: Mentor, 1972.

Valdez, Luis, with Stan Steiner, eds. *Aztlán: An Anthology of Mexican-American Literature*. New York: Alfred A. Knopf, 1972.

Yinger, Winthrop. *César Chávez: The Rhetoric of Nonviolence*. Hicksville, N.Y.: Exposition, 1975.

BIOGRAPHIES

Bruns, Roger. *Cesar Chavez: A Biography*. Westport, Conn.: Greenwood Press, 2005.

Dunne, John Gregory. *Delano: The Story of the California Grape Strike*. Introduction by Ilan Stavans. Berkeley: University of California Press, 2008.

Etilian, Richard W., ed. *Cesar Chavez: A Brief Biography with Documents*. Boston: Bedford/St. Martin's, 2002.

Ferriss, Susan, with Ricardo Sandoval. *The Fight in the Fields: Cesar Chavez and the Farmworkers Movement*. New York: Harcourt Brace, 1997.

Griswold del Castillo, Richard, with Richard A. Garcia. *César Chávez: A Triumph of the Spirit*. Norman: University of Oklahoma Press, 1995.

Levy, Jacques E. *Cesar Chavez: Autobiography of La Causa*. New York: W.W. Norton, 1975.

Matthiessen, Peter. *Sal Si Puedes: Cesar Chavez and the New American Revolution*. Foreword by Ilan Stavans. Berkeley: University of California Press, 2000.

Muller, Jean-Marie, with Jean Kalman. *César Chavez: Un combat non-violent*. Paris: Fayard/Le Cerf, 1977.

Pitrone, Jean Maddern. *Chavez: Man of the Migrants*. Staten Island, N.Y.: Alba House, 1977.

Ross, Fred. *Conquering Goliath: Cesar Chavez at the Beginning*. Keene, Calif.: United Farm Workers, 1989.

Steinbacher, John A. *Bitter Harvest*. Whittier, Calif.: Orange Tree Press, 1970.

Taylor, Ronald B. *Chavez and the Farm Workers*. Boston: Beacon Press, 1975.

CRITICAL STUDIES

Calavita, Kitty. *Inside the State: The Bracero Program, Immigration, and the INS.* N.Y.: Routledge, 1992.

Dalton, Frederick John. *The Moral Vision of Cesar Chavez.* Maryknoll, N.Y.: Orbis Books, 2003.

Gómez-Quiñonez, Juan. *Mexican-American Labor, 1790–1990.* Albuquerque: University of New Mexico Press, 1994.

La Botz, Dan. *Cesar Chavez and La Causa.* New York: Pearson Longman, 2006.

London, Joan, with Henry Anderson. *So Shall Ye Reap.* New York: Crowell, 1970.

Pouty, Marco G. *César Chávez, the Catholic Bishops, and the Farmworkers' Struggle for Social Justice.* Tucson: University of Arizona Press, 2006.

DOCUMENTARIES

Galán Productions. *Chicano!: A History of the Mexican-American Civil Rights Movement.* Four videos. Los Angeles: NLCC Educational Media and KCET, 1996.

Telles, Ray, with Rick Tejada-Flores, dirs. *The Fight in the Fields: Cesar Chavez and the Farm Workers' Struggle.* DVD New York: Cinema Guild, 1996.

Chronology

March 31, 1927: Cesario Estrada Chavez is born on a small farm near Yuma, Arizona, to Librado and Juana Chavez.

August 29, 1937: The state takes possession of Librado Chavez's ranch.

1938: Librado Chavez leaves home in August with several relatives to look for work in California. He soon finds a job threshing beans in Oxnard, a small town near the coast about fifty-five miles north of Los Angeles. Librado writes home to Juana telling her to come with the children. The Chavezes become a family of migrant workers.

1941: Chavez has his first contact with a union when a CIO member comes to the Chavez house to talk to Librado and his brother about organizing with other workers.

1942: Chavez quits school after the eighth grade. He begins full-time work in the fields to help his father support the family.

1946: At the age of nineteen, Chavez is tired from the physical strain of sugar beet thinning. He joins the navy to get away from farm labor where he works as a deck hand, a job assigned to most Mexican Americans in the navy. He will serve in the western Pacific. While visiting his home in Delano on a seventy-two-hour leave, Chavez and his friends go to a local theater. He is arrested after refusing to give up his seat in the left hand section reserved for Anglos and Japanese customers.

1948: Chavez marries Helen Fabela, with whom he eventually has eight children. In the late forties, Chavez and his family join the congregation of Father Donald McDonnell in their San Jose barrio Sal Si Puedes. Father McDonnell introduces Chavez to the writings of the Encyclicals, St. Francis, and Gandhi as well as to the transcripts of the Senate La Follette Committee hearings, which were held from 1936 to 1940.

1952: In June, while Chavez is working in an apricot orchard outside San Jose, Fred Ross, founder of the Community Service Organization (CSO), recruits him to become an active member of CSO.

1952–62: Chavez and Fred Ross organize twenty-two CSO chapters across California. With the help of Chavez's leadership, CSO is the most effective Latino civil rights group of its day. Chavez and his organizers help Latinos become citizens and gain the right to vote.

March 31, 1962: Chavez resigns from the CSO to dedicate himself full-time to organizing farmworkers. He and his family move to Delano so that he can start building the foundations of his organization.

September 30, 1962: The first convention of Chavez's National Farm Workers Association (NFWA) convenes in an abandoned theater in Fresno. About one hundred and fifty delegates and their families attend the convention. Members vote to organize the farmworkers, elect temporary officers, agree to lobby for a minimum wage law covering farmworkers, and adopt "¡Viva La Causa!" as a motto.

1962–65: Chavez works incessantly to build up the membership of his union. In spring 1965, the NFWA organizes its first strike, against the rose growers. On September 16, the association joins a strike against the grape growers in the Delano area. Twelve hundred workers join the strike on the first day. The Delano Grape Strike lasts five years. NFWA begins a grape boycott in the months of November and December. Members follow grape trucks and set up picket lines wherever grapes are sold.

1966: To draw interest in the farmworkers' cause, Chavez and strikers from the NFWA and AWOC embark on a 340-mile pilgrimage from Delano to the steps of the capitol in Sacramento in March and April. Organizers of the NFWA devise "El Plan de Delano" (The Plan of Delano) to outline the rights of farmworkers. During the march, and four months into the grape boycott, Schenley Vineyards signs a contract with the NFWA. It's the first between a grower and a farmworker's union in United States history. The NFWA calls a strike and a boycott against DiGiorgio Fruit Corp. that lasts from the spring to the summer. The union forces the grower to hold an election among its workers. In response, the company brings in the Teamsters to oppose Chavez's NFWA. The NFWA and AWOC decide to merge and create the United Farm Workers Association (UFWA), and DiGiorgio workers vote for the UFWA. During the DiGiorgio struggle, Martin Luther King Jr. sends a telegram to Chavez offering fellowship and goodwill. In it, Dr. King wishes Chavez and his members continuing success in their fight for equality.

1967: The UFWA goes after Giumarra, the largest table-grape grower. Nearly all of Giumarra's workers join in the strike, but many workers return to the field days later. The UFWA then imposes a boycott of Giumarra products, but when the boycott begins to become effective, Giumarra changes its labeling. The UFWA decides to boycott all California table grapes.

1968: In February, after several discouraged strikers begin to contemplate the use of violence against growers, Chavez embarks on his first fast to encourage his members to adhere to nonviolence. Eight thousand farmworkers as well as Senator Robert F. Kennedy attend a mass to break Chavez's twenty-five-day fast. Kennedy gives Chavez a piece of bread and calls him "one of the heroic figures of our time." Six days after the fast ends Robert Kennedy announces his candidacy for the presidency of the United States.

1967–70: The grape boycott is in the international spotlight. Grape strikers spread across North America in an effort to impose an international grape boycott.

1970: Most California table-grape growers sign UFWA contracts in the spring and summer. Chavez calls for a national boycott of lettuce after Salinas Valley growers sign contracts with the Teamsters Union to help keep the UFWA out of the fields. On December 10, the UFWA singles out Bud Antle on the lettuce boycott. Chavez is arrested and jailed for ignoring the injunction prohibiting the UFWA from boycotting him. Coretta Scott King, widow of the Reverend Martin Luther King Jr., and Ethel Kennedy, widow of Robert Kennedy, pay Chavez a visit in jail.

1971: UFWA membership grows to eighty thousand. Headquarters for the union moves to La Paz, in Keene, California.

1972: The UFWA becomes an independent affiliate of the AFL-CIO. The UFWA turns into the United Farm Workers of America (UFWA). To avoid a possible attack by the UFWA, the American Farm Bureau Federation, along with other grower organizations and extreme right-wing groups, start legislation in California and other states outlawing boycotting and strikes at harvest time, and setting up election procedures geared to allow only a few people to decide whether a union will be welcome. Bills are passed in Kansas, Idaho, and Arizona. Between May 11 and June 4, Chavez fasts in Phoenix to protest the recent legislation.

1973: Rather than renew their three-year contract with the UFWA, table-grape growers sign contracts in the spring and summer with the Teamsters without an election. In the Coachella and San Joaquin valleys, thousands of grape workers begin a three-month strike. Strikers are arrested, beaten, and shot for violating antipicketing injunctions. To prevent further violence, Chavez calls off the strike and begins a second grape boycott.

1973–75: A Louis Harris poll shows that millions of Americans are boycotting grapes, Gallo wine, and lettuce. In June 1975 growers agree to a state law guaranteeing California farmworkers the right to organize and bargain with their employers. Chavez gets the Agricultural Labor Relations Act through the state legislation once Jerry Brown becomes governor. In the mid-to-late seventies, the UFWA wins the majority of the elections it participates in. It signs contacts with a large number of growers. The Teamsters Union signs a "jurisdictional" agreement with the UFWA, agreeing to leave the fields.

1978: The UFWA calls off its boycotts of grapes, Gallo wine, and lettuce.

1979: From January to October, the UFWA continues to strike growers to negotiate better wages and benefits. Striker Rufino Contreras is shot dead in a lettuce field by a foreman. Chavez delivers Contreras's eulogy. In the early eighties, with the aid of one million dollars in growers' contributions, George Deukmejian is elected governor of California.

1983–90: Governor Deukmejian stops enforcing California's farm labor law. As a result, thousands of farmworkers lose their UFWA contracts and their jobs. In 1983 worker René López is shot after voting in a Union election. In 1984 Chavez declares a third grape boycott. To make the public aware of pesticide poisoning of grape workers and their children, he launches the "Wrath of Grapes" campaign. Between July and August 1988, Chavez, at the age of sixty-one, embarks on his last and longest fast, for thirty-six days. In the early nineties, he continues the third grape boycott.

1992: Chavez and the UFWA's vice president, Arturo Rodriguez, lead vineyard walkouts from the spring to the summer in the Coachella and San Joaquin valleys. With the help of the walkout, grape workers win their first industry-wide pay hike in eight years.

April 23, 1993: Chavez dies in his sleep. On April 29, forty thousand mourners march behind Chavez's pine casket in Delano.

1994: On the anniversary of Chavez's passing, UFWA president Arturo Rodriguez leads a march retracing Chavez's pilgrimage from Delano to Sacramento. Seventeen thousand farmworkers join on the steps of the state capitol to kick off another UFWA contract-negotiating campaign. On August 8, President Bill Clinton presents the Medal of Freedom, America's highest civilian honor, to Cesar Chavez posthumously. Helen Chavez receives the medal at a White House ceremony.

A Note on the Text

Cesar Chavez's papers are housed in the Farm Workers Archive, Walter P. Reuther Library, College of Urban, Labor and Metropolitan Affairs, Wayne State University, in Detroit, Michigan. A vast number of boxes containing letters, speeches, interviews, and news clippings chronicle his quest for justice and self-determination. Additional material is found in the San Joaquin Valley Farm Workers Collection, Special Collections Department, Fresno State University Library, in Fresno, California. The selections in this volume come from disparate sources, predominantly periodicals, anthologies, and transcriptions at the archives. I benefited substantially from the archival and editorial research in *The Words of Cesar Chavez*, edited by Richard J. Jensen and John C. Hammerback (Texas A&M University Press, 2002). All speeches, notes, letters, interviews, and other writings are the property of the Cesar E. Chavez Foundation, with the exception of those listed below. Grateful acknowledgement is made for permission to reprint the material:

"Marcher," an interview with Cesar Chavez by Daniel Chasan, first published in *The New Yorker*, May 27, 1967. Used by permission of Daniel Jack Chasen.

"Sharing the Wealth," by Cesar Chavez, first published in *Playboy*, January 1970. Used by permission of *Playboy Enterprises, Inc.*

"Forty Acres," by Cesar Chavez, first published as the introduction to *Forty Acres: Cesar Chavez and the Farm Workers*, by Mark Day. New York: Praeger, 1971. Used by permission of Greenwood Publisher Group, Inc.

xliv   A NOTE ON THE TEXT

This edition would not have been possible without Elda Rotor at Penguin Classics, New York, whose rigorous attention carried the manuscript through the editorial process. Paul E. Parks, Esq., vice president and general counsel of the Cesar E. Chavez Foundation, has been a friend and supporter for years. His help in procuring the rights for the material is invaluable. Kathleen Schmeling, Interim Associate Director of the Walter P. Reuther Library, College of Urban, Labor and Metropolitan Affairs, at Wayne State University, expeditiously responded to my queries. As always, I benefited from the advice of my friends Verónica Albin, Harold Augenbraum, Martín Carrera, Martín Espada, and Luis Leal. Bobbie Helinski and Elizabeth Eddy at Amherst College helped with secretarial work, Xeroxes, and permissions. My student assistants Adriana Fazzano and Rachel S. Edelman provided invaluable research and critical perspective.

The Cesar E. Chavez Foundation is located at 500 North Brand Boulevard, Suite 1650, Glendale, California 91203. Visit www.ChavezFoundation.org.

A final word about accent marks in Cesar Chavez's name. César Chávez carries accents in Spanish but not in English. Bibliographical listings are inconsistent in their usage. Since this volume is meant primarily for an American audience, I've eliminated the accents. In the section of Suggestions for Further Reading, I've only used them in a reference if that is the original author's intent.

An Organizer's Tale

We Shall Overcome

Published in El Malcriado *on September 16, 1965, Mexican Independence Day. Chavez's National Farm Workers Association joined with the Agricultural Workers Organizing Committee in the Delano Grape Strike. The Delano Grape Strike lasted five years and had an impact on the table grape industry, bringing fair wages to farmworkers through collective bargaining.*

In a 400-square-mile area halfway between Selma and Weedpatch, California, a general strike of farm workers has been going on for six weeks. The Filipinos, under AWOC AFL-CIO, began the strike for a $1.40 per hour guarantee and a union contract. They were joined by the independent Farm Workers Association, which has a membership of several thousand Mexican Americans.

Filipino, Mexican American and Puerto Rican workers have been manning picket lines daily for 41 days in a totally non-violent manner. Ranchers in the area, which include DiGiorgio Fruit, Schenley, and many independent growers, did not take the strike seriously at first. By the second or third week, however, they began taking another look and striking back. Mechanized agriculture began picketing the pickets, spraying them with sulfur, running tractors by them to create dust storms, building barricades of farm machinery so that scabs could not see the pickets. These actions not only increased the determination of the strikers, but convinced some of the scabs that the ranchers were, in fact, less than human. Scabs quit work and the strike grew.

The growers hired security guards for $43 a day. They began driving their Thunderbirds, equipped with police dogs and rifles, up and down the roads. The people made more picket signs, drew in their belts, and kept marching.

Production was down 30 percent and the growers began looking for more and more scabs. They went to Fresno and Bakersfield and Los Angeles to find them. They didn't tell the workers that they would be scab crews. The pickets followed them into every town and formed ad hoc strike committees to prevent scabbing. They succeeded in these towns. Within two weeks, only one bus, with half a dozen winos escorted by a pearl gray Cadillac, drove into the strike zone. A new plan was formed. The ranchers would advertise in South Texas and Old Mexico. They bring these workers in buses and the workers are held in debt to the rancher before they even arrive in town. We have a new and more difficult task ahead of us with these scabs.

As our strike has grown, workers have matured and now know why and how to fight for their rights. As the strike has grown into a movement for justice by the lowest paid workers in America, friends of farm workers have begun to rally in support of *La Causa*. Civil rights, church, student and union groups help with food and money.

We believe that this is the beginning of a significant drive to achieve equal rights for agricultural workers. In order to enlist your full support and to explain our work to you, I would like to bring some of our pickets and meet with you.

On the NFWA

At the beginning of the Delano Grape Strike, Chavez was hard at work garnering public support for the NFWA and the AWOC. In December 1965, he addressed a statewide meeting of the Student Nonviolent Coordination Committee as a part of that effort, speaking on his experiences in community organizing. The speech was published in Movement.

I have been asked to discuss some of my thoughts on community organizing. Labor organizing, as I know it, has a lot of community organizing in it. When you read of labor organizing in this country you can say there is a point where labor "is organized." But in community organizing there never is a point where you can say "it is organized."

In community organizing you need a continuous program that meets the needs of the people in the organization. I have seen many groups attempt community organization and many have failed. The biggest reason for this is that there is a big emphasis on meetings and discussion and writing up programs and not on working with the people. Many organizers get lost in the shuffle of going to meetings, and somehow those who are being organized are lost. Too often we see as a remedy to this, people suggesting that you should have a survey or a study made.

Anyone who has done any community organizing would agree with me that you can't have a program until you have the people organized. I don't mean you have to wait until you're fully organized, but how can you write a program without the participation of those you are trying to organize?

Community organization is very difficult. You can't put it in the freezer for a couple of years and then thaw it out and you're in business again. Or even a month. Community organization can disintegrate right from under you. This is why we see so many other kinds of groups—church and labor—and so few community organizations formed.

There are a lot of different ideas of what community organization is. When I think of a community, I think not of Fresno, but of Negroes or Mexican Americans or poor workers.

BUILDING POWER

Anyone who thinks they can organize a community and then join with the power structure is in for an awful surprise. And a disappointment because things don't happen that way. When you speak of community organization you are also speaking, really, of power. If you haven't the power to do things, you're not going to do anything. Some organizers I know say, "All I need is a good public relations man." This is a lot of nonsense. The only PR the opposition knows is power, and having the power to strike him where it hurts him, political and economic. You're building power based not on the prestige of your group, but on how many actual bodies you have with you and how many bodies can be united and directed. In many cases community organizations have been started just because there was money available to have them started. This is another real problem in getting something permanent.

MONEY

I was in CSO for many years. In some ways we were successful, but in one of the most important aspects we were a complete failure, and this was in getting the group to generate its own finances so it becomes permanent. I remember many times stopping organizing so we could go organize another part of the community to raise money. In most cases when you get money, though this varies in degree, you have some strings attached. We got a lot of money for CSO and we made very clear to the donors that there could be no strings attached.

But there's always one string attached—that is when people give money, they expect miracles. Then your staff or Executive Board starts compromising between a well-thought-out long-range program and something that will show immediate progress.

WHAT IS AN ORGANIZER?

When there's another problem, people say, "I'm just an organizer." An organizer is an outsider in many cases—there's nothing wrong in that. But then he assumes a sort of special position in that program. If you organize a good group, pretty soon you find yourself hoping, "I wish I had a vote in this outfit."

If you're going to do community organizing, you'll find out in the course of doing your job, some of the good people and some of the bad people invariably get hurt.

Another problem is respectability. If a minority group does "nice" things, like taking a petition to the Mayor, or having tea parties with the PTA, it's going to become respectable. And once you become a respectable group, you're not going to fight anymore. I've had a lot of experience in that. So if your group is going to City Hall or the Police Department and fight with the Police Chief, and someone on your Executive Board is friends with him, you're going to think twice before attacking him.

If an organizer comes looking for appreciation he might as well stay home. He's not going to get any, especially out of a group that's never been organized or had any power before.

In the Association, to get 100 members, we had a heck of a time. When we were over that, some joined. It wasn't because an organizer or an officer told him to join, but because another worker was right beside him in the fields telling him about it. So if you get a small group, they become the organizers. The only way I know is to spend an awful lot of time with each individual—hours and hours—until he understands and you've got him going.

HOW NFWA BEGAN

It was a major decision for me to leave Los Angeles and the CSO. CSO was the only organization I had ever known; it was my whole world. So it was difficult to quit and go out on my own. To go a little further back:

I was working in the fields when CSO came to San Jose. I was in the orchards, apricots and peaches. I talked to their organizer, Fred Ross, and the first thing I asked him was "How is the CSO going to help the farmworker?" And he told me—if we get strong enough, we're going to build a union. And I said, "That's for me." And of course I had a lot of hatred for the cops and that was one of the main issues of CSO in LA.

And so it was just perfect for me; I was learning a lot of things. But after a while, it was growing too fast, and it was making a name for itself, and it was attracting a lot of people who were not farm workers, but who were semiprofessional and professional Mexican Americans. It developed a verbal commitment to farm workers, but no action, just legislation.

BEST MOTEL IN TOWN

There were other problems. It was unheard of that CSO would meet in a room like this (a meeting room in a low-rent housing project). It had to meet in the best motel in town, very expensive, and it cut off all the farm workers who couldn't afford to be there. The reason given was—we have to build prestige. The politicians have to know who we are; we can't take them to a dump. We have to take them to the best place in town and then we can relate to them about farm workers. I was naive about farm workers. I was naive enough in the beginning to buy that.

So we ended up just with farm workers who had gone to school or who weren't farm workers anymore. They just thought that going to school gave them the right to be leaders—which incidentally isn't the case; I'll debate that with anyone.

OUT OF TOUCH

Pretty soon we developed conflict between the people with problems in the cities, whether to help them or the farm workers. Then somehow we got messed up with programs that meant little or nothing to the worker. For example—legislation. Too remote. The farm worker isn't trained to understand the processes of government, so having a big fight for unemployment insurance or a minimum wage [he or she] had no idea how laws were made.

We'd constantly get into situations where we'd explain about legislation and a guy would get up in the back and say, "I've been a farm worker all my life. This is a lot of nonsense. Let's go directly to the President." Or "The Governor should issue a statement saying we should get paid more." And we'd have to explain that the Governor couldn't do that; and we lost him.

Or, when the officers of CSO were semiprofessional or professional it became a problem of communicating with the workers. In most cases the leadership had more to lose than the workers; they'd say, "We should fight, but we should be moderate."

SPLIT

We couldn't get them to organize a union—they felt that farm workers were outside the jurisdiction of CSO—it was a "labor" problem. Some of us in the movement felt the only way to get it was to force the issue and if we lost move out and create a group that would serve only farm workers. We felt if we had nothing but farm workers in their own group, a lot of ills we had known in CSO would not be present.

So in April 1962 I moved out of LA and came down to Delano. A lot of people have asked me—why Delano, and the answer is simple, I had no money. My wife's family lived there, and I have a brother [in Delano]. And I thought if things go very bad we can always go and have a meal there. Any place in the Valley would have made no difference.

I had some ideas of what should be done. No great plans; just that it would take an awful lot of work and also that it was a gamble. If I can't organize them to a point where they can carry on their own group, then I'm finished, I can't do it, I'd move on and do something else.

I went around for about eleven months, and I went to about eighty-seven communities and labor camps and in each place I'd find a few people who were committed to doing something; something had happened in their lives and they were ready for it. So we went around to the towns, played the percentages, and came off with a group.

FIRST MEETING

We had a convention here in Fresno, the first membership meeting, to set up a union—about 230 people from as many as 65 places. We knew the hardest thing would be to put across a program that would make them want to pay the $3.50 (monthly dues), because we were dependent on that. I felt that organizing couldn't be done on outside money.

We had signed up about 1,100 people. The first month 211 paid. At the end of three months we had 10 people paying. Talk about being scared! But we went back and kept at it. By this time Dolores (Huerta) was helping me up in the northern part of the Valley, and I was getting help from Gilbert Padilla, both of whom are Vice Presidents now. Gradually the membership was increasing.

At the end of six months we were up to about two hundred members. Instead of going all over the Valley as I did at first, I started staying in one place long enough for them to get in touch with me if they wanted to. We put a lot of emphasis on the people getting members.

HOUSE MEETINGS

We had hundreds of house meetings. Sometimes two or three would come, sometimes none. Sometimes even the family that called the house meeting would not be there.

I wasn't trying to prove anything to a board or a grant. I don't think it would have worked. In the first place, I had to get the dues in order to eat. I suspect some of the members were paying dues because they felt sorry for me.

A guy who's paid his dues for a year or three years has a stake in the Association. In CSO if I was making a report, and there were five people in the room and I mentioned four of them, the fifth would take off—it's very sensitive. We never got any arguments, any debate in CSO. Here there are a lot of questions about how the money is spent. It should be that way.

At the beginning of the strike we had $85 in the treasury. We had the problem of people going out on strike and having no way to support them. So we had a big drive to get workers to go outside the area to work so they wouldn't be strikebreakers.

ROLE OF ORGANIZER

The organizer has to work more than anyone else in that group. Almost no one in a group is totally committed. And in the initial part of the movement there's the fear that when the organizer leaves, the movement will collapse. So you have to be able to say, I'm not going to be here a year, or six months, but an awful long time. So until when they get rid of me, they'll have leaders to do it themselves.

A Penitential Procession

Written in March 1966. As a part of the grape boycott, the NFWA organized a 250-mile march from Delano to Sacramento in 1966. The march signified the union's growing power and the growers' waxing fear of the union. The march took on the spirituality of a pilgrimage, attracting a great deal of attention and sympathy for farmworkers. This selection was reprinted in César Chávez: The Rhetoric of Nonviolence *by Winthrop Yinger.*

In the "March from Delano to Sacramento" there is a meeting of cultures and traditions; the centuries-old religious tradition of Spanish culture conjoins with the very contemporary cultural syndromes of "demonstration" springing from the spontaneity of the poor, the downtrodden, the rejected, the discriminated-against baring visibly their need and demand for equality and freedom.

In every religious orientated culture "the pilgrimage" has had a place, a trip made with sacrifice and hardship as an expression of penance and of commitment—and often involving a petition to the patron of the pilgrimage for some sincerely sought benefit of body or soul. Pilgrimage has not passed from Mexican culture. Daily at any of the major shrines of the country, and in particular at the Basilica of the Lady of Guadalupe, there arrive pilgrims from all points—some of whom may have long since walked-out the pieces of rubber tire that once served them as soles, and many of whom will walk on their knees the last mile or so of the pilgrimage. Many of the "pilgrims" of Delano will have walked such pilgrimages themselves in their lives—perhaps as very small children even; and cling to the memory of the day-long marches, the camps at night, streams forded, hills climbed, the sacral aura of the sanctuary and the "fiesta" that followed.

But throughout the Spanish-speaking world there is another tradition that touches the present march, that of the Lenten penitential processions, where the penitentes would march through the streets, often in sack cloth and ashes, some even carrying crosses as a sign of penance for their sins, and as a plea for the mercy of God. The penitential procession is also in the blood of the Mexican American, and the Delano march will therefore be one of penance—public penance for the sins of the strikers, their own personal sins as well as their yielding perhaps to feelings of hatred and revenge in the strike itself. They hope by the march to set themselves at peace with the Lord, so that the justice of their cause will be purified of all lesser motivation.

These two great traditions of a great people meet in the Mexican American with the belief that Delano is his "cause," his great demand for justice, freedom, and respect from a predominantly foreign cultural community in a land where he was first. The revolutions of Mexico were primarily uprisings of the poor, fighting for bread and for dignity. The Mexican American is also a child of the revolution.

Pilgrimage, penance, and revolution. The pilgrimage from Delano to Sacramento has strong religio-cultural overtones. But it is also the pilgrimage of a cultural minority who have suffered from a hostile environment, and a minority who means business.

The Plan of Delano

Published in El Malcriado, *March 17, 1966. The "Plan de Delano" was a long-considered series of actions that outlined the NFWA's goals for the Delano Grape Strike. Coauthored by Chavez and Dolores Huerta, with help from playwright Luis Valdez, the Plan traced the roots of* La Causa *to the Mexican Revolution.*

PLAN for the liberation of the Farm Workers associated with the Delano Grape Strike in the State of California, seeking social justice in farm labor with those reforms that they believe necessary for their well-being as workers in these United States.

We the undersigned, gathered in Pilgrimage to the capital of the State in Sacramento in penance for all the failings of Farm Workers, as free and sovereign men, do solemnly declare before the civilized world which judges our actions, and before the nation to which we belong, the propositions we have formulated to end the injustice that oppresses us.

We are conscious of the historical significance of our Pilgrimage. It is clearly evident that our path travels through a valley well known to all Mexican farm workers. We know all of these towns of Delano, Madera, Fresno, Modesto, Stockton, and Sacramento, because along this very same road, in this very same valley, the Mexican race has sacrificed itself for the last hundred years. Our sweat and our blood have fallen on this land to make other men rich. This Pilgrimage is a witness to the suffering we have seen for generations.

The Penance we accept symbolizes the suffering we shall have in order to bring justice to these same towns, to this same valley. The Pilgrimage we make symbolizes the long historical road we have traveled in this valley alone, and the long road we have yet to travel, with much penance, in order to bring about the Revolution we need, and for which we present the propositions in the following PLAN:

1. This is the beginning of a social movement in fact and not in pronouncements. We seek our basic, God-given rights as human beings. Because we have suffered—and are not afraid to suffer—in order to survive. We are ready to give up everything, even our lives in our fight for social justice. We shall do it without violence because that is our destiny. To the ranchers, and to all those who oppose us, we say, in the words of Benito Juárez, "EL RESPETO AL DERECHO AJENO ES LA PAZ." Respect for others brings peace.

2. We seek the support of all political groups and protection of the government, which is also our government, in our struggle. For too many years we have been treated like the lowest of the low. Our wages and working conditions have been determined from above, because irresponsible legislators who could have helped us, have supported the rancher's argument that the plight of the Farm Worker was a "special case." They saw the obvious effects of an unjust system, starvation wages, contractors, day hauls, forced migration, sickness, illiteracy, camps, and subhuman living conditions, and acted is if they were irremediable causes. The farm worker has been abandoned to his own fate— without representation, without power—subject to mercy and caprice of the rancher. We are tired of words, of betrayals, of indifference. To the politicians we say that the years are gone when the farm worker said nothing and did nothing to help himself. From this movement shall spring leaders who shall understand us, lead us, be faithful to us, and we shall elect them to represent us. WE SHALL BE HEARD.

3. We seek, and have, the support of the Church in what we do. At the head of the Pilgrimage we carry LA VIRGEN DE LA GUADALUPE (the Virgin of Guadalupe) because she is ours, all ours, Patroness of the Mexican people. We also carry the Sacred Cross and the Star of David because we are not sectarians, and because we ask the help and prayers of all religions. All men are brothers—sons of the same God; that is why we say to all men of good will, in the words of Pope Leo XIII, "Everyone's first duty is to protect the workers from the greed of speculators who use human beings as instruments to provide themselves with money. It is neither just nor human to oppress

men with excessive work to the point where their minds become enfeebled and their bodies worn out." GOD SHALL NOT ABANDON US.

4. We are suffering. We have suffered, and we are not afraid to suffer in order to win our cause. We have suffered unnumbered ills and crimes in the name of the law of the land. Our men, women, and children have suffered not only the basic brutality of stoop labor, and the most obvious injustices of the system; they have also suffered the desperation of knowing that that system caters to the greed of callous men and not to our needs. Now we will suffer for the purpose of ending the poverty, the misery, and the injustice, with the hope that our children will not be exploited as we have been. They have imposed hungers on us, and now we hunger for justice. We draw our strength from the very despair in which we have been forced to live. WE SHALL ENDURE.

5. We shall unite. We have learned the meaning of UNITY. We know why these United States are just that—united. The strength of the poor is also in union. We know that the poverty of the Mexican or Filipino worker in California is the same as that of all farm workers across the country, the Negroes and poor whites, the Puerto Ricans, Japanese, and Arabians; in short, all of the races that comprise the oppressed minorities of the United States. The majority of the people on our Pilgrimage are of Mexican descent, but the triumph of our race depends on a national association of all farm workers. The ranchers want to keep us divided in order to keep us weak. Many of us have signed individual "work contracts" with the ranchers or contractors, contracts in which they had all the power. These contracts were farces, one more cynical joke at our impotence. That is why we must get together and bargain collectively. We must use the only strength that we have, the force of our numbers. The ranchers are few; we are many. UNITED WE SHALL STAND.

6. We will strike. We shall pursue the REVOLUTION we have proposed. We are sons of the Mexican Revolution, a revolution of the poor seeking bread and justice. Our revolution will not be armed, but we want the existing social order to dissolve; we want a new social order. We are poor, we are humble, and our

only choice is to strike in those ranches where we are not treated with the respect we deserve as working men, where our rights as free and sovereign men are not recognized. We do not want the paternalism of the rancher, we do not want the contractor; we do not want charity at the price our dignity. We want to be equal with all the working men in the nation; we want a just wage, better working conditions, a decent future for our children. To those who oppose us, be they ranchers, police, politicians, or speculators, we say that we are going to continue fighting until we die, or we win. WE SHALL OVERCOME.

Across the San Joaquin Valley, across California, across the entire Southwest of the United States, wherever there are Mexican people, wherever there are farm workers, our movement is spreading like flames across a dry plain. Our PILGRIMAGE is the MATCH that will light our cause for all farm workers to see what is happening here, so that they may do as we have done. The time has come for the liberation of the poor farm workers.

History is on our side.

MAY THE STRIKE GO ON! VIVA LA CAUSA!

An Organizer's Tale

Written in July 1966. Chavez describes how he rose to the challenge of labor organizing, coming to terms with what it means to be a leader of a marginalized group.

It really started for me 16 years ago in San Jose, California, when I was working on an apricot farm. We figured he was just another social worker doing a study of farm conditions, and I kept refusing to meet with him. But he was persistent. Finally, I got together some of the rough element in San Jose. We were going to have a little reception for him to teach the gringo a little bit of how we felt. There were about 30 of us in the house, young guys mostly. I was supposed to give them a signal—change my cigarette from my right hand to my left—and then we were going to give him a lot of hell. But he started talking and the more he talked, the more wide-eyed I became and the less inclined I was to give the signal. A couple of guys who were pretty drunk at the time still wanted to give the gringo the business, but we got rid of them. This fellow was making a lot of sense, and I wanted to hear what he had to say.

His name was Fred Ross, and he was an organizer for the Community Service Organization (CSO) which was working with Mexican Americans in the cities. I became immediately really involved. Before long I was heading a voter registration drive. All the time I was observing the things Fred did, secretly, because I wanted to learn how to organize, to see how it was done. I was impressed with his patience and understanding of people. I thought this was a tool, one of the greatest things he had.

It was pretty rough for me at first. I was changing and had to take a lot of ridicule from the kids my age, the rough characters I worked with in the fields. They would say, "Hey, big shot. Now that you're a *politico*, why are you working here for 65 cents an hour?" I might add that our neighborhood had the highest percentage of San Quentin graduates. It was a game among the *pachucos* in the sense that we defended ourselves from outsiders, although inside the neighborhood there was not a lot of fighting.

After six months of working every night in San Jose, Fred assigned me to take over the CSO chapter in Decoto. It was a tough spot to fill. I would suggest something, and people would say, "No, let's wait till Fred gets back," or "Fred wouldn't do it that way." This is pretty much a pattern with people, I discovered, whether I was put in Fred's position, or later, when someone else was put in my position. After the Decoto assignment I was sent to start a new chapter in Oakland. Before I left, Fred came to a place in San Jose called the Hole-in-the-Wall and we talked for half an hour over coffee. He was in a rush to leave, but I wanted to keep him talking; I was that scared of my assignment.

Those were hard times in Oakland. First of all, it was a big city and I'd get lost every time I went anywhere. Then I arranged a series of house meetings. I would get to the meeting early and drive back and forth past the house, too nervous to go in and face the people. Finally I would force myself to go inside and sit in a corner. I was quite thin then, and young, and most of the people were middle-aged. Someone would say, "Where's the organizer?" And I would pipe up, "Here I am." Then they would say in Spanish— these were very poor people and we hardly spoke anything but Spanish—"Ha! This *kid*?" Most of them said they were interested, but the hardest part was to get them to start pushing themselves, on their own initiative.

The idea was to set up a meeting and then get each attending person to call his own house meeting, inviting new people—a sort of chain letter effect. After a house meeting I would lie awake going over the whole thing, playing the tape back, trying to see why people laughed at one point, or why they were for one thing and against another. I was also learning to read and write, those late evenings. I had left school in the 7th grade after attending 67 different schools, and my reading wasn't the best.

At our first organizing meeting we had 368 people: I'll never forget it because it was very important to me. You eat your heart out; the meeting is called for 7 o'clock and you start to worry about 4. You wait. Will they show up? Then the first one arrives. By 7 there are only 20 people; you have everything in order, you have to look calm. But little by little they filter in and at a certain point you know it will be a success.

After four months in Oakland, I was transferred. The chapter was beginning to move on its own, so Fred assigned me to organize the San Joaquin Valley. Over the months I developed what I used to call schemes or tricks—now I call them techniques—of making initial contacts. The main thing in convincing someone is to spend time with him. It doesn't matter if he can read, write or even speak well. What is important is that he is a man and, second, that he has shown some initial interest. One good way to develop leadership is to take a man with you in your car. And it works a lot better if you're doing the driving; that way you are in charge. You drive, he sits there, and you talk. These little things were very important to me; I was caught in a big game by then, figuring out what makes people work. I found that if you work hard enough you can usually shake people into working too, those who are concerned. You work harder and they work harder still, up to a point and then they pass you. Then, of course, they're on their own.

I also learned to keep away from the established groups and so-called leaders, and to guard against philosophizing. Working with low-income people is very different from working with the professionals, who like to sit around talking about how to play politics. When you're trying to recruit a farm worker, you have to paint a little picture, and then you have to color the picture in. We found out that the harder a guy is to convince, the better leader or member he becomes. When you exert yourself to convince him, you have his confidence and he has good motivation. A lot of people who say OK right away wind up hanging around the office, taking up the workers' time.

During the McCarthy era in one Valley town, I was subjected to a lot of redbaiting. We had been recruiting people for citizenship classes at the high school when we got into a quarrel with the naturalization examiner. He was rejecting people on the grounds that they were just parroting what they learned in citizenship class. One day we had a meeting about it in Fresno, and I took along some of the leaders of our local chapter. Some redbaiting official gave us a hard time, and the people got scared and took his side. They did it because it seemed easy at the moment, even though they knew that sticking with me was the right thing to do. It was disgusting. When we left the building they walked by themselves ahead of me as if I had some kind of communicable disease. I had been working with these people for three months and I was very sad to see that. It taught me a great lesson.

That night I learned that the chapter officers were holding a meeting to review my letters and printed materials to see if I really was a Communist. So I drove out there and walked right in on their meeting. I said, "I hear you've been discussing me, and I thought it would be nice if I was here to defend myself. Not that it matters that much to you or even to me, because as far as I'm concerned you are a bunch of cowards." At that they began to apologize. "Let's forget it," they said. "You're a nice guy."

But I didn't want apologies. I wanted a full discussion. I told them I didn't give a damn, but that they had to learn to distinguish fact from what appeared to be a fact because of fear. I kept them there till two in the morning. Some of the women cried. I don't know if they investigated me any further, but I stayed on another few months and things worked out.

This was not an isolated case. Often when we'd leave people to themselves they would get frightened and draw back into their shells where they had been all the years. And I learned quickly that there is no real appreciation. Whatever you do, and no matter what reasons you may give to others, you do it because you want to see it done, or maybe because you want power. And there shouldn't be any appreciation, understandably. I know good organizers who were destroyed, washed out, because they expected people to appreciate what they'd done. Anyone who comes in with the idea that farm workers are free of sin and that the growers are all bastards either has never dealt with the situation or is an idealist of the first order. Things don't work that way.

For more than 10 years I worked for the CSO. As the organization grew, we found ourselves meeting in fancier and fancier motels and holding expensive conventions. Doctors, lawyers and politicians began joining. They would get elected to some office in the organization and then, for all practical purposes, leave. Intent on using the CSO for their own prestige purposes, these "leaders," many of them, lacked the urgency we had to have. When I became general director I began to press for a program to organize farm workers into a union, an idea most of the leadership opposed. So

I started a revolt within the CSO. I refused to sit at the head table at meetings, refused to wear a suit and tie, and finally I even refused to shave and cut my hair. It used to embarrass some of the professionals.

At every meeting I got up and gave my standard speech: We shouldn't meet in fancy motels, we were getting away from the people, farm workers had to be organized. But nothing happened. In March of '62 I resigned and came to Delano to begin organizing the Valley on my own.

I drew a map of all the towns between Arvin and Stockton—86 of them, including farming camps—and decided to hit them all to get a small nucleus of people working in each. For six months I traveled around, planting an idea. We had a simple questionnaire, a little card with space for name, address and how much the worker thought he ought to be paid. My wife, Helen, mimeographed them, and we took our kids for two- or three-day jaunts to these towns, distributing the cards door-to-door and to camps and groceries.

Some 80,000 cards were sent back from eight Valley counties. I got a lot of contacts that way, but I was shocked at the wages the people were asking. The growers were paying $1 and $1.15, and maybe 95 percent of the people thought they should be getting only $1.25. Sometimes people scribbled messages on the cards: "I hope to God we win" or "Do you think we can win?" or "I'd like to know more." So I separated the cards with the pencilled notes, got in my car and went to those people.

We didn't have any money at all in those days, none for gas and hardly any for food. So I went to people and started asking for food. It turned out to be about the best thing I could have done, although at first it's hard on your pride. Some of our best members came in that way. If people give you their food, they'll give you their hearts. Several months and many meetings later we had a working organization, and this time the leaders were the people.

None of the farm workers had collective bargaining contracts, and I thought it would take ten years before we got that first contract. I wanted desperately to get some color into the movement, to give people something they could identify with, like a flag. I was reading some books about how various leaders discovered what colors contrasted and stood out the best. The Egyptians had found that a red field with a white circle and a black emblem in the center crashed into your eyes like nothing else. I wanted to use the Aztec eagle in the center, as on the Mexican flag. So I told my cousin Manuel, "Draw an Aztec eagle." Manuel had a little trouble with it, so we modified the eagle to make it easier for people to draw.

The first big meeting of what we decided to call the National Farm Workers Association was held in September 1962, at Fresno, with 287 people. We had our huge red flag on the wall, with paper tacked over it. When the time came, Manuel pulled a cord ripping the paper off the flag and all of a sudden it hit the people. Some of them wondered if it was a Communist flag, and I said it probably looked more like a neo-Nazi emblem than anything else. But they wanted an explanation, so Manuel got up and said, "When that damn eagle flies—that's when the farm workers' problems are going to be solved."

One of the first things I decided was that outside money wasn't going to organize people, at least not in the beginning. I even turned down a grant from a private group—$50,000 to go directly to organize farm workers—for just this reason. Even when there are no strings attached, you are still compromised because you feel you have to produce immediate results. This is bad, because it takes a long time to build a movement, and your organization suffers if you get too far ahead of the people it belongs to. We set the dues at $42 a year per family, really meaningful dues, but of the 212 families we got to pay, only 12 remained by June of '63. We were discouraged at that, but not enough to make us quit.

Money was always a problem. Once we were facing a $180 gas bill on a credit card I'd got a long time ago and was about to lose. And we *had* to keep that credit card.

One day my wife and I were picking cotton, pulling bolls, to make a little money to live on. Helen said to me, "Do you put all this in the bag, or just the cotton?" I thought she was kidding and told her to throw the whole boll in so that she had nothing but a sack of bolls at the weighing.

The man said, "Whose sack is this?" I said, well, my wife's, and he told us we were fired. "Look at all that crap you brought in," he said.

Helen and I started laughing. We were going anyway. We took

the $4 we had earned and spent it at a grocery store where they
were giving away a $100 prize. Each time you shopped they'd give
you one of the letters of M-O-N-E-Y or a flag: you had to have
M-O-N-E-Y plus the flag to win. Helen had already collected the
letters and just needed the flag. Anyway they gave her the ticket.
She screamed, "A flag? I don't believe it," ran in and got the $100.
She said, "Now we're going to eat steak." But I said no, we're
going to pay the gas bill. I don't know if she cried, but I think
she did.

It was rough in those early years. Helen was having babies and I
was not there when she was at the hospital. But if you haven't got
your wife behind you, you can't do many things. There's got to be
peace at home. So I did, I think, a fairly good job of organizing
her. When we were kids, she lived in Delano and I came to town as
a migrant. Once on a date we had a bad experience about segregation at a movie theater, and I put up a fight. We were together then,
and still are, I think I'm more of a pacifist than she is. Her father,
Febela, was a colonel with Pancho Villa in the Mexican Revolution.
Sometimes she gets angry and tells me, "These scabs—you should
deal with them sternly," and I kid her, "It must be too much of that
Febela blood in you."

The Movement really caught on in '64. By August we had a
thousand members. We'd had a beautiful 90-day drive in Corcoran, where they had the Battle of the Corcoran Farm Camp 30
years ago, and by November we had assets of $25,000 in our
credit union, which helped to stabilize the membership. I had gone
without pay the whole of 1963. The next year the members voted
me a $40-a-week salary, after Helen had to quit working in the
fields to manage the credit union.

Our first strike was in May of '65, a small one but it prepared
us for the big one. A farm worker from McFarland named Epi-
fanio Camacho came to see me. He said he was sick and tired of
how people working the roses were being treated, and was willing
to "go the limit."

I assigned Manuel and Gilbert Padilla to hold meetings at Camacho's house. The people wanted union recognition, but the real
issue, as in most cases when you begin, was wages. They were
promised $9 a thousand, but they were actually getting $6.50 and
$7 for grafting roses. Most of them signed cards giving us the

right to bargain for them. We chose the biggest company, with about 85 employees, not counting the irrigators and supervisors, and we held a series of meetings to prepare the strike and call the vote. There would be no picket line; everyone pledged on their honor not to break the strike.

Early on the first morning of the strike, we sent out 10 cars to check the people's homes. We found lights in five or six homes and knocked on the doors. The men were getting up and we'd say, "Where are you going?" They would dodge. "Oh, uh . . . I was just getting up, you know."

We'd say, "Well, you're not going to work, are you?" And they'd say no. Dolores Huerta, who was driving the green panel truck, saw a light in one house where four rose workers lived. They told her they were going to work, even after she reminded them of their pledge. So she moved the truck so it blocked their driveway, turned off the key, put in it her purse and sat there alone.

That morning the company foreman was madder than hell and refused to talk to us. None of the grafters had shown up for work. At 10:30 we started to go to the company office, but it occurred to us that maybe a woman would have a better chance. So Dolores knocked on the office door, saying, "I'm Dolores Huerta from the National Farm Workers Association."

"Get out!" the man said, "you Communist. Get out!" I guess they were expecting us, because as Dolores stood arguing with him the cops came and told her to leave. She left.

For two days the fields were idle. On Wednesday they recruited a group of Filipinos from out of town who knew nothing of the strike, maybe 35 of them. They drove through escorted by three sheriff's patrol cars, one in front, one in the middle and one at the rear with a dog. We didn't have a picket line, but we parked across the street and just watched them go through, not saying a word. All but seven stopped working after half an hour, and the rest had quit by mid-afternoon.

The company made an offer the evening of the fourth day, a package deal that amounted to a 120 percent wage increase, but no contract. We wanted to hold out for a contract and more benefits, but a majority of the rose workers wanted to accept the offer and go back. We are a democratic union so we had to support what they wanted to do. They had a meeting and voted to settle. Then we had a problem with a few militants who wanted to hold out. We had to convince them to go back to work, as a united front, because otherwise they could be canned. So we worked— Tony Oredain and I, Dolores and Gilbert, Jim Drake and all the organizers—knocking on doors till two in the morning, telling people, "You have to go back or you'll lose your job."

And they did. They worked.

Our second strike, and our last before the big one at Delano, was in the grapes at Martin's Ranch. The people were getting a raw deal there, being pushed around pretty badly. Gilbert went out to the field, climbed on top of a car and took a strike vote. They voted unanimously to go out. Right away they started bringing in strikebreakers, so we launched a tough attack on the labor contractors, distributed leaflets portraying them as really low characters. We attacked one so badly that he just gave up the job, and he took 27 of his men out with him. All he asked was that we distribute another leaflet reinstating him in the community. And we did. What was unusual was that the grower would still talk to us. The grower kept saying, "I can't pay. I just haven't got the money." I guess he must have found the money somewhere, because we were asking $1.40 and we got it.

We had just finished the Martin strike when the Agricultural Workers Organizing Committee (AFL-CIO) started a strike against the grape growers, DiGiorgio, Schenley liquors and small growers, asking $1.40 an hour and 25 cents a box. There was a lot of pressure from our members for us to join the strike, but we had some misgivings. We didn't feel ready for a big strike like this one, one that was sure to last a long time. Having no money—just $87 in the strike fund—meant we'd have to depend on God knows who.

Eight days after the strike started—it takes time to get 1,200 people together from all over the Valley—we held a meeting in Delano and voted to go out. I asked the membership to release us from the pledge not to accept outside money, because we'd need it now, a lot of it. The help came. It started because of the close, and I would say even beautiful, relationship that we've had with the Migrant Ministry for some years. They were the first to come to our rescue, financially and in every other way, and they spread the word to other benefactors.

We had planned, before, to start a labor school in November. It never happened, but we have the best labor school we could ever have, in the strike. The strike is only a temporary condition, however. We have over 3,000 members spread out over a wide area, and we have to service them when they have problems. We get letters from New Mexico, Colorado, Texas, California, from farm workers saying, "We're getting together and we need an organizer."

It kills you when you haven't got the personnel and resources. You feel badly about not sending an organizer because you look back and remember all the difficulty you had in getting two or three people together, and here *they're* together. Of course, we're training organizers, many of them younger than I was when I started in CSO. They can work 20 hours a day, sleep four and be ready to hit it again; when you get to be 39 it's a different story.

The people who took part in the strike and the march have something more than their material interest going for them. If it were only material, they wouldn't have stayed on the strike long enough to win. It is difficult to explain. But it flows out in the ordinary things they say. For instance, some of the younger guys are saying, "Where do you think's going to be the next strike?"

I say, "Well, we have to win in Delano."

They say, "We'll win, but where do we go next?"

I say, "Maybe most of us will be working in the fields."

They say, "No, I don't want to go and work in the fields. I want to organize. There are a lot of people that need our help."

So I say, "You're going to be pretty poor then, because when you strike you don't have much money." They say they don't care much about that.

And others are saying, "I have friends who are working in Texas. If we could only help them."

It is bigger, certainly, than just a strike. And if this spirit grows within the farm labor movement, one day we can use the force that we have to help correct a lot of things that are wrong in this society. But that is for the future. Before you can run, you have to learn to walk.

There are vivid memories from my childhood—what we had to go through because of low wages and the conditions, basically because there was no union. I suppose if I wanted to be fair I could say that I'm trying to settle a personal score. I could dramatize it by saying that I want to bring social justice to farm workers. But the truth is that I went through a lot of hell, and a lot of people did. If we can even the score a little for the workers then we are doing something. Besides, I don't know any other work I like to do better than this. I really don't, you know.

Recapping the Mission

Chavez delivered this speech at Solidarity House, in Lansing, Michigan, on April 1, 1967, as an effort to spread the word of the Delano strike and to foster public sympathy and support for farmworkers.

Brother [Walter] Reuther and friends: I am very happy to be here with you this evening. I'd like to take what time I have to bring to you, at least in part, the story of the strikers in the Delano Area. There is one difficulty in getting up to speak before groups. On one hand, I've had not too much experience and on the other hand I've had some bad experiences with instruments. I've been in jail three times recently as a consequence of the strike and each time I've been in jail because I've been using microphones to talk to scabs in the fields. So every time I get to speak before people and I see these things in front of me, I get somewhat uneasy.

The workers in Delano asked me to be very sure to tell all the members of the U.A.W., Brother Reuther, all of the leadership, how much they sincerely appreciate all of the help that has been given in our efforts to organize in California and Texas. And a little while later I will tell you of some of the specific things that they have done for us. So much help and so many things that I can't begin to tell you everything that has been done for our struggle by the U.A.W. But there are some important things, in my opinion, that should be shared with you.

Have you ever considered land, a lot of land, a lot of free water and a lot of cheap labor. Have you ever considered what this combination can do and is doing in the West? Because of the combination of these three elements, there are growers in California and the western part of this country that are not only rich but are very powerful. These are the growers, these are the people that control and have a say in what legislation is going to be enacted or not going to be enacted especially when it deals with agriculture and with farm labor. And they have been doing this for years. And this is, I suppose, one of the biggest difficulties in organizing workers. It all started seventy or eighty years ago. And it was probably quite by accident that it started this way.

Soon after the railroads had been built, according to history, and there were a lot of Chinese workers that had been laid off the railroads and had gone into the cities of San Francisco and Stockton and Sacramento and other cities waiting for some work, the growers began to develop and use the system which even up to this day they follow. And this is the system of the farm labor contractor. Among the Chinese there were those who were looking ahead and began to recruit workers in San Francisco and bring them into the Valley. We have the same thing even today. But this was the early beginning. Soon after the Chinese had gone to work in the fields and they understood that there was no real future for them, they moved into the cities and began to go into small businesses—restaurants and laundries and so forth.

The growers realizing full well that this was a very good arrangement that they had with the Chinese and wanting to keep that, they went to Japan and made the same arrangement with the Japanese. And after a few years of working, the Japanese began to develop the slow-down, attempts to organize, but they did something else. They went out and bought their own land and they became small growers. And then the growers sent to India for the Indians, but that didn't work out too well. Then they got the Filipino and they worked out very well. And lastly they got the Mexican. The Negro they didn't have to import. He had already been imported many years before. And with the Mexican, we see with the beginning of the Mexican Revolution when thousands of families were fleeing from the conflict there; they came to the States and also were put to work in the fields. And when a lot of people in this group were moving out of agriculture, then they went and devised somehow the infamous Bracero Program. And here they were able, first of all because of the manpower shortages during the Second World War, they were able to keep this program until up to just a few years ago. The exploitation that these workers suffered is something that is very difficult to understand and quite difficult to explain. But while all of these things were taking place there were attempts to organize workers.

And while we sometimes are not fully satisfied with the American labor movement in their attempts to organize workers, we realize that they have made some very valiant attempts. Back in 1913 in Wheatland, California, the hub of the cotton belt, the pickers had a strike. And as we read history, depending on who writes the history, if it is someone who is partial to labor it is usually called a great and glorious strike that failed, that was called by the I.W.W. [Industrial Workers of the World]. On the other hand, if the history was written by someone who was not so partial to labor, then it was a great and a big and nasty riot. And through the years during the first part of the century these attempts persisted and every time the union would start in, every time that workers wanted to organize those attempts were broken and they were never able to succeed.

And we in the union, even before we started to organize, wanted to know really everything that was written and talk to everyone available that had been involved in past strikes and to find out why they had failed so often. No victories. We came up with some parallels as we talked to people, as we read what had been written about the strikes and so forth. We saw some parallels. First of all, that the unions in organizing were trying to do two jobs at once. They were trying to organize on the one hand and they were trying to strike at the very same time. And as you know it's a very big job.

Now it is only so because as farm workers we are excluded from protection of the National Labor Relations Act. We can't go to the employer and say we got 30 percent or 50 percent or 100 percent of the workers signed up and we want you to recognize our union. Or we couldn't go to the Board and ask for an election. We can't do either one. We may have a thousand percent signed but they won't give us that protection. And so while they were trying to strike and organize at the same time, it seemed to us that they were losing that valuable time that must be spent by the organizer to be able to do a real job of developing an understanding, the brotherhood, the solidarity of the workers to be able to stick together. And best of all to be able to understand what the opposition is.

Then, the other problem was that in all the attempts to organize, the ones that we could see, there was the International Union, the C.I.O. [Congress of Industrial Organizations], the

A.F.L. [American Federation of Labor], and the AFL-CIO—[all] came in with great expectations and with some money. And organizing farm workers takes quite a bit of money—thousands and thousands of dollars. And after they had spent the money, they saw that things were not really going any place. The International Unions had to pull out because they had spent more than what they had intended to spend in the first place. On the attempts of the AFL as we see in some attempts back in the mid-thirties, and the CIO had a very large attempt which also failed.

We also saw in examining the failures that in most cases the unions were going out to the fields to organize workers after the workers had revolted. The workers were out on strike—on one of those suicide strikes, and they couldn't put the thing together to hold it, to give it permanence. And we also saw then in most of the reports that the people felt that the union had sold them out and the leaders felt that the people didn't really want a union. And so we had just a number of failures to contend with and we wanted to change that around.

First of all, we were convinced that because of the exclusion from the law and not having that protection, we wanted to convince ourselves that workers really wanted a union this time. They had to show us that they wanted a union, and we had to help them to do that, by their paying for the initial organizing drive. So we began on April 10, 1962, a very small operation called the National Farm Workers Association (NFWA). There was no reference to a union in the name and we were a scab outfit. The AWOC [Agricultural Workers Organizing Committee], under the AFL-CIO, didn't like us at all. We knew that sooner or later we would have to get together with them, but we also knew that we wanted time to try out some ideas we had, basic attempts to see if they would work, and sure enough, as it turned out, now both groups are one and the same. But during those first few years it was a very difficult thing to organize on the one hand and then have to be confronted every time you met someone from the other union and be called a scab. And we saw that workers if they were told what the whole idea was and they were permitted to participate and they were told that the only way that it could be done was that they had to pay for it. When we met, they voted for a dues of $3.50 a month without collective bargaining agreements, without really anything. It was just the idea.

We went out to try to implement the $3.50 a month dues and it was a very difficult thing to do, but we gradually succeeded. And I think if any one thing is said about any success that we've had, the fact that we got people to put up their own money, however little it was, to do the initial organizing was what got them together. Because, you see, they had an investment now. They were coming to the meetings, if for nothing else, but to see what was happening with their money that they were paying. And while they were there, we were taking advantage of educating them.

But it seems to me that one other reason that it was difficult to organize was that for some time back and more so today, people tend to romanticize the poor people. Or romanticize the Negro or the Mexican or anybody who was discriminated against. And we say that to help someone help themselves we have to look at him as a human being. And we cannot romanticize his race or his poverty if we are really going to deal with the problem and to help him as a human being.

So we went along for almost four years and we came to September 1965 when the AWOC called a strike in Delano. Eight days later we called our membership together, we took a vote, and we struck for the same things. We wanted recognition and we wanted a wage increase and a written contract. The growers were paying then from $1.10 to $1.15 an hour. We were demanding $1.40, recognition, and a written contract. Most of us in the NFWA had no idea of what a written contract was but my experience in organizing had been strictly, at that point, in community organizing.

In trying to put the union together, when the other union was organizing workers, we felt that they were approaching the organization of farm workers just on those issues that the workers were confronting with their employers and that they weren't doing anything on the community part of it. We wanted to do both things. We wanted to have a community union. We didn't have that name for it at the time, but we wanted first of all to deal with the community problems, get the people together, show them that there is some power in numbers, win some small personal victories, pull all those things together, begin some programs and gradually move that into a union setting, striking and really confronting the employer. And all these four and a half years we had a lot of time to do this. Only once did the press find out what we were doing. Only once did it get through—but for four and a half years no one knew what we were doing except our most immediate friends. And we kept building and building until that September. When we took the vote on September 26, 1965, it was a unanimous vote to strike. We wanted to strike Schenley and the workers said—No, let's strike them all at once. And we struck forty.

We had also read in the many attempts to organize workers that violence had played a large part in suppression of the union. We knew that the moment we struck that justice was going to be about 20 percent for us and 80 percent for the opposition. And we know that because of the violence of which strikers had been accused and convicted, for things that they had never committed. So I asked the workers to take a vote to consider that this strike be a nonviolent strike. And many of them didn't know what a nonviolent strike meant. But many of them did know that there was another group in the country that had been making a lot of progress for human rights and that was also committed to nonviolence, and this was the civil rights movement.

And so we went out that first day to the picket lines, and the moment we hit the picket lines at 5:30 in the morning we began to have reaction from the growers. They had guns and they took shots at us on two or three occasions. They were poor shots and didn't hit us. And in a period of seven days we had fourteen incidents where they actually fired a gun at the strikers. And not even in one case were we able to get the District Attorney to take that case. They wouldn't take it.

When we went on strike there were some very great miscalculations. First of all, we thought we were striking the growers. The strike was only against the growers, and we were convinced that the other forces in the community, at the worst, would probably tend to say that they were neutral or to say that they didn't like the strike but we can't do anything about it. As it turned out we were dead wrong. Within twenty-four hours from the moment that we had hit the picket lines, the City Council had passed a resolution condemning the Red ties. The High School Board and the Elementary School Board had done the same thing. And the Chamber of

Commerce did it also with the exception that their statement was a lot more wordy. And three days later when everything seemed to be against us the Church had not yet acted. And we thought, this is the group that is going to be the conciliator. And for the first time as I know it, the first time in the history of Delano, the [Protestant] Ministerial Association agreed to meet with the three priests in the town. They got together and passed a resolution condemning the strike. At that point we were cut off completely. We had no friends in Delano except the workers. We had no money. Our union was so poor that we had only $70.00 in the treasury when the strike started. And we had no way of getting labor support because we were a scab group. We had no way of getting anyone to give us money except some friends that we had in the Church. Immediately when the strike started, I called on the Migrant Ministry. It is a group that had been around California for about forty years trying to do something for workers, and it was that group that gave us the first $500.00 to use for the strike. And things went very badly for us during the first two or three months. We were having difficulty in letting the rest of the country know about our strike difficulty—raising money—all sorts of difficulties. We were not getting together with the other union although we stood for the same things. Things looked very bad for us.

At this time the AFL-CIO was having its convention in San Francisco and we were hoping that someone from that convention would come and talk to us, at least be present with us for a short while to show that the great American labor movement was behind us. We didn't know how but we thought if someone would come that we would be able to get some help. Maybe it would scare the growers into signing a contract. On December 15, there were rumors that Walter Reuther was coming to Delano. The City Council thought it was going to be a demonstration so they passed a resolution prohibiting demonstrations and marching on the street. And we had a copy of the resolution delivered by the Chief of Police to my office saying that "this was just passed today and we mean to enforce it."

And so on December 17, Walter Reuther did come to Delano. He arrived at the local airport and there were a lot of people from all over. It seemed that all the farm workers in the Valley had come down to greet him. And we got into our cars and marched over to the local picket line. We were picketing the local railroad yard. We didn't know anything about secondary boycotts and injunctions— we were picketing. And it sounded very strange to us that AWOC wouldn't join us in the picketing, and when they did they would carry our NFWA signs and not their own. And they wouldn't carry their own signs. And we couldn't understand these things.

Well anyway, Walter Reuther came and he got off at the picket line. It was December and it was cold. And he said, "Does this picket line ever march?" And the people said, "No. Yes." And he said, "Well, let's march." And before I could say that we had a regulation against it, he started marching and we followed. And everybody started marching. And the chief of police who saw all these people couldn't do anything except to direct traffic for us as we're marching through the streets. That same evening we had one of the largest meetings we had in Delano since the strike had begun and Brother Reuther spoke. People were very happy that he was there and we felt that now that we had some backing, that we were going to do things.

The Mayor of the town, who was also a dentist and who was very much against the strike, came to the hall to hear Walter Reuther, and then he invited him to meet with some of the growers at their homes. But while he was talking, Walter was explaining to us what your union, those of you who are in the UAW, had gone through. And I began to think that really this wasn't something very different, that if we kept insisting and working and striking that we too might get there. But there was something else very important to us. We were a scab union even then. When he pledged his help, Walter Reuther didn't say that you were going to help the AFL-CIO union and that we were going to get a little bit or nothing because you happen not to be in the family of labor. He said we are going to give you money and we are going to cut it right down the middle. Now to us this was great recognition and, of course, a lot of help because we needed the money very badly. And from that time a lot of things began to happen.

First of all we had to go down to the other union office because the money was coming there and we had to go there to pick up our share. And so soon we began to talk to them and became friendly. And we began to see that they were people just like us. They were on strike and wanted to win just as badly as we did. And to make a very long story short, we did merge in August of 1966.

I would like to point out some of the other things because we don't have too much time. You haven't eaten and I haven't eaten. There are some things that I would like to leave with you to give you an idea of what we are going through.

For the first nine days of the strike things were very quiet from the police side. They weren't really harassing us. They were calling us Mr. Chavez and Mr. Garcia and so forth. The first day of the strike seventeen Deputy Sheriffs came to Delano. And the Sergeant, I shall never forget his name, Sergeant Dodd, came and told me that the Sheriff of the County had sent this group of deputies to protect the strikers. I had never been in a strike before and I thought this was really great. And I thanked him kindly. Two days later he called me to an emergency conference. So I went to his office in the morning. Sergeant Dodd was sitting there with three other officers and two police dogs. Sergeant Dodd said, "I want to ask a very special favor of you." And I asked, "What is it?" And he said, "Well, we want to keep our relationship. We want to have a nice clean strike. Would you do me a favor?" And I said, "Yes." "Well, the poor people working in the fields." And I said, "Well, they are strikebreakers and we call them worse than that sometime." He said, "Well, I've had a lot of complaints that you are shouting *huelga* (strike) at them and its annoying a lot of them. And if you stop doing this I think it would be a lot of help to all of us."

I called a membership meeting that evening and I asked for permission to do that and for their approval. And the members weren't too happy about it, but they took a vote after our discussion and it was decided that the next day instructions would be given not to shout *huelga* at the people in the fields.

So two or three days later, Sergeant Dodd called me to his office again. He wasn't satisfied because although we had stopped shouting *huelga* we were still calling out "*huelga*" in a normal tone of voice to the strikebreakers and they objected to that. By this time I said, "Well, what is your objection to the word. It is only a word." And he said, "Well, first of all, we live in America and English is the official language and we want you to use the English language." And I said, "I understand that." And even then I wasn't aware of what he was trying to do. And I continued, "Yes, but most of the people who are breaking the strike come from Mexico. They are green-carders and they don't understand English. We want them to understand us so we say *huelga*." Sergeant Dodd said, "Well, you can't do that. Also, there are rumors here that the only reason that you are using *huelga* is because you want to be best understood by the Communist Party in Latin America." This was just too much for me and I began to argue with him. And after a big argument with him about how I was a citizen and although I wasn't blond I was still an American, and about my rights and the Constitution, the Supreme Court decisions and so forth, he said to me, "You can't convince me. All of the arguments that you have for your work and all the arguments that we have against it: I have an additional argument. That word sounds downright nasty."

So I called the workers and that evening we had another meeting and a great debate, and I asked them not to use *huelga*, and perhaps coin another word. Let's do something else, because we have a strike to win. The members told me to go back to the picket line.

The next day we went out, forty-four workers including my wife and six or seven ministers. They went out, spaced themselves fifty feet apart and shouted *huelga* at the top of their lungs and sure enough, Sergeant Dodd kept his promise. They arrested every one of them. I got the call in the office that forty-four people were in jail—at the County Jail in Bakersfield and for me to come quickly. I didn't have the money and I didn't quite know what to do. I got in the car and instead of going south where the strikers were I traveled about 300 miles to Berkeley to the campus. I spoke to the students at noon and I said, "Look, what I want is your money—your lunch money because we have forty-four people in jail and we don't have any money to bail them out."

The students gave us $6,600 that afternoon and we went to Bakersfield and bailed the strikers out of jail. We got an attorney. Every single case was dismissed but we spent about $10,000 on that case.

We've had over 150 arrests (some of the strikers have been arrested five times), and we have had only one conviction.

Then the winter came and there was very little activity in Delano. We wanted to keep the movement moving and so we decided to have a pilgrimage from Delano to Sacramento. It was during this pilgrimage, on April 6, that we arrived in Stockton, California, and a telephone call came from a man claiming to be an attorney for Schenley saying that they wanted to settle. It was so unexpected that I thought it was another crank trying to pull my leg so I hung up the phone and started to walk out. The phone rang again and I picked it up. It was the same man. He identified himself. The next day we met in Los Angeles and Schenley gave us a recognition agreement. It was just a very simple document about two-thirds of a letter-sized paper saying that they recognized us and were prepared to give the workers a thirty-five cent an hour across-the-board wage increase. It was some weeks later that I showed this to Paul Schrade of the UAW in Los Angeles, and he told me that in the history of the UAW that they had gotten less than that. They just got a recognition agreement and no wage increase when they won their first battle.

We then moved into the DiGiorgio conflict. And this was open war. By this time we had another union which had come in and was, with the aid of the Company, trying to form a company union. We were having great difficulties and we had just ended the Schenley Boycott and we had people all over the country and we didn't have any money to bring them back. Some were proposing to hitchhike, while others were thinking of U-Drive cars that you can rent.

And it was in San Francisco at this time that I again met Walter Reuther. I told him we were having problems. He asked me what kinds of problems. I told him that we had to get our organizers who were all over the country back to Delano to organize and beat DiGiorgio. Also we don't have any automobiles. We need money to bring our people back and we need automobiles. And the response to that, although I expected something, didn't quite come up to what he said. He said, "Anything you need." Now I've had a lot of friends in my life who have said, "If there's anything you need, Cesar, just call on me." Walter turned to Jack Conway and said, "Jack, work out with him the arrangements." And sure enough, two days later we had seven cars in Delano and in less than twenty-four hours later we had all of our people right back in Delano working on the strike.

This is the kind of support. . . . You know that somehow if you persist and if you continue the support that we are going to move forward and build a union.

I have one grave concern about the American Labor Movement, and it comes to me mostly because I don't quite understand it yet. I'm very new in it yet. But it seems to me that the capitalists are at least twenty-five years ahead of most of the unions in this country. Coming from a background of not knowing anything about injunctions and Taft-Hartley and so forth, it seems to me very difficult to understand. For instance, if I am on strike here, how come my brother who belongs to this other union cannot do something in direct action to help me or vice versa. I couldn't understand this. And we went to some of the other unions that were supplying DiGiorgio with materials that were needed for packing, transportation, and so forth. And they said they couldn't help us. And we said, if we place our pickets here would you help, and they said they couldn't because they would get in trouble. And it seems to me that by legislation, by agreement, and I guess just by laxity more than anything else that we are permitting the public, all of us, to let the labor movement be divided in such a way that we can't understand it. For instance, why do we have so many laws to control the activities of unions. For instance, if you have a railroader you have one kind of law; if you are industrial workers, you have another kind of law; if you are a public employee, another kind of law; if you are a farm worker, no law at all.

While money is a very important help during a strike as all of us know and other technical advice and help, I don't think we will ever see in America again a general strike. And I know that some real great battles have been won when the workers say that although I am not on strike I'm going to support my brothers. And I don't know where we are going to go. But I'm just frightened that more laws, more restrictions are being placed that the situation will be such that although the workers would really want to help that they wouldn't be able to do it.

We're in a bit of trouble, you know, for not believing that things are as they are. We started picketing the chain of Mayfair Stores in California—three hundred stores. And we picketed for five weeks, and they couldn't remove the Perelli-Minetti Liquors. We told the people, "Don't buy at Mayfair. We don't care about secondary boycotts. We don't want you to buy at Mayfair." And today I received the news that the Board is prepared to get an injunction against us. And what is so very difficult to understand is that, on the one hand, they will enjoin us. They will use the law to enjoin us but, on the other hand, we petitioned the Board three times for an election on the Perelli-Minetti dispute, and they said they couldn't handle it because it is out of their jurisdiction. On the other hand, they are going to enjoin us. It is very difficult to understand.

I am happy to be with you. We have many fond memories of the UAW. Many fine memories of that fine convention in Long Beach, and we have come to understand that when the UAW says that they are going to help, they mean it.

Marcher

This comment on Chavez, published in The New Yorker *on May 27, 1967, shows the obviously endearing qualities he had that attracted so many farmworkers when he began to organize. His principles were clear and simple, if not always apparent to everyone. The Delano Grape Strike became a nationwide boycott of table grapes in 1967, turning the public eye to Chavez and the NFWA.*

When we heard that Cesar Chavez, the man who organized the Delano, California, grape-pickers' strike, was in town, we recalled that in March, 1966, Mr. Chavez had led sixty-five striking grape pickers, joined eventually by ten thousand sympathizers, three hundred miles, from Delano to Sacramento—the longest major protest march in recent memory—and we decided he was the ideal person to talk with about the current state of American protest. We met Mr. Chavez after a 10:30 P.M. television interview (he had arrived on a noon plane, and had already survived an interview, three speeches, and a reception) outside Channel 13's basement studio, at 345 East Forty-sixth Street. We had expected, if not a Mexican-American Lenin, at least a young, hard, intense man bristling with revolutionary zeal. Instead, we found Mr. Chavez to be a stocky man of forty, about five feet seven, with Indian features, brown skin darkened by television makeup, and a pleasant, earnest manner. He wore a blue cardigan, much like a high-school varsity sweater, with two white bands around the left sleeve, and a yellow-gray plaid sports shirt, gray slacks, and scuffed black shoes. His feet and hands were conspicuously small. On the left breast of his sweater was a red-on-black button that read "Delano—Grapes of Wrath."

Mr. Chavez led us upstairs to an empty two-room office. The outer room had a big tiger skin on the floor, and the inner room, in which we settled, contained a map of Africa, several African wood carvings, and a red fez; from the inner room we could see the United Nations and two big red neon signs on the Queens shore.

As we sat down, Mr. Chavez said with surprise, "All of a sudden I have a terrible craving for candy." Then he grasped the arms of his chair and leaned forward for our first question.

We asked him about the New Left.

"I don't know what the New Left is," he said, with a very slight Spanish accent. "But I do know there's a tremendous change going on in this country. There are things happening in America, such as anti-war rallies and civil-rights demonstrations, that no one has ever seen before. There are very few countries in which such things *could* happen, but they *can* happen here, and that's what gives our system its strength. In most countries, all change goes in the other direction, and eventually you end up with an armed revolution. The beautiful thing here is that it's happening in an orderly way." He smiled, then continued, "One reason for the protest—of course, it's not the only reason, but I think it's a contributing factor—is that our kids are taught in school about justice and equality; then they find out the world isn't run by justice and equality, and they want to do something about it. Another reason is simply the level of sophistication that our society has attained. Of course, the people who protest now aren't ideological. They're protesting against regimentation, so how could they be ideological?"

We asked Mr. Chavez whether activism had really replaced ideology, and he said he thought it had. Then he cocked his head to one side and said, "The trouble with activists is that movements grow old for them very quickly, and they move on." But he added that in his own experience the current activists have much in their favor. "These students are the first people who have ever come to us without a hidden agenda," he said. "They just want to help us—to be servants—and that's a really beautiful thing. In the past, the people who have come to us have always been ideological, and they have always had a hidden agenda; they have said, 'We'll help you if you believe in our ideology.' The trouble with ideologies is that they make politics the most important thing, and they make people lose sight of the *human* values."

An Age of Miracles

Following his first fast in 1968, Cesar Chavez used the public attention he received to get more people involved in the fight for farmworkers' rights. He gave this speech at an interfaith lunch at Calvary Episcopal Church in Manhattan.

We are not in the age of miracles, and yet it is surprising that we can attract, and keep, and increase the type of support that is needed to keep our economic struggle going for thirty-three months. It is a struggle in which the poorest of the poor and weakest of the weak are pitted against the strongest of the strong. We are fighting not against the family farm, not against agriculture, but against agribusiness.

When we think of powerful interests, we think of General Motors and other great corporations. But we must turn our minds to the power of the land. It is hard to think that agribusiness could have such tremendous power as it has in California—it is worth $5 billion in our state alone. We must see it as it is, a similar situation to Latin America. The interests can control not only the land but everything that moves, everyone that walks in the land. They control even the actions of the Congress of the United States, even some church groups. Right up to today, some groups in the churches think we are a bunch of Communists. I can take the credit for one of the first ecumenical actions of the churches in the Delano area. Some ministers and priests got together to make a statement denouncing us as outside agitators.

You must have some of the background of agriculture in California to understand what we have been doing. The three basic elements, people, poor people, to provide the cheap labor.

We know how the land was acquired. The railroads, the Union Pacific and the Southern Pacific, got large tracts of land, and so did the Bank of America. Who would think that the Bank of America is a grower, but it is.

When the land was reclaimed, water had to be brought in from great distances, even six hundred to seven hundred miles. Your taxes are paying for this water supply today. Ours are not, right now, because we are on strike. Back in the early part of this century, legislators began to see that the family farm should be helped. So water was to be supplied to 160-acre farms. This was never enforced. The water went to the larger tracts.

One thing was necessary to the success of the exploitation of California land: workers. The whole cry to get poor people to do the work of the land is a story in itself. When the Southern Pacific and Union Pacific railroads were completed, the Chinese were left without work to do. They went to the cities. The growers who needed workers dealt with contractors who supplied the Chinese. The contractors, who were Chinese themselves, began to sell their brothers for profit. When the Chinese wanted to own their own land, we had the Chinese Exclusion Act. The Chinese land workers could not own land nor could they marry Caucasian women, so they left agriculture for the cities.

The growers went to Congress for special legislation. Tailor-made immigration laws made it possible for them to recruit labor from Japan. When the Japanese used the slow-down (they had no unions and could not strike) to get better conditions, the growers began to get rid of them. The Japanese could not own land either but began to rent it. In time they began to exploit the laborers.

The growers even went to India for labor, and in the early twenties they were recruiting in the Philippines. When they saw that many Mexicans were leaving their country because of the Revolution, they saw an opportunity. One grower explained that Mexicans were good for California land work because they were short and close to the ground. The growers went further than they ever went before. During World War II, our own government became the recruiter for laborers, "braceros." Even today, as I stand here talking to you, we cannot choke off production on the great farms for one simple reason. The regulations on immigration are not being enforced. Our own government is the biggest strikebreaker against the union. The biggest weapon in the hands of the growers is the "green card" commuter.

You can live in Mexico and come in to work for a season and then go back home. This is not like the regulations covering immigrants from Europe. Hundreds of thousands of people are recruited and put into employers' camps. We cannot reach them there. They are like concentration camps. If the laws were enforced, we would not have to boycott. Employers are not supposed to recruit workers while labor disputes are in progress.

We have to play the game without any rules or procedures. In New York, the rights of unions are enforced, but in our case 95 percent of the workers were signed up with the union, but the producer of table grapes, Giumarra, refused to sit down with us for representation procedures. We were willing to abide by the results of the election. The employers would not talk to us. The only approach left to us is the strike and the boycott.

Now that the growers are hurting, they want an election. Their strikebreakers are inside. Who can win an election this way? This is the predicament we are in. We say to Giumarra, you are not going to get two bites at the same apple. You will have to sign an agreement under pressure. With Edison, we called off the strike and the boycott and we had a contract. Then the land was sold to another grower and we are out of a contract. The day the contract is concluded with Giumarra, that day we take off the pressure.

Even if you have an election—without rules or procedures or protection—what do you have but the law of the jungle? The Board says we have no protection, but when we institute a boycott, the growers go the Board and get protection.

People raise the question: Is this a strike or is it a civil rights fight?

In California, in Texas, or in the South, anytime you strike, it becomes a civil rights movement. It becomes a civil rights fight.

The local courts say we have no right to use an amplifier to reach strikebreakers who are a quarter of a mile away. In every case, the growers get an injunction against us immediately. Then we go up to the Appellate Court and up to the Supreme Court. Justice is very expensive sometimes.

We go further. We take advantage of modern technology. I even went up in a plane with two priests to broadcast to the strikebreakers from seven hundred feet up. As soon as we came down, the growers were there to protest.

We have had priests with us before, during and after the strike. The priests of the California Migrant Ministry, Chris Hartmire and Jim Drake, have been with us from the beginning. They took losses in their church because of the Migrant Ministry and the suffering they accepted was for the migrants and for justice. It was from them that we learned the importance of the support of the church in our struggle. The church is the one group that gives help and never qualifies it or asks for favors.

The priests and ministers do everything from sweeping floors to giving out leaflets. They developed a true worker-priest movement. In the field and in the center, a minister and a worker joined together. The importance of Christian teachings to the worker and to his struggle for dignity becomes clear. Now we have a Franciscan priest working full-time with us.

The three most important issues at this time are these.

First, union recognition by the employers. We have certain rights as human beings. Every law is for this recognition—except when it comes to farm workers. Recognizing the union is recognizing us as human beings. Second, an increase in wages is important. Third, in my opinion and in the opinion of the workers, is safety. The whole question of pesticides and insecticides must be met. The men who work to apply these poisons should have protection. Two or three weeks after working with pesticides a man begins to have trouble with his sight. In some cases, he begins to lose his fingernails. It does not happen immediately. Someday our government will have to undertake real research to determine the effects of these poisons, not only on the workers who are in direct contact with them, but on the consumers. Millions of dollars are spent in the research on the effectiveness of the poisons in destroying pests and insects on plants. This is from the business angle. Millions must also be spent on the effects of the same poisons on human beings.

There is a fine dust that nature puts on grapes. It is called bloom. The contamination from the insecticides remains in this fine dust.

I don't eat grapes because I know about these pesticides. You can stop eating grapes for your safety as well as for the boycott. Even our strongest supporters are afraid of the boycott of table grapes. The key to the success of this boycott is right here in New York. Action is necessary. If you don't do anything, you are permitting the evil. I would suggest that labor take a page in the largest newspaper and make the issue clear to all, and I would suggest that the clergy also take a page. The message of the clergy should be different, bringing out the morality of our struggle, the struggle of good people who are migrants, and therefore the poorest of the poor and the weakest of the weak.

Chicanos and the Church

*Delivered in Sacramento, California, on March 8–10, 1968.
Chavez was in the middle of his twenty-five-day fast when he gave
this speech on his own spiritual experience to the Second Annual
Mexican American Conference.*

It is common knowledge that the Catholic Church is a block of
power in society and that the property and purchases of the
Church rate second only to the government. True Christianity demands that this institutional power and wealth of the Church be
brought to bear in solving the current Chicano urban and rural
crisis. The religious dollar must be invested, without return expected, in the barrios.

The Church must come to realize that her commitment to serve
the poor today means the investment of land and seed money for
La Raza's self-help projects such as housing development corporations, management development corporations, small business corporations, credit unions, and coops, the profit from which will be
used to further our own barrios. . . .

Spanish surnamed clergy and laity should determine the priorities of goals and objectives in a given barrio. Financial assistance
must be provided without stringent controls and bureaucratic at-
tachments.

Because of the incredibly high dropout rate among Mexican
American students, tutorial services, study halls, bilingual programs, programs for dropouts, etc., must be initiated and funded.

In conclusion, to build power among Mexican Americans presents a threat to the Church; to demand reform of Anglo-controlled
institutions stirs up dissension. However, if representatives of the
Church are immobilized and compromised into silence, the Church
will not only remain irrelevant to the real needs and efforts of La
Raza in the barrios, but our young leaders of today will continue to
scorn the Church and view it as an obstacle to their struggle for social, political and economic independence.

After the Fast

After fasting for twenty-five days, Chavez broke his fast with a Mass on March 10, 1968. Too weak to speak, he still felt commitment to his fellow union members and repeated his belief in suffering for others and for the pursuit of justice.

I have asked the Rev. James Drake to read this statement to you because my heart is so full and my body too weak to be able to say what I feel. My warm thanks to all of you for coming today. Many of you have been here before, during the fast. Some have sent beautiful cards and telegrams and made offerings at the Mass. All of these expressions of your love have strengthened me and I am grateful.

We should all express our thanks to Senator [Robert] Kennedy for his constant work on behalf of the poor, for his personal encouragement to me, and for taking time to break bread with us today.

I do not want any of you to be deceived about the fast. The strict fast of water only which I undertook on February 16 ended after the twenty-first day because of the advice of our doctor, James McKnight, and other physicians. Since that time I have been taking liquids in order to prevent serious damage to my kidneys.

We are gathered here today not so much to observe the end of the fast but because we are a family bound together in a common struggle for justice. We are a union family celebrating our unity and the nonviolent nature of our movement. Perhaps in the future we will come together at other times and places to break bread and to renew our courage and to celebrate important victories.

The fast has had different meanings for different people. Some of you may still wonder about its meaning and importance. It was not intended as a pressure against any growers. For that reason we have suspended negotiations and arbitration proceedings and relaxed the militant picketing and boycotting of the strike during this period. I undertook the fast because my heart was filled with grief and pain for the sufferings of farm workers. The fast was first for me and then for all of us in this union. It was a fast for nonviolence and a call to sacrifice.

When we are really honest with ourselves we must admit that our lives are all that really belong to us. So it is how we use our lives that determines what kind of men we are. It is my deepest belief that only by giving our lives do we find life. I am convinced that the truest act of courage, the strongest act of manliness is to sacrifice ourselves for others in a totally nonviolent struggle for justice. To be a man is to suffer for others. God help us to be men!

Before the Senate Committee on Labor and Public Welfare

This testimony, delivered on April 16, 1969, served to alert the Senate to labor abuses happening in America and to start the process of legislative involvement in the rights of farmworkers.

My name is Cesar E. Chavez. I am Director of the United Farm Workers Organizing Committee, AFL-CIO, a labor organization whose office is Post Office Box 130, Delano, California 93215.

It is indeed a privilege to address this body, so many of whose members have distinguished themselves over the years by their genuine concern for the welfare of farm workers. For this we are grateful. What has impressed us most is your open-mindedness, your desire to explore our problems in depth. Unwilling to believe what you have heard or read about the farm worker, some of you have even come to our valley to see for yourselves and experience at first hand our deprivation, our frustration, and our struggle for social justice.

We welcome the decision of this subcommittee to hold hearings on S.8 in order to explore still further the question of whether and in what way farm workers should be covered by the National Labor Relations Act, as amended. The fact that so many Senators have joined in co-sponsoring S.8—and that so many members of the other House have co-sponsored a somewhat similar measure—demonstrates at least that much. No one any longer seriously argues that the issue of labor relations legislation for agriculture can be resolved simply by striking the exclusion of "agricultural laborer" from the definition of "employee" in section 2(3) of the act.

Perhaps because of certain similarities between our employment situation and that of the building trades, some have been led in their search for the right answer to experiment with the construction industry exemptions of section 8(f). We do resemble the building trades in certain characteristics of our employment, though not in others—a matter I shall return to later.

First, let me say that we too have been learning. In the no-nonsense school of adversity, which we did not choose for ourselves, we are learning how to operate a labor union. The difficulty of our struggle, together with the growing possibility of labor relations legislation for agriculture, has led us to challenge again and again the assumption that coverage under the NLRA would prove the ultimate salvation of the farm worker.

This much at least is certain. His salvation will not be found in sloganeering.

Through long hours of discussion and debate, officers of our union have tried to envision just what real trade union life would be like under various provisions of the NLRA. At times we have wondered whatever led our friends to say we had been denied the "protections" of that act.

Our conclusion is that we do support coverage under the NLRA, but with certain amendments, for not every kind of amendment will really benefit the farm worker.

The need is for amendments that will make strong, effective labor unions realistically possible in agriculture.

I say "make realistically possible" because laws cannot deliver a good union any more than laws can bring an end to poverty. Only people can do that through hard work, sacrifice, and dedicated effort.

The end to be achieved, and therefore the starting point of the debate, is the elimination of rural poverty in America. How can the nation, how can the Congress help the farm worker close the yawning gap between his own social and economic condition and that of other wage earners, even those of comparable skill in other industries such as manufacturing and construction?

Answer? Through strong, effective, well-run unions. The road to social justice for the farm worker is the road to unionization. Our cause, our strike against table grapes, and our international boycott are all founded upon our deep conviction that the form of collective self-help which is unionization holds far more hope for the farm worker than any other approach, whether public or private. This conviction is what brings spirit, high hope, and optimism to everything we do.

No one has said it better than President George Meany of the AFL-CIO: "The United Farm Workers Organizing Committee already has awakened the nation's conscience. Even more important, it has demonstrated to farm workers across the country that they can obtain first-class membership through self-organization."

Repressive legislation is not the answer to strikes during harvest time and boycotts of farm products. The farm worker has learned that his sub-human existence is not inevitable. He has awakened to the realization that something better is possible for himself and his family. Laws are not going to stop strikes and boycotts so long as his honest, law-abiding efforts to improve his condition are met with massive, hostile grower resistance. Such resistance will only feed the fires of his own burning frustration. The best insurance against strikes and boycotts lies not in repressive legislation, but in strong unions that will satisfy the farm worker's hunger for decency and dignity and self-respect.

Unionization cannot make progress in the face of hostile employee attitudes unless it receives effective governmental support. Despite a resigned acceptance by some farm employers that collective bargaining under law is inevitable, grower attitude on the whole remains exceedingly hostile. If farm unionism is to make progress, we need sufficient economic power under law to be able to wrench signed agreements from unwilling hands of growers who still refuse to admit that unionization and collective bargaining have a rightful place to take in agriculture for the genuine long-run benefit of all concerned. Coverage under the present NLRA would not give us the needed economic power, and it would take away what little we have.

As Senators well know, there are times when legislative proposals become part of the strategy of calculated retreat. We urge a hard, questioning look at any farm labor proposal designed to make union recognition easier than ever while keeping all the economic power where it has always been—in the hands of the grower.

Under the complex and time-consuming procedures of the National Labor Relations Board, growers can litigate us to death; forced at last by court order to bargain with us in good faith, they can bargain in good faith—around the calendar if need be—unless we are allowed to apply sufficient economic power to make it worth their while to sign.

We want to be recognized, yes, but not with a glowing epitaph on our tombstone. Union recognition is of value only in terms of what it leads on to. At the end of the trail we seek:

—not recognition, but signed contracts;
—not recognition, but good wages;
—not recognition, but a strong union.

And these things are not primarily a matter of elections and representation procedures, or even of court orders, but of economic power.

To equalize the inequality of bargaining power—this was the high legislative purpose of both Wagner and Taft-Hartley, was it not? The more basic reason why we oppose coverage under the present Taft-Hartley, without more, is that it would not correct the inequality of bargaining power between growers and ourselves.

In the last Congress, the House Special Subcommittee on Labor chaired by Rep. Frank Thompson of New Jersey, which will also hold hearings soon on this subject, published a report entitled "National Labor Relations Act Remedies: The Unfulfilled Promise."

The report quotes Mr. William L. Kircher, Director of Organization of the AFL-CIO, as saying: "It is very natural for workers to unionize because unionism and the collective bargaining process enable them to increase their wages and obtain that dignity and self-respect which comes with job security."

Mr. Kircher testified that when there is no employer opposition to the desire for unionization, the union almost always wins the election. In 29 representation elections held over a 13-month period, unions won 28 and tied the other. In all but seven cases the margin of victory was in excess of 2 to 1.

The burden of the report, however, was that "in campaign after campaign in the southeastern, southwestern, and midwestern parts of the United States" the union encounters all-out organized opposition not only from the employer, but also from the police, the local courts, and the business and political leadership of the community.

What the report said about the trials of the textile, retail clerks, and other unions could have been written as well about our own experience with the table grape industry in California. Anyone who thinks coverage under the present NLRA would be a tremendous favor to farm workers should study the Thompson Report and ponder its contents as well.

How then did it happen that so many people for so long a time made so much of NLRA "protections" for farm workers?

To better understand this, I think we must go back 34 years in time to 1935, when Congress passed the original NLRA, the Wagner Act. We almost made it that time, but not quite, and people concerned about the plight of the farm worker began to say we had been denied the protections of the act. They said it for 12 years when it could fairly be called a pro-labor act. They kept on saying it after the Taft-Hartley revision of 1947 and the Landrum-Griffin amendments of 1959 converted into an anti-labor act.

The policy of the original Wagner Act and its administration for the succeeding 12 years was to promote unionization of the unskilled and semi-skilled workers in mass production industry. Its aim was to quiet widespread industrial unrest and to meet the social and economic challenges of the Great Depression.

Senators will recall that when the 80th Congress passed the Taft-Hartley Act over President Truman's veto, labor leaders called it a "slave labor act." They were ridiculed by their enemies at the time, and they were ridiculed later when their unions survived. But what survived? Large, well-established unions which had ongoing collective bargaining relationships with employers who were by that time accustomed to dealing with labor unions. That's what survived.

Taft-Hartley did, however, accomplish the purpose of its sponsors in that it effectively decelerated the pace of union organizing, as annual union membership statistics will show. History will record that Taft-Hartley and Landrum-Griffin, together with continuing business community determination to oppose unions at nearly every turn, succeeded in checking the progress of labor organization in America before it had accomplished half its job.

Even today, some of the most striking gains in union membership are occurring among teachers and other public employees who, like us, must operate without benefit of labor relations law. Public employee unions were greatly helped, it is true, by the executive order of the late President John F. Kennedy and by similar policies adopted by certain state and local governments.

Where would the large industrial unions be today in Congress had "protected" them from the beginning, not with the Wagner Act, but with the Taft-Hartley Act in its present form?

We too need our decent period of time to develop and grow strong under the life-giving sun of a favorable public policy which affirmatively favors the growth of farm unionism.

Of utmost importance is an exemption for a time from the Taft-Hartley and Landrum-Griffin restrictions on traditional union activity. The bans on recognition and organizational picketing and on the so-called secondary boycott would be particularly harmful, and the mandatory injunction in both cases makes them truly disastrous.

How does it happen that the law provides no mandatory injunctions against employer unfair labor practices, such as discharges for union activity or promotion of company unions?

As to the secondary boycott, it is shameful that the richest nation on earth, confronted with the moral challenge of farm worker deprivation, should create a legal fiction of "innocent neutrality" for those who reap a monetary profit from the sale of scab grapes. Union security is most essential in an industry like agriculture, which is marked by seasonal and casual employment and where a work force can build up from a few hundred to several thousand in a few short days and just as quickly disappear.

While the nation is busy fighting poverty in all its forms, let us not create new situations where nonunion farm worker poverty in "right to work" Texas or Arizona will become a threat to the small measure of union farm worker prosperity in California.

We therefore urge that farm workers and their unions be exempted from section 14(b), which makes misnamed state "right to work" laws operative interstate commerce.

All of labor ought to be liberated from section 14(b), but this much at least. It makes no sense for Congress to labor hard at making collective bargaining possible for farm workers if it leaves untouched that major obstacle which is 14(b). Railroad employees are not subject to "right to work" laws and we see no reason why we should be.

Regarding section 14(c), we are opposed to any exemption of small growers whether legislative or administrative.

It is a matter of principle with us that the single employee of a small grower is as entitled to his union as anyone else, and if a union cannot represent him under a regulatory law, then it will have to proceed as we do at the present, without benefit of a specific law.

It is perhaps but natural that small growers should see the coming of unionism only in terms of wage cost. We think that the problem is much more complex than that.

If Congress passes a bad law, making us worse off than we are at present, but exempts small growers from coverage, then we might have to concentrate most of our organizing effort for a time on small growers and let the big agribusiness corporations go until we can get the law changed.

If on the other hand Congress passes a law which really makes it possible to get contracts with the big growers, but which exempts the small ones, something else is apt to happen. We would certainly begin by going after the big growers. Then I suspect that internal union politics would have the tendency to force a concentration on getting higher and higher wages from the big corporations while ignoring both the small growers and their employees completely.

This might be a welcome prospect to the small grower who thinks he can find competent, efficient workmen at nonunion wage rates and so continue to compete effectively. We think such a view highly unrealistic if one considers what is going on in the world of agriculture—the mass exodus of small farmers to the cities, the increasing concentration of more and more farmland in fewer and fewer hands. This is taking place without the presence of labor unions in any significant sector of agriculture, and without any consideration of union vs. nonunion farm wages. What will happen if unions are permitted to organize big corporate agribusiness but not small growers is this: Big agribusiness will get the benefit of better workers attracted by higher union wages, of higher union worker productivity, and of whatever benefit derives from political alliance with the union when there is a question of union employers against nonunion employers. This could affect such issues as support payments and other forms of federal subsidy, federal money for retraining employees to operate new farm machines, and so on.

Let me say right here that all of this is a prospect which the leadership of our union does not relish at all. Our natural sympathy is to favor the small grower and to help him in every way we can to remain in business and to prosper. We do not want to be forced into a political and economic alliance with large growers against small growers. We are, however, trade unionists and our first obligation is to our members. Our cooperation must be reserved for those employers who believe in unions, or who are at least willing to tolerate unions, and who sign fair union contracts.

We urge small growers to give the matter a great deal of thought before pressing for an exemption from NLRA coverage.

If we could have our own way, what we would really like to see is a family living wage for every farm worker, a family living income for every family-sized farm owner, and a fair return on investment for every grower, whether he is an employer or not.

To this end we urge Congress to give favorable consideration to the proposed National Agricultural Bargaining Act of 1969, or whatever legislative assistance may be needed so that all agricultural producers can obtain a fair price for their produce in the various commodity markets.

Concerning section 302, our only objection is to the requirement of subsection (c)(5)(B) that employers have equal representation with employers in administration of the funds. These monies are for the benefit of the workers, who have elected to take part of their negotiated pay increase in the form of pension or health-welfare or other benefits. We believe that the trust agreement offers sufficient protection for these funds and that unilateral administration by employee representatives should be legally possible under the act.

Some unions, notably the building trades, derived little benefit from the original Wagner Act, but all of them in some way had something else going for them. The skilled trades, together with the professions, enjoy first of all a natural limitation on labor supply in that their members possess some kind of skill or formal training. In addition, they have been permitted by public policy to restrict freedom of entry to the occupation, or freedom of access to the needed training.

Where would they be today if they had to contend with the same economic forces that we do?

The seasonal farm worker does not possess extensive skills. While experience accounts on the farm as well as anywhere, he is scarcely called upon to do anything that cannot be learned passably well in half a day.

Our potential competition appears almost unlimited as thousands upon thousands of green carders pour across the border during peak harvest seasons. There are people who, though lawfully admitted to the United States for permanent residence, have not now, and probably never have had, any bona fide intention of making the United States of America their permanent home. They come here to earn American dollars to spend in Mexico where the cost of living is lower. They are natural economic rivals of those who become American citizens or who otherwise decide to stake out their future in this country.

In abolishing the bracero program, Congress has but scotched the snake, not killed it. The program lives on in the annual parade of thousands of illegals and green carders across the United States–Mexico border to work in our fields.

To achieve law and order in any phase of human activity, legislators must apply heed to other laws not made by man, one of which is the economic law of supply and demand. We are asking Congress to pay heed to this law in the light of some hard facts about farm labor supply along our southern border. Otherwise, extension of NLRA coverage to farm workers in that part of the country will not produce much law and order.

What we ask is some way to keep the illegals and green carders from breaking our strikes—some civil remedy against growers who employ behind our picket lines those who have entered the United States illegally and, likewise, those green carders who have not permanently moved their residence and domicile to the United States.

An especially serious problem in agricultural employment is the concerted refusal of growers even to discuss their use of economic poisons or pesticides. There are signs that several members of Congress are becoming increasingly aware of the dangers posed by economic poisons to human life and to wildlife, to the air we breathe and the water we drink. Senator Gaylord Nelson of Wisconsin is to be congratulated for proposing a federal ban on DDT.

For us the problem is before all else one of worker health and safety. It is aggravated in California by the refusal of county agricultural commissioners to disclose their records of pesticide application and by state court injunctions against such public disclosure.

The economic poison threat is a major reason why we need strong unions and collective bargaining in agriculture. Growers who try to pass our complaints off as a cheap smear campaign for consumer benefit reveal thereby that they are not very well acquainted with the daily anxieties and sufferings of their field workers.

Some there may be who dread the adjustments they think may be required by the coming of unionism to ranch and farm. Our leadership has given much thought to this matter.

Perhaps Congress could create a temporary Joint Committee on Family Living Farm Income, along the lines of the Joint Committee on Labor Management Relations set in 1947 by the old Taft-Hartley Title IV. The new committee would have such time as Congress deems expedient to study and report on such subjects as these: methods for improving employer-employee relations in agriculture; conditions necessary to produce a family living wage for farm workers and a family living income for farm owner; requisites for a national policy of enabling and encouraging farm workers to become self-sustaining family-sized farm owners; requisite sizes for various kinds of self-sustaining family-sized farms; structural changes needed to enhance the bargaining power of agricultural producers in the various commodity markets; suitable methods for expanding agricultural production to meet the challenge of hunger at home and abroad; training programs needed to equip unemployed and underemployed persons, both urban and rural, to fill the new jobs created by such expanded production; methods for reversing the current trend toward concentration of more and more agricultural land in fewer and fewer hands.

As one looks at the millions of acres in this country that have been taken out of agricultural production; and at the millions of additional acres that have never been cultivated; and at the millions of people who have moved off the farm to rot and decay in the ghettoes of our big cities; and at all the millions of hungry people at home and abroad; does it not seem that all these people and things were somehow made to come together and serve one another? If we could bring them together, we could stem the mass exodus of rural poor to the big city ghettoes and start it going back the other way; teach them how to operate new farm equipment; and put them back to work on those now uncultivated acres to raise food for the hungry. If a way could be found to do this, there would be not only room but positive need for still more machinery and still more productivity increase. There would be enough employment, wages, profits, food, and fiber for everybody. If we have any time left over after doing our basic union job, we would like to devote it to such purposes as these.

Walter P. Reuther, President of the United Automobile Workers, described the right order of priorities for us in these words: "The journey of farm workers and their families into the mainstream of American life has begun with a struggle to build their own community unions and through them to reach out for the elementary rights so long denied them."

Eventually, we will reach out for the rights denied us, such as full and equal coverage under minimum wage laws and the various forms of social insurance. But first things first. Today we ask the American people and the Congress to help us build our union with some special help in the face of some especially stubborn opposition of long standing. Give us that and the rest will come in due time.

Thirty-four years ago a nation groping its uncharted course through the seas of the Great Depression faced the threatening storms of social and economic revolution.

The late President Franklin D. Roosevelt met the challenge with the Wagner Act and with other New Deal measures, then considered quite revolutionary, such as Social Security, unemployment insurance, and the Fair Labor Standards Act.

While these measures modified the existing capitalistic system somewhat, they also saved the nation for free enterprise.

They did not save the farm worker. He was left out of every one of them. The social revolution of the New Deal passed him by. To make our union possible with its larger hope that the farm worker will have his day at last, there was required a new social revolution.

The relief we seek from Congress today, however, is neither new nor very revolutionary. It has proved beneficial to the nation in the past when unions were weak and industry strong. We need and favor NLRA amendments along the lines of the original Wagner Act, but we oppose for this period in history the restrictions of Taft-Hartley and Landrum-Griffin.

Good Friday Letter

This letter was written to E. L. Barr Jr., who was the president of the California Grape and Tree Fruit League, a growers' organization, following accusations of violence on the part of the strikers. Chavez was greatly troubled by these accusations, and the letter, written in Delano, was published in Christian Century *on April 23, 1969.*

DEAR MR. BARR:

I am sad to hear about your accusations in the press that our union movement and table grape boycott have been successful because we have used violence and terror tactics. If what you say is true, I have been a failure and should withdraw from the struggle. But you are left with the awesome moral responsibility, before God and man, to come forward with whatever information you have so that corrective action can begin at once.

If for any reason you fail to come forth to substantiate your charges then you must be held responsible for committing violence against us, albeit violence of the tongue. I am convinced that you as a human being did not mean what you said but rather acted hastily under pressure from the public relations firm that has been hired to try to counteract the tremendous moral force of our movement. How many times we ourselves have felt the need to lash out in anger and bitterness.

Today on Good Friday 1969 we remember the life and the sacrifice of Martin Luther King, Jr., who gave himself totally to the nonviolent struggle for peace and justice. In his Letter from Birmingham Jail, Dr. King describes better than I could our hopes for the strike and boycott: "Injustice must be exposed, with all the tension its exposure creates, to the light of human conscience and the air of national opinion before it can be cured." For our part I admit that we have seized upon every tactic and strategy consistent with the morality of our cause to expose that injustice and thus to heighten the sensitivity of the American conscience so that farm workers will have without bloodshed their own union and the dignity of bargaining with their agribusiness employers.

By lying about the nature of our movement, Mr. Barr, you are working against nonviolent social change. Unwittingly perhaps, you may unleash that other force that our union by discipline and deed, censure and education has fought to avoid; that panacean short cut: that senseless violence that honors no color, class, or neighborhood.

You must understand—I must make you understand—that our membership and the hopes and aspiration of the hundreds of thousands of the poor and dispossessed that have been raised on our account, are above all, human beings, no better no worse than any other cross section of human society; we are not saints because we are poor but by the same measure neither are we immoral. We are men and women who have suffered and endured much and not only because of our abject poverty but because we have been kept poor. The color of our skins, the languages of our cultural and native origins, the lack of formal education, the exclusion from the democratic process, the numbers of our slain in recent wars—all these burdens generation after generation have sought to demoralize us, to break our human spirit. But God knows that we are not beasts of burden, we are not agricultural implements or rented slaves, we are men. And mark this well, Mr. Barr, we are men locked in a death struggle against man's inhumanity to man in the industry that you represent. And this struggle itself gives meaning to our life and ennobles our dying.

As your industry has experienced, our strikers here in Delano and those who represent us throughout the world are well trained for this struggle. They have been under the gun, they have been kicked and beaten and herded by dogs, they have been cursed and ridiculed, they have been stripped and chained and jailed, they have been sprayed with the poisons used in the vineyards. They have been taught not to lie down and die or to flee in shame, but to resist with every ounce of human endurance and spirit. To resist not with retaliation in kind but to overcome with love and compassion, with ingenuity and creativity, with hard work, and longer hours, with stamina and patient tenacity, with truth and public appeal, with friends and allies, with mobility and discipline, with politics and law, and with prayer and fasting. They were not trained in a month or even a year; after all, this new harvest season will mark our fourth full year of strike and even now we continue to plan and prepare for the years to come. Time accomplishes for the poor what money does for the rich.

This is not to pretend that we have everywhere been successful enough or that we have not made mistakes. And while we do not belittle or underestimate our adversaries, for they are the rich and the powerful and possess the land, we are not afraid nor do we cringe from the confrontation. We welcome it! We have planned for it. We know that our cause is just, that history is a story of social revolutions, and that the poor shall inherit the land.

Once again, I appeal to you as the representative of your industry and as a man. I ask you to recognize and bargain with our union before the economic pressure of the boycott and strike takes an irrevocable toll; but if not, I ask you to at least sit down with us to discuss the safeguards necessary to keep our historical struggle free of violence. I make this appeal because as one of the leaders of our nonviolent movement, I know and accept my responsibility for preventing, if possible, the destruction of human life and property. For these reasons and knowing of Gandhi's admonition that fasting is the last resort in place of the sword, during a most critical time in our movement last February 1968 I undertook a 25-day fast. I repeat to you the principle enunciated to the membership at the start of the fast; if to build our union required the deliberate taking of life, either the life of a grower or his child, or the life of a farm worker or his child, then I choose not to see the union built.

Mr. Barr, let me be painfully honest with you. You must understand these things. We advocate militant nonviolence as our means for social revolution and to achieve justice for our people, but we are not blind or deaf to the desperate and moody winds of human frustration, impatience, and rage that blow among us. Gandhi himself admitted that if his only choices were cowardice or violence, he would choose violence. Men are not angels and the time and tides wait for no man. Precisely because of these powerful human emotions, we have tried to involve masses of people in their own struggle. Participation and self-determination remain the best experience of freedom; and free men instinctively prefer democratic change and even protect the rights guaranteed to seek it. Only the enslaved in despair have need of violent overthrow.

This letter does not express all that is in my heart, Mr. Barr. But if it says nothing else it says that we do not hate you or rejoice to see your industry destroyed; we hate the agribusiness system that seeks to keep us enslaved and we shall overcome and change it not by retaliation or bloodshed but by a determined nonviolent struggle carried on by those masses of farm workers who intend to be free and human.

Sincerely Yours,
Cesar E. Chavez

Creative Nonviolence

*Chavez believed strongly in the tradition of nonviolence exempli-
fied by Mahatma Gandhi and the Reverend Martin Luther King Jr.
In this brief comment for* The Catholic Worker, *June 1969, he describes his belief that violence is for the weak. He distinguished his
views from those of King by emphasizing a nonracial message.*

Many people feel that an organization that uses nonviolent methods to reach its objectives must continue winning victories one after another in order to remain nonviolent. If that be the case then
a lot of efforts have been miserable failures. There is a great deal
more involved than victories. My experience has been that the
poor know violence more intimately than most people because it
has been a part of their lives, whether the violence of the gun or
the violence of want and need.

I don't subscribe to the belief that nonviolence is cowardice, as
some militant groups are saying. In some instances nonviolence
requires more militancy than violence. Nonviolence forces you to
abandon the shortcut, in trying to make a change in the social order. Violence, the shortcut, is the trap people fall into when they
begin to feel that it is the only way to attain their goal. When
these people turn to violence it is a very savage kind.

When people are involved in something constructive, trying to
bring about change, they tend to be less violent than those who are
not engaged in rebuilding or in anything creative. Nonviolence
forces one to be creative; it forces any leader to go to the people
and get them involved so that they can come forth with new ideas.
I think that once people understand the strength of nonviolence—
the force it generates, the love it creates, the response that it brings
from the total community—they will not be willing to abandon it
easily.

Before the House of Representatives

On September 29, 1969, Chavez testified about the hazards from pesticides in the fields before the Migratory Labor Subcommittee of the Senate Committee on Labor and Public Welfare. His comments were reprinted in the Congressional Record *on October 3, 1969.*

On August 1st, 1969, after testifying concerning the misuse of economic poisons by table grape growers, our general counsel, Jerry Cohen, submitted to the staff of the Senate Subcommittee on Migratory Labor a Laboratory test from C. W. England Laboratories in Washington, D.C. which indicated that table grapes which were purchased by Manuel Vasquez at a Safeway store in northeast Washington contained an Aldrin residue of 18 parts per million. Subsequent to that time Senator George Murphy abused his privilege of senatorial immunity by making false accusations regarding the testimony of the United Farm Workers Organizing Committee. The innuendo in Senator Murphy's remarks in the *Congressional Record* of August 12, 1969, is that the farm workers tampered with the grapes. I can assure you that this is false.

I am confident that our position will be vindicated in this hearing and that the reports which have been received concerning the fact that Safeway conducted its own independent tests which confirmed our tests and subsequently cancelled its contract with Bianco are accurate reports.

The real issue involved here is the issue of the health and safety not only of farm workers but of consumers and how the health and safety of consumers and farm workers are affected by the gross misuse of economic poisons.

The issue of the health and safety of farm workers in California and throughout the United States is the single most important issue facing the United Farm Workers Organizing Committee. In California the agricultural industry experiences the highest occupational disease rate. This rate is over 50 percent higher than the second place industry. It is also three times as high as the average rate of all industry in California. Growers consistently use the wrong kinds of economic poisons in the wrong amounts in the wrong places in reckless disregard of the health of their workers in order to maximize profits. Advancing technological changes in agriculture have left the industry far behind in dealing with the occupational hazards of workers which arise from the use of economic poisons. This problem is further compounded by the fact that commonplace needs such as clean drinking water and adequate toilet facilities are rarely available in the fields and are also deficient in many living quarters of farm workers, especially of those workers who live in labor camps provided by the employer.

In California an estimated 3,000 children receive medical attention annually after having injested pesticides. There are over 300 cases of serious nonfatal poisonings annually, most of which occur in agriculture. There are some fatal poisonings which occur annually in agriculture. In addition to this, literally thousands of workers experience daily symptoms of chemical poisoning which include dermatitis, rashes, eye irritation, nausea, vomiting, fatigue, excess sweating, headaches, double vision, dizziness, skin irritations, difficulty in breathing, loss of fingernails, nervousness, insomnia, bleeding noses, and diarrhea.

The misuse of pesticides is creating grave dangers not only to farmworkers but to their children as well. Dr. Lee Mizrahi at the Salud Clinic in Tulare County has recently conducted a study relating to nutrition, parasites, and pesticide levels. Dr. Mizrahi chose his samples by inviting every fifth family who came to his clinic to participate in a free complete study of their children. Sixty families participated to date and 170 children have been tested. Dr. Mizrahi has reported to the United Farm Workers Organizing Committee that though the results of the test are not complete, based on the findings already received there are pesticide levels which can only be described as epidemic.

Thus far, on 29 children tested, 32 of the 84 reported values have fallen outside normal limits. Dr. Mizrahi has informed me that as a practicing physician he would be greatly worried if he found 10 percent of reportedly normal children outside normal limits. In this case he is frightened. These farm worker children are suffering from high levels of DDT in their blood and from low cholinesterase levels in their blood plasma.

Recently the state director of public health. Dr. Thomas Milby, said that there is ample evidence of many unreported poisonings in agriculture. Dr. Milby is currently conducting an investigation in an attempt to get an accurate picture of pesticide poisonings among the workers. The state of California is not releasing the data from this investigation. As an article in the *Fresno Bee* by Ron Taylor claims this study is headed by Mr. Henry Anderson who would not answer questions concerning the factual findings of the study to date because "the subject is too controversial." According to Mr. Taylor's article an undisclosed number of farm workers are reporting symptoms of pesticide poisoning. Many of these workers do not go to the doctors ordinarily but suffer in silence what they feel is an occupational hazard. The adverse effects of chemical poisons are so pervasive that they are considered by farm workers to be part of their way of life. They are accepted. One of the interviewers who is helping the state to conduct this investigation has informed the United Farm Workers Organizing Committee that of the 774 workers who filled out questionnaires which are now in the possession of th e state, 469 of the workers had worked in the grapes and 295 had not worked in the grapes. Among the 774 farm workers, the following symptoms caused by pesticide poisonings were reported:

One hundred and fifty-four of the workers reported having one of the above symptoms, 144 reported two of the symptoms, 109 reported three, 83 reported four, and 163 reported five or more symptoms. Only 121 of the 774 workers studied reported none of the above symptoms. This study was limited to a relatively small county, Tulare, which is immediately north of Delano.

Dr. Irma West, who works in the State Department of Public Health, has written many articles concerning the occupational hazards of farm workers. Some of the examples of injuries are as follows:

On a large California ranch in the fall of 1965 a group of Mexican-American workers and their families were picking berries. None could understand or read English. A three-year-old girl and her four-year-old brother were playing around an unattended spray rig next to where their mother was working. The four-year-old apparently took the cap off a gallon can of 40 percent tetraethyl phyrophosphate (TEPP, a phosphate ester cholinesterase inhibitor) pesticide left on the rig. The three-year-old put her finger in it and sucked it. She vomited immediately, became unconscious, and was dead on arrival at the hospital where she was promptly taken. TEPP is the most hazardous of all pesticides in common use in agriculture in California. The estimated fatal dose of pure TEPP for an adult is one drop orally and one drop dermally. This child weighed about 30 pounds.

Because of engine trouble, an agricultural aircraft pilot attempted a forced landing in an unplanted field. The plane rolled into a fence and turned over. The hopper of the airplane contained a dust formula of TEPP, another of the phosphate ester pesticides. The estimated adult fatal dose for TEPP concentrate is one drop orally or dermally. The pilot was not injured but was covered with dust. He walked a distance of 50 feet to a field worker, stated he felt fine, and asked for a drink of water. After drinking the water, he began to vomit and almost immediately became unconscious. By the time the ambulance arrived, the pilot was dead and the ambulance driver, the pathologist, and the mortician became ill from handling the body.

During this past summer in the grapes alone and largely in the Delano area the following incidents have been brought to the attention of our legal department.

On May 16th, 1969, Mrs. Dolores Lorta was working for labor contractor Manuel Armendariz in a table grape vineyard owned by Agri-Business Investment Company. Without warning, an Agri-Business spray rig sprayed the row she was working on, and Mrs. Lorta was sprayed all over her body with an unknown mixture of chemicals. Shortly thereafter, she experienced difficulty in breathing. She told her forelady, who responded that the spraying had nothing to do with that; that she must have had that difficulty before.

The next day she felt quite sick and large red blotches had appeared on her skin. She went to work that day but was unable to continue and hasn't been well enough to work since. She has suffered from continuing sores and rashes all over her body, headaches, dizziness, loss of weight, and her condition still continues. She has received no compensation from her employer as yet, and she has had to pay for her medical care herself.

Mr. and Mrs. Abelardo de León, and their teenage children, Juan and María, worked picking grapes for labor contratcor Manuel Armendariz in vineyards owned by Agri-Business Investment Company during July and August of 1969. From the start of their work there, Mr. de León suffered rashes all over his body, which lasted until they quit. Mrs. de León began to suffer extremely irritated and swollen eyes as soon as they started working there and one eye is still somewhat swollen. The irritation ceased when she quit, and has not reoccurred though she has returned to work in a different crop since then. Both the de León children, along with their mother, suffered eye irritation while working for Armendariz, and often their eyes would water profusely throughout the working day. When this was brought to the attention of Armendariz, he laughed and called them cry babies. He did not suggest that medical help was available for the family under the workman's compensation program, and as a result they had to make do with drugs and home remedies. Though the de Leons were not sprayed on directly, there was a heavy white dust on the vines and grapes which they picked. They saw no signs warning of the ill effects of this chemical spray, nor did they receive any warning or advice about it whatsoever. The de León family eventually stopped working for Armendariz because of the ill effects they were suffering from the chemical poisons on the grapevines.

Mr. Gregorio Sisneros was engaged in spraying a vineyard in the Selma area in 1968. According to directions which came with it, he mixed one quart of economic poison with a large quantity of water. But his employer told him to add in another quart of poison, and so he did. After spraying this mixture for a short while he became ill and had to be taken to a doctor immediately. After receiving medical treatment he was confined to his home and unable to work for some days. Since then he has been sensitive to chemical spray and has become ill several times.

While working the vineyards of George A. Lucas & Sons this summer, Mrs. Beatrice Roman developed trouble breathing, sore throat, difficulty in speaking, and stomach pain. Each day her condition would improve as she left the vineyards, and it would worsen as she began work the following morning. There was a heavy white powder on the vines which she was working among. Mrs. Roman has worked in other crops without experiencing such illness. She has been informed by her physician that it is due to the spray residues on the vines. She stopped working for Lucas, because of the illness caused by the sprays, on August 4, 1969. She has been unable to work more than very little since then because of the continuing effects of the illness.

Mr. Mauro Roman (Beatrice's husband), along with his son, José, and a neighboring family all worked picking grapes in the vineyards of Lamanuzzi and Pantaleo in August 1969. All suffered severe skin rashes over their bodies, with cracked and peeling skin. All left this work after several weeks, and improved sharply as soon as they left. There was a very heavy white powder on the vines and grapes they were picking there.

After working in the vineyards of D. M. Steele for several days, Mr. Juan Q. López developed trouble breathing, rashes on his neck and face, numbness in his left arm and upper left chest, headache, and irritated eyes. There was a white powder on the vines. Mr. Lopez's condition began to improve when he stopped working in these fields.

While working picking grapes in a Caric vineyard about 10 days ago, Mr. Abelardo Hernández ate some grapes from the vine. Shortly thereafter, he began to vomit and to bleed from the nose. His foreman refused to take him to a doctor until other workers finally convinced his to do so. The doctor who treated him said his illness was due to the grapes and the chemicals on them. He has suffered from this illness on and off since then.

During this season, Mrs. Dominga F. Medina has worked in vineyards near Richgrove. She has seen spray rigs spraying liquid preparations on the vineyards only a short distance from where she and the other members of her crew were working. She has suffered from bloody nose, eye irritation, and headache while working in these vineyards.

Aurelio de la Cruz worked with Giumarra Vineyards in the spring of 1969. On more than one occasion he saw spray rigs spraying right ahead of the crew he was working in; his crew was told to work in the sprayed areas shortly after the spraying was concluded. He suffered eye irritation and skin rashes on these occasions.

Mr. Claro Runtal suffered very severe rashes and dermatitis on his legs and neck while working in vineyards of Richard Bagdasarian from December 1968 to June 1969. Many of the other men in the crew suffered skin irritations during the same period from the chemical dusts which had been applied to the vines.

Juanita Chavera was working in the Elmco vineyards in the spring of 1969 when she developed, as a result of the spray residue on the vines, skin rash, eye irritation, and hands swollen so badly that her ring had to be cut off. Other women in the crew including Mrs. Chovera's sister, Linda Ortiz, suffered similar symptoms.

María Serna also working in the Elmco vineyards in May 1969, where she developed irritated eyes, headaches, and severe dizziness. Her daughter, Alicia Ramona, suffered rashes and eye irritation.

Frances Barajas also worked in the Elmco vineyards this spring. While she was working there, a tractor spraying a liquid economic poison came through the vineyard in which she was working. She ran out of the field because she did not want to get sprayed, but a foreman ordered her to go back in and get back to work. She later talked to the tractor driver, who said he had been ordered to spray there by one of the Elmco supervisors. While working there she developed skin rashes and eye irritations that led to a serious eye infection. She has been afraid to complain about the poisons for fear of being fired.

Rafaela Ayala worked in the Elmco vineyards in the same crew as Mrs. Barajas. When the tractor sprayed the field they were working in she immediately began to vomit and her eyes became very irritated; they are still sore. She stopped working for Elmco as a result.

Mrs. Celestina Pereales was working in the Elmco vineyards in May 1968 when a tractor spray rig approached the row her crew was working in. Her supervisor told them to hunch down under the vines while the spray rig sprayed them. Not knowing better at the time, she did so. Her eyes became red and watery right away, and became persistently irritated, and she has had eye trouble ever since.

Mrs. Josephine C. Moreno was working in a crew leafing vines in the Elmco vineyards this spring. A spray rig came through the vineyard one row away from where the crew was working, and she and other women got sprayed soaking wet, but were put back to work after five minutes.

Petra Sisneros was working in the Elmco vineyards, tipping grape bunches, in May 1969, when four tractor driven spray rigs came into the field. Without any warning, one of them came right over the spot she was working in, spraying her soaking wet and blinding her to the point that she almost fell under the spray rig. Other women workers dragged her away from the danger of the spray rig. Her supervisor did not take her to a doctor until she became visibly sick. Until then she had merely been told to sit in the shade under the vine. She was vomiting a great deal by this time. After she was taken to a doctor, who gave her an injection and bathed her eyes, she was returned to the vineyards where she had to wait for a ride home until her co-workers were finished for the day. She was extremely ill for the next 10 days with vomiting, nausea, trembling, dizziness, headache, difficulty in breathing, tightness of chest, and difficulty in sleeping. To date she has received no compensation from her employer. She is still suffering from the aftereffects of this illness. When she asked her supervisor and foreman what kind of chemical she had been sprayed with, they claimed they didn't know and said it was not their fault she had been sprayed.

Alfonso Pedraza was also sprayed by an Elmco spray rig while working in its vineyards in the summer of 1969. The spray hit him on his back. When he saw a doctor three days later, his back was very red and the skin was cracked. The rash spread all over his body, and he developed muscle stiffness and eye irritation as well.

The carelessness with which economic poisons are applied in this area is such that farm workers are endangered outside the fields as well as within. About a month ago, while Petra Ojeda was working in a Tulare County orchard, the grower's tractor driven spray rigs sprayed her car and the cars of other workers which were parked along the road nearby. Mrs. Ojeda's young child was in the car asleep, along with food for lunch for the entire family. The child was covered by a blanket, but her bottle was covered with spray. The entire car was white with the chemical spray.

The James Morning family didn't even have to leave their home in order to be sprayed with economic poisons. In May 1969, their country home was sprayed by an airplane which was applying poison to a nearby field. All six members of the family were hit with the spray, causing rashes, cracked skin, and irritated eyes.

The United Farm Workers Organizing Committee is attempting to solve this pervasive problem by the collective bargaining process. We have recently attained what is for farm workers an historic breakthrough in our negotiations with the Perelli-Minetti Company. We have completed negotiating a comprehensive health and safety clause which covers the subject of economic poisons. It includes the following protections:

HEALTH AND SAFETY

A. The Health and Safety Committee shall be formed consisting of equal numbers of worker's representatives selected by the bargaining unit and P–M representatives. The Health and Safety Committee shall be provided with notices on the use of pesticides, insecticides, or herbicides, as outlined in Section D 1, 2, and 3.

The Health and Safety Committee shall advise in the formulation of rules and practices relating to the health and safety of the workers, including, but not limited to, the use of pesticides, insecticides, and herbicides; the use of garments, materials, tools, and equipment as they may affect the health and safety of the workers and sanitation conditions.

B. The following shall not be used: DDT, Aldrin, Dieldrin, and Endrin. Other chlorinated hydrocarbons shall not be applied without the necessary precautions.

C. The Health and Safety Committee shall recommend the proper and safe use of organic phosphates including, but not limited to parathion. The Company shall notify the Health and Safety Committee as soon as possible before the application of organic phosphate material. Said notice shall contain the information set forth in Section D below. The Health and Safety Committee shall recommend the length of time during which farm workers will not be permitted to enter the treated field following the application of organic phosphate pesticide. If P–M uses organic phosphates, it shall pay for the expense for all farm workers, applying the phosphates, of one baseline cholinesterase test and other additional such tests if recommended by a doctor. The results of all said tests shall be immediately given by P–M to the Health and Safety Committee.

D. P–M shall keep the following records and make them available to each member of the Health and Safety Committee:

(1) A plan showing the size and location of fields and a list of the crops or plants being grown.

(2) Pesticides, insecticides, and herbicides used, including brand names plus active ingredients, registration number on the label, and manufacturer's batch or lot number.

(a) Dates and time applied or to be applied.

(b) Location of crops or plants treated or to be treated.

(c) Amount of each application.

(d) Formulation.

(e) Method of application.

(f) Person who applied the pesticide.

(3) Date of harvest.

SANITATION

A. There shall be adequate toilet facilities, separate for men and women, in the field, readily accessible to workers, that will be maintained in a clean and sanitary manner. These may be portable facilities and shall be maintained at the ratio of one for every 35 workers.

B. Each place where there is work being performed shall be provided with suitable, cool, potable drinking water convenient to workers. Individual paper drinking cups shall be provided.

C. Workers will have two (2) relief periods of fifteen (15) minutes which, insofar as practical, shall be in the middle of each work period.

TOOLS AND PROTECTIVE EQUIPMENT

Tools and equipment and protective garments necessary to perform the work and/or to safeguard the health of or to prevent injury to a worker's person shall be provided, maintained, and paid for by P–M.

The Union and the Strike

This undated speech reiterates the goals of the NFWA in striking against growers, linking its goals to fundamental and indisputable human rights issues. Chavez's faith in the power of unions is demonstrated forcefully.

WHAT IS THIS STRIKE?

This strike is all the farm workers standing up together and saying FROM THIS DAY WE DEMAND TO BE TREATED LIKE THE MEN WE ARE! We are not slaves and we are not animals. And we are not alone.

This strike is good men standing side by side and telling the growers WE WILL NO LONGER WORK FOR LOW WAGES! We are not afraid of the growers because we are strong. We want a union contract that will guarantee us our jobs.

This strike is all farm workers telling the growers WE WILL NO LONGER WORK FOR YOU UNTIL WE CAN SHARE IN THE GREAT DEAL OF MONEY YOU HAVE MADE! You live in big, warm homes and we live in boxes. You have plenty to eat while our children work in your fields. You wear good clothing while we are dressed in rags. Your wives are free to make a good home while our wives work in the fields. We do the work and you make most of the money. THIS GREAT INEQUALITY MUST END!

This strike is to force the growers to RECOGNIZE THE UNION OF FARM WORKERS! We will not work in the growers' fields until they sign a contract that shows they respect us as men and that they respect our union. This strike is a great sacrifice for all farm workers, but WE ARE MAKING THIS SACRIFICE BECAUSE WE KNOW OUR ONLY HOPE IS IN THE STRENGTH OF A UNION!

WHAT IS THIS UNION?

This union is a group of farm workers who have joined together to win for themselves the high wages and the decent working conditions they have already earned. This union is the proof of the strength of good men who realize that the growers are strong and rich, and WE MUST BE EVEN STRONGER IF WE ARE TO MAKE THE GROWERS RESPECT US! We must be strong if we are to win decent wages and decent living conditions and a better life for our wives and children.

This is A UNION OF FARM WORKERS! More of our brothers learn of the union every day, and come and join with us. We know OUR ONLY HOPE IS IN THE STRENGTH OF THE UNION AND WE MUST TEACH OUR BROTHERS WHO DO NOT YET KNOW!

We are showing our unity in our strike. Our strike is stopping the work in the fields. Our strike is stopping ships that would carry grapes. Our strike is stopping the trucks that would carry the grapes. OUR STRIKE WILL STOP EVERY WAY THE GROWER MAKES MONEY UNTIL WE HAVE A UNION CONTRACT THAT GUARANTEES US A FAIR SHARE OF THE MONEY HE MAKES FROM OUR WORK!

We are a union and we are strong and we are striking to force the growers to respect our strength!

Sharing the Wealth

In this essay for Playboy, *published in January 1970, Chavez reminds the public, as well as the President, directly about the force driving the effort to change farming practices: poverty.*

How can we narrow the gap between the wealthy and the poor in this country? What concrete steps can be taken *now* to abolish poverty in America? There are a number of things that President Nixon could do immediately, if he wanted to. In terms of our own grape pickers' strike, he could tell the Pentagon to stop shipping extraordinary amounts of grapes to Vietnam—the Government's most obvious tool in its attempt to break our strike. And he could improve the lot of *all* the farmworkers in the Southwest—easily, under existing legislation—by putting an end to the importing and exploitation of cheap foreign labor. The Immigration Service has allowed almost 500,000 poor Mexicans to flood across the border since 1965. Absorbing this number of resident aliens would not be detrimental if they actually became residents, but most of these workers return to Mexico after each harvest season, since their American wages go much farther there than they would in this country. They have no stake in either economic or political advances here; it is the domestic farmworker who wants our union, who wants better schools, who wants to participate in the political system. Our poor Mexican brothers who are allowed to come across the border for the harvest are tools in the Government's and the growers' attempts to break our strike.

In the still larger framework of all the country's poor, President Nixon should acknowledge that the War on Poverty programs of the Sixties have failed. The Office of Economic Opportunity pumped out propaganda about "community action programs" through which the poor were supposedly going to have a say in the solution of their own problems. Then, just as the communities were organizing for meaningful change through these programs, the money was suddenly yanked away. Washington seemed to realize that if it lived up to its rhetoric, it would actually be encouraging real political participation and building real economic power among the poor, and got cold feet. The Government and the power class will never allow their money to be used to build another power class—especially if they are convinced, however wrongly, that their own economic security and self-interest would be jeopardized.

It might be expected for me to propose that the anti-poverty programs be continued but with better financing and with complete control over them given to representatives of the communities and the people involved. I could also plead for the money that has been spent in the past few years on anti-poverty programs to be simply distributed among the poor. But neither of these sensible alternatives is going to come to pass under an Administration that made it perfectly clear last fall that it intended to channel all Federal funds through local governments, no matter how corrupt.

Nothing is going to happen until we, the poor, can generate our own political and economic power. Such a statement sounds radical to many middle-class Americans, but it should not. Though many of the poor have come to see the affluent middle class as its enemy, that class actually stands between the poor and the real powers in this society—the administrative octopus with its head in Washington, the conglomerates, the military complex. It's like a camel train: The herder, way up in front, leads one camel and all the other camels follow. We happen to be the last camel, trudging along through the leavings of the whole train. We see only the camel in front of us and make him the target of our anger, but that solves nothing. The lower reaches of the middle class, in turn, are convinced that blacks, Mexican Americans, Puerto Ricans, Indians and poor whites want to steal their jobs—a conviction that the power class cheerfully perpetuates. The truth of the matter is that, even with automation, there can still be enough good-paying jobs for *everyone* in this country. If all of us were working for decent wages, there would be a greater demand for goods and services, thus creating even more jobs and increasing the gross national product. Full and fair employment would also mean that taxes traceable to welfare and all the other hidden costs of poverty—presently borne most heavily by middle-income whites—would inevitably go down.

At one time, we would have searched for ways to bring about a direct change in the course of the camel driver. That was the situation in the Thirties, when President Roosevelt initiated such massive programs as the Works Progress Administration and the Civilian Conservation Corps. At that time, *most* Americans were poor, white and nonwhite alike; but most were white. The union movement was fighting to win gains for its members, then an underclass. (Now it feels it has to fight to protect the economic independence it has since achieved.) And there was only a relatively small upper class trying to frustrate change. But today the majority of Americans—most of them still white—are relatively well off financially. The country's policies naturally respond to the desires of the majority, and that majority—having joined the comfortable middle class—is no longer motivated to eliminate poverty.

The forces in control today at the top, furthermore, are so immense, powerful and interlocked that it would be absurd to expect dramatic change from them. The Pentagon, for example, has a hand-in-glove relationship with the same industrialists who manufacture tractors, reapers and mechanical grape harvesters. How can we expect the Defense Department to do anything *but* undermine our battle with the growers? The poor today, finally, are not only impoverished; most of them are also members of minority races. Thus, as a class, we are racially as well as economically alienated from the mainstream.

Despite this alienation, however, and despite the magnitude of the forces opposing us, the poor have tremendous potential economic power, as unlikely as that may seem. That power can derive from two facts of life: First, even though our numbers are much smaller than they were in the Thirties, we are still a sizable group—some 30,000,000. Perhaps even more important, we have a strong sense of common indignation; the poor always identify with one another more than do the rich. What instruments can we use to win this power? Perhaps the most effective technique is the boycott. Most Americans realize that the black civil rights revolution of the late Fifties and early Sixties effectively began with Dr. Martin Luther King's successful bus boycott in Montgomery, Alabama. This tool is being perfected, for blacks, by the Reverend Jesse Jackson in Chicago. Our own nationwide grape boycott is hurting corporate agriculture so much that the growers are eventually going to have to deal with us, no matter how hard the power class tries to weaken the boycott's effectiveness.

Another powerful tool is the strike. Attacking the unions is fashionable today, but the labor movement, for all its faults, is one of the few institutions in the country that I see even *trying* to reach down to us. The universities, thanks to some student organizations, and the churches, thanks to a few radical groups, are the only other institutions making a real attempt to alleviate our plight. With their help, we farmworkers are now trying to build our own union, a new kind of union that will actively include people rather than exclude them. A man is a man and needs an organization even when—in fact, especially when—a machine displaces him. The poor are also beginning to experiment with cooperatives of all kinds and with their own credit unions—that is, with the creation of our own institutions, the profits from which can go to us rather than to the wealthy. And, at least in the Southwest, we are looking at ways to give the farmworkers plots of land they can call their own, because we know that power always comes with landownership.

We need greater control of important noneconomic institutions, too. We have very little to say, for example, about the attitude of our churches to economic and political problems. We are looking for ways to get the church involved in the struggle, to make it relevant to our needs. The poor also need control of their schools and medical facilities and legal defenses; but these advances are all subsidiary, in my opinion, to the need for developing strictly economic power. Economic power has to precede political power. Gandhi understood this when, in 1930, he and his followers resolved to defy the British government's salt monopoly by making their own salt from the sea; this boycott was one of the crucial steps in the Indian fight for independence. We, the poor of the United States, have not yet hit upon the specific issue around which we can bring all of our boycotting and striking capabilities to bear. But we will.

The poor are badly prepared to participate in the political arena. Entire nations of us, such as the American Indians, have never had more than token representation in Federal, state, county or city government. Migratory farmworkers are almost always disenfranchised by voter-registration residency requirements.

Minority immigrants face long waits for citizenship papers and the additional barrier of literacy tests. And even if they qualify, it is prohibitively expensive for many of the poor to vote. A farm-worker putting in long hours simply can't afford to take half or all of a weekday off to travel to the polls.

In a society that truly desired full participation, all 18-year-olds and convicts would be given the franchise; the whole practice of voter registration would be scrapped; immigrants would automatically be given a citizenship certificate at the end of one year if their record was clean, whether or not they were literate in English or in their own language; elections would last up to 72 hours and would include Saturdays and Sundays.

These are some of the simpler things that could be done to increase participation. But they aren't being done and they won't be done unless the poor can change the political *status quo*. Our vote simply doesn't matter that much today. Once we give it away, we lose it because we can't control the men we elect. We help elect liberals and then they pass civil rights bills that defuse our boycotts and strikes, taking the steam out of our protest but leaving the basic problems of injustice and inequality unsolved. Or, worse, we elect a candidate who says he will represent us and then discover that he has sold out to some special interest.

I propose two reforms that would go a long way toward a cure. First, the whole system of campaign financing should make it as easy for a poor man as for a millionaire to put his case before the people. Second, the various minority groups—as well as such pockets of poor whites as the Appalachians, who make up a distinct economic subculture—should be given a proportionate number of seats in every governing body affecting them. Black people should have 43 or 44 seats in the House of Representatives and 10 or 11 seats in the Senate. In California, where ten percent of the population is Mexican American, eight seats in the state assembly should be set aside for us; there is now only one Mexican American assemblyman. This same procedure should be followed all the way down the line, through the county level down to the school and water districts. In each case, the electorate would be allowed to vote for whomever they pleased—even if he weren't of the same race as the majority of voters—but the representative would clearly be an advocate of their needs. Though this system may seem alien to many Americans, something like it already works in the cities, where tickets are often drawn up to reflect the racial balance of the community. And the idea of special representation for minority political groups is common in foreign countries. Once the minority group or the economic subculture is completely assimilated, of course, the need for special representation will wither away.

These are the kinds of reforms we will work for once we have an economic base established; they certainly aren't going to come about as long as we remain powerless. But we will remain powerless until we help ourselves. I know that there are men of good conscience in the affluent society who are trying to help. Many of them are middle-class people who remember the Depression, or unionists who wear scars of the battle to liberate workingmen. They are like a large army of guerrillas within the establishment. We are depending on them to hear our cry, to respect our picket lines and to support our grape boycott, the Reverend Ralph Abernathy's Poor People's Campaign and the Reverend Jesse Jackson's Operation Breadbasket. And we hope that they will understand how crucial it is that the vote become truly universal. As long as democracy exists mainly as a catchword in politicians' speeches, the hopes for *real* democracy will be mocked.

In the final analysis, however, it doesn't really matter what the political system is; ultimately, the results are the same, whether you have a general, a king, a dictator or a civilian president running the country. We don't need perfect political systems; we need perfect participation. If you don't participate in the planning, you just don't count. Until the chance for political participation is there, we who are poor will continue to attack the soft part of the American system—its economic structure. We will build power through boycotts, strikes, new unions—whatever techniques we can develop. These attacks on the *status quo* will come not because we hate but because we know America *can* construct a humane society for all of its citizens—and that if it does not, there will be chaos.

But it must be understood that once we have substantial economic power—and the political power that follows in its wake—our work will not be done. We will then move on to effect even more fundamental changes in this society. The quality of compassion seems to have vanished from the American spirit. The power class and the middle class haven't done anything that one can truly be proud of, aside from building machines and rockets. It's amazing how people can get so excited about a rocket to the moon and not give a damn about smog, oil leaks, the devastation of the environment with pesticides, hunger, disease. When the poor share some of the power that the affluent now monopolize, we *will* give a damn.

No More Cathedrals

Written on February 11, 1970. Chavez was raised in a strict Catholic household. But, as he acknowledges here, the Catholic Church was reticent to accept Chicanos and other Latino groups as full members of the Church, and failed to support them in their battles for social justice. Chavez challenges the Church to uphold the doctrines it taught him. This piece appeared in Aztlán: An Anthology of Mexican-American Literature.

The place to begin is with our own experience with the Church in the strike which has gone on for thirty-one months in Delano. For in Delano the Church has been involved with the poor in a unique way which should stand as a symbol to other communities. Of course, when we refer to the Church we should define the word a little. We mean the whole Church, the Church as an ecumenical body spread around the world, and not just its particular form in a parish in a local community. The Church we are talking about is a tremendously powerful institution in our society, and in the world. That Church is one form of the Presence of God on Earth, and so naturally it is powerful. It is powerful by definition. It is a powerful moral and spiritual force which cannot be ignored by any movement. Furthermore, it is an organization with tremendous wealth. Since the Church is to be servant to the poor, it is *our* fault if that wealth is not channeled to help the poor in our world.

In a small way we have been able, in the Delano strike, to work together with the Church in such a way as to bring some of its moral and economic power to bear on those who want to maintain the status quo, keeping farm workers in virtual enslavement. In brief, here is what happened in Delano.

Some years ago, when some of us were working with the Community Service Organization, we began to realize the powerful effect which the Church can have on the conscience of the opposition. In scattered instances, in San Jose, Sacramento, Oakland, Los Angeles and other places, priests would speak out loudly and clearly against specific instances of oppression, and in some cases, stand with the people who were being hurt. Furthermore, a small group of priests, Frs. McDonald, McCollough, Duggan and others, began to pinpoint attention on the terrible situation of the farm workers in our state.

At about that same time, we began to run into the California Migrant Ministry in the camps and fields. They were about the only ones there, and a lot of us were very suspicious, since we were Catholics and they were Protestants. However, they had developed a very clear conception of the Church. It was called to serve, to be at the mercy of the poor, and not to try to use them. After a while this made a lot of sense to us, and we began to find ourselves working side by side with them. In fact, it forced us to raise the question why OUR Church was not doing the same. We would ask, "Why do the Protestants come out here and help the people, demand nothing, and give all their time to serving farm workers, while our own parish priests stay in their churches, where only a few people come, and usually feel uncomfortable?"

It was not until some of us moved to Delano and began working to build the National Farm Workers Association that we really saw how far removed from the people the parish Church was. In fact, we could not get any help at all from the priests of Delano. When the strike began, they told us we could not even use the Church's auditorium for the meetings. The farm workers' money helped build that auditorium! But the Protestants were there again, in the form of the California Migrant Ministry, and they began to help in little ways, here and there.

When the strike started in 1965, most of our "friends" forsook us for a while. They ran, or were just too busy to help. But the California Migrant Ministry held a meeting with its staff and decided that the strike was a matter of life or death for farm workers everywhere, and that even if it meant the end of the Migrant Ministry they would turn over their resources to the strikers. The political pressure on the Protestant Churches was tremendous and the Migrant Ministry lost a lot of money. But they stuck it out, and they began to point the way to the rest of the Church. In fact, when 30 of the strikers were arrested for shouting Huelga, 11 ministers went to jail with them. They were in Delano that day at the request of Chris Hartmire, director of the California Migrant Ministry.

Then the workers began to raise the question: "Why ministers? Why not priests? What does the Bishop say?" But the Bishop said nothing. But slowly the pressure of the people grew and grew, until finally we have in Delano a priest sent by the new Bishop, Timothy Manning, who is there to help minister to the needs of farm workers. His name is Father Mark Day and he is the Union's chaplain. *Finally,* our own Catholic Church has decided to recognize that we have our own peculiar needs, just as the growers have theirs.

But outside of the local diocese, the pressure built up on growers to negotiate was tremendous. Though we were not allowed to have our own priest, the power of the ecumenical body of the Church was tremendous. The work of the Church, for example, in the Schenley, DiGiorgio, Perelli-Minetti strikes was fantastic. They applied pressure—and they mediated.

When poor people get involved in a long conflict, such as a strike, or a civil rights drive, and the pressure increases each day, there is a deep need for spiritual advice. Without it we see families crumble, leadership weaken, and hard workers grow tired. And in such a situation the spiritual advice must be given by a *friend,* not by the opposition. What sense does it make to go to Mass on Sunday and reach out for spiritual help, and instead get sermons about the wickedness of your cause? That only drives one to question and to despair. The growers in Delano have their spiritual problems . . . we do not deny that. They have every right to have priests and ministers who serve their needs. BUT WE HAVE DIFFERENT NEEDS, AND SO WE NEEDED A FRIENDLY SPIRITUAL GUIDE. And this is true in every community in this state where the poor face tremendous problems.

But the opposition raises a tremendous howl about this. They don't want us to have our spiritual advisors, friendly to our needs. Why is this? Why indeed except that THERE IS TREMENDOUS SPIRITUAL AND ECONOMIC POWER IN THE CHURCH. The rich know it, and for that reason they choose to keep it from the people.

The leadership of the Mexican-American Community must admit that we have fallen far short in our task of helping provide spiritual guidance for our people. We may say, "I don't feel any such need. I can get along." But that is a poor excuse for not helping provide such help for others. For we can also say, "I don't need any welfare help. I can take care of my own problems." But we are all willing to fight like hell for welfare aid for those who truly need it, who would starve without it. Likewise we may have gotten an education and not care about scholarship money for ourselves, or our children. But we would, we should, fight like hell to see to it that our state provides aid for any child needing it so that he can get the education he desires. LIKEWISE WE CAN SAY WE DON'T NEED THE CHURCH. THAT IS OUR BUSINESS. BUT THERE ARE HUNDREDS OF THOUSANDS OF OUR PEOPLE WHO DESPERATELY NEED SOME HELP FROM THAT POWERFUL INSTITUTION, THE CHURCH, AND WE ARE FOOLISH NOT TO HELP THEM GET IT.

For example, the Catholic Charities agencies of the Catholic Church has millions of dollars earmarked for the poor. But often the money is spent for food baskets for the needy instead of for effective action to eradicate the causes of poverty. The men and women who administer this money sincerely want to help their brothers. It should be our duty to help direct the attention to the basic needs of the Mexican Americans in our society . . . needs which cannot be satisfied with baskets of food, but rather with effective organizing at the grass roots level.

Therefore, I am calling for Mexican-American groups to stop ignoring this source of power. It is not just our right to appeal to the Church to use its power effectively for the poor, it is our duty to do so. It should be as natural as appealing to government . . . and we do that often enough.

Furthermore, we should be prepared to come to the defense of that priest, rabbi, minister, or layman of the Church, who out of commitment to truth and justice gets into a tight place with his pastor or bishop. It behooves us to stand with that man and help him see his trial through. It is our duty to see to it that his rights of conscience are respected and that no bishop, pastor or other higher body takes that God-given, human right away.

Finally, in a nutshell, what do we want the Church to do? We don't ask for more cathedrals. We don't ask for bigger churches or fine gifts. We ask for its presence with us, beside us, as Christ among us. We ask the Church to *sacrifice with the people* for social change, for justice, and for love of brother. We don't ask for words. We ask for deeds. We don't ask for paternalism. We ask for servanthood.

At Harvard

In March 1970, four years into the Delano Grape Strike, Chavez spoke at Harvard, focusing on the hardships of the men and women involved in the strike and how their struggle was undermined by the Department of Defense's purchase of grapes. He highlights the growth in support for La Causa *as a result of the grape strike's publicity. It was published in* Metanoia *in March 1970.*

You know the struggle to organize the farm workers and particularly the boycott has received a lot of attention lately—so much so that it is frightening some groups we have in our society. And some of these groups have gone so far as to change the priority as to what is more dangerous for our country. Did you know that some groups in America today have said that sex education is the number one menace to society? I would like to announce tonight that the John Birch Society now rates the grape boycott as number one and sex as number two! We knew it was very important and thus knew what we were heading for.

It is very important to farm workers. The whole question of gaining independence and freedom to be able to form their own associations and to get employers to deal with those associations as other workers have done for so long. And this is one of the key issues that we are confronted with, the right of workers to have their own unions without the interference of their employers, and certainly without the interference to the point where they attempt to break every attempt of the workers to organize.

You know, we have had a long historical struggle in the fields of California to form unions. Very little has been recorded, very little has been written about it, because in most cases this struggle has been waged by immigrant groups. In many cases those groups made very little achievement, but for the last seven years there have been basic struggles to organize, and for seven years these attempts have been thwarted and broken by the overwhelming power of the employer groups.

Today in Delano we have a group of men and women who have done outstanding work to try and liberate themselves through their collective action to get those things in life that other workers have had so long. They have gone to great expense and personal selfless dedication and work just to stay alive as a group. We ourselves frequently ask: What causes a man to give up his paycheck for forty-eight months—forty-nine months now—however small it may be, for the right to have a living? Or what would cause a woman striker to picket and demonstrate, peacefully and non-violently, and then be arrested as a common criminal? Or what would cause men and women in the struggle to suffer the painful separation from family and be sent across the country to all the major cities and Canada, to bring the word of the boycott and the struggle of the farm workers? We often ask ourselves: What would cause teenage boys and girls to school without a new pair of shoes or go to school with the same old clothes and do without noon lunch? What causes this greatest personal sacrifice? Why are they going insane? Or what would cause still little children who are too small to understand the struggle, to do without milk, to do without the basic necessities of life because their parents are involved in what is getting to be perhaps the longest and, perhaps, we hope, the most successful strike of farm workers ever in the history of our country? We say that what causes this is what causes other people in other parts of the world and in our own country— a spirit of independence and freedom, the spirit that they want to change things and that they want to be independent and they want to be able to run their own lives. This is the cause why these workers are so willing to bear the sacrifices and all the personal suffering that go with the strike and boycott.

You know, organizing farm workers is very different from organizing any other workers in the country today. Here we don't have any rules, any regulations. We don't have any prescribed methods, no precedents. There is no law for farm labor organizing, save the law of the jungle. The citizens and their rights for seven years have been ignored and the employers have seen to it that they don't survive. Agriculture in this country is not a family with a small plot of land. That is not agriculture, that is not where the fruits and the vegetables, the nuts and the grapes are produced. They are produced in large factory farms, huge corporate farms. They themselves have adopted a new name: they call themselves "agro-business."

It is against agro-business, in such combinations as they have going now with the Defense Department, that we have to deal. For we had cut the sales of grapes nationally thirty percent. The Defense Department, on the other hand, is increasing its purchases to the extent that they are now shipping to Vietnam eight hundred percent more grapes than they were in the beginning of the boycott. When we complained to the Defense Department about the increased purchases, they sent us back a letter saying that it was true that they were buying the grapes, but there was nothing unusual, their role in life was to remain neutral! We sent another letter back asking them if they are going to continue to buy grapes, how did they justify it. Why did they continue doing it? They wrote back and they told us that they were buying grapes because there had been a sudden craving for grapes among servicemen in Vietnam. We reported this to the strikers in Delano after we received the letter. One of the ladies of the strike found it very difficult to understand and after the meeting she approached me and asked me, "Did you say that the servicemen in Vietnam are craving for grapes?" And I told her that that is what the Defense Department said in their letter. She looked at me mystified and said, "I only thought expectant mothers could have a craving for grapes!"

But it is no joke that the Defense Department is in a deal with agro-business for the sole purpose of breaking the strike. And the eight hundred percent only takes us to the end of the last fiscal year. As the report comes from the first quarter of this new fiscal year; we don't know what the percentage may be. We can very well guess that it will probably be about a thousand percent. That means they are sending to Vietnam now about eight pounds of grapes per man. Imagine what happens over there when a fellow doesn't like grapes gets that much!

But in the face of this overwhelming power, enough to wipe out literally any attempt of a group of people to organize, we will continue to work, we will continue to spread our strike and boycott to many parts of the world. We have been able to enlist the support of the transport workers throughout the world, the support of the metal-workers, all the labor movements in Canada and the labor movement here, the church supporting us in a manner to be marvelled at, and the liberal community. But it was not like this always. There was a time at the beginning of the strike when people were afraid of us. There was a time at the beginning of the strike when we stood alone with the workers and when no one dared to come near us. No one dared to come near us because we were being red-baited. And it did not come to be what it is today, except for today, thank God—and we thank them a million times— the students who came to our support right from the beginning. So there is sympathy of the worker in this struggle for students whoever they may be.

The love of this people for justice and for organization and for a union is so great that they have shown us in many ways their dedication. Willing at all times to work day and night, willing to eat once a day if need be, willing to picket now forty-eight months—forty-nine months—day in and day out, morning, noon, and evening.

I know that one of the great attributes we have is the people's willingness: first of all, to do the work; and secondly, that the only way we can progress and the only way we can effectively conduct our strike, our boycott, and our whole effort, is to do it nonviolently. We have had over four years of experience with many examples where willingness not to strike back has paid handsome dividends for the furtherance of our movement. And every day we learn that the nonviolence expected of us, both from the leadership and the membership, requires all the creativity that may be within us, and to pull that creativity out and not resort to violence. We have learned that nonviolence needs the maximum of one's patience. And we know that nonviolence is always a constant reminder that the essence of it is our capacity to love not only ourselves and our friends, but the opposition. And believe me that is difficult! But if ever we can come to that, there is no force on this earth that could stop this movement or any other movement!

We need your help as you have given it to us in the past when we began. We need you to do your work, our work, to end the war in Vietnam. Please don't forget us. People need to be reminded.

Please remind the people that the Pentagon is not only killing the Vietnamese, but our soldiers are being fed with our grapes of wrath. And also your friends, and more especially your grocer. We are very happy to have you go into a store and when there are grapes sold to call the manager and call his attention to it. He, I am sure, is not going to appreciate the time he has to spend with you just to receive the advice that he should stop selling grapes in his store. In this way it may become for him so expensive that he will not sell them any more.

It becomes our conviction that there has developed in our country not only in our movement, but in the movement for the poor and the oppressed a real desire, beginning with the students and young people, to eradicate poverty and bring justice to our people. Our voices and your voices are being heard all over—you can be assured of that!

It is our belief that in working together we are going to be able to bring justice to an important group in our land. In working together, whether white or black or brown—it really doesn't matter because we really are just one people. In working together we will be able to bring justice to all of these people who suffer the pains of injustice. In working together as one people, we will someday be proud to know that it was our generation who was responsible for eliminating the inhuman treatment of workers and other minorities and other poor people. In working together, we know that we will be able to accomplish much more than that because the farm worker is not organized today, and if the farm worker ever gets organized, he is going to become a powerful force in our society, whereby he will work with you in those things we all share so dearly like peace.

Jesus's Friendship

In this undated speech, Chavez talks about his Catholic vision of beatitude and engagement with Christ's teachings.

The beatitudes make natural good sense to the poor. We, of course, do not analyze the words and the meanings in the way that scholars do. Jesus's words fit his life and therefore, the meaning of his words appear to be obvious to us. He spent his life with the poor, the sick, the outcasts, the powerless people. He attacked the wealthy and the powerful. He is with us! We feel that he is our friend, our advocate, our leader. (Of course it is for that reason that we expect the Church of Jesus to be with us.) It may be too simple to say that Jesus is on our side; but we tend to feel that way and perhaps his identification with the oppressed is so clear to us because we do not have to rationalize our wealth and possessions and fit Jesus's deeds and words into the world view of the power and the affluent.

The beatitudes make natural good sense to the poor and the oppressed. They come through to us as Good News: "Blessed are you poor," "Blessed are you who mourn," "Blessed are you meek." It is a message unlike anything we have heard from a society that sees poverty and color as signs of weakness and inferiority. Jesus turns society's standards upside down. His words point to a whole new way of looking at life. He seems to be saying: "Forget what those with earthly power have taught you. This is the way life really is: those who think they have it made have missed the point of life. The rich and the powerful will have their reward; but true happiness is reserved for those of you who are poor, who are merciful, who are peacemakers!" That is good news indeed, especially for those who have been treated with contempt by the powerful structures and the "successful" people of this world.

"Blessed are you who hunger and thirst for righteousness for you shall be satisfied." Jesus was a worker, a man of plain words. He said what was on his mind and his words were meaningful because they were drawn from the real life of the people. His listeners knew what it meant to be hungry and thirsty. They could feel the feeling because they had been there. To be hungry and thirsty was in one sense a sign of life: at least you were healthy enough to yearn for food and drink. To be hungry and thirsty also included a primitive passion for food and water that had to do with survival itself. To be hungry and thirsty was a part of life but it was also a reminder of death. In a very real way it was a matter of life and death.

In this beatitude Jesus is saying that one life-and-death matter has to do with righteousness: "Blessed are you who have an unrelenting passion for what is right and just for you shall be satisfied." Some who listened to Jesus may have concluded that the "righteousness" message was not for them since they were already poor, the victims of someone else's *un*rightousness. Others surely believed that their own rise to affluence was a clear enough sign of God's righteousness. Still others must have felt that their whole way of life was being challenged by this prophet from Galilee. For those who had ears to hear, Jesus's message was strength for their spirits, an affirmation of life as they had chosen to live it. . . . Good News!

Jesus's life and words are a *challenge* at the same time that they are Good News. They are a challenge to those of us who are poor and oppressed. By his life he is calling us to give ourselves to others, to sacrifice for those who suffer, to share our lives with our brothers and sisters who are also oppressed. He is calling us to "hunger and thirst after justice" in the same way that we hunger and thirst after food and water: that is, by putting our yearning into practice! It is not good enough to know why we are oppressed and by whom. We must join the struggle for what is right and just! Jesus does not promise that it will be an easy way to live life and his own life certainly points in a hard direction; but he does promise that we will be "satisfied" (not stuffed, but satisfied). He promises that by giving life we will find life—full, meaningful life as God meant it to be.

When I first started organizing a farm workers' union in 1962, I was looking for those farm workers who were most hungry and thirsty for justice. If we were going to have our own union we would have to pay for it so that we could control it. We set the dues at $3.50 per month with $2.00 of that amount going toward a death benefit insurance plan that was very important to the members. One of my jobs as organizer was to collect the dues. I hated it and at the same time I knew it was essential. I remember many incidents when I went to collect dues. I want to tell you just one. I went to a worker's home in McFarland, seven miles south of Delano. It was a dark, rainy night in the middle of winter. There was no work for farm workers and there would not be any for weeks. As I knocked on the door, the father of the house was going to the store with $5.00 for groceries. It was all the money he had. I told him that he was two months behind in his dues and that he would have to pay at least one month to keep his membership active. He thought a little while. I don't know what was going through his mind but he must have said to himself what we all knew in our hearts: "we have been hungry before and we are going to be hungry again; nothing will ever change unless some of us make sacrifices." He gave me the $5.00. We went to the store together and got change. I stayed with him while he bought $1.50 of groceries for his family and gave $3.50 to his union. In many of the hard days that followed I thought about that farm worker. With his kind of faith there was no person or group who could stop us from having our own union!

Since 1962, I have met many, many farm workers and friends who love justice and who are willing to sacrifice for what is right. They have a quality about them that reminds me of the beatitude. They are living examples that Jesus's promise is true: they have been hungry and thirsty for righteousness and they have been satisfied. They are determined, patient people who believe in life and who give strength to others. They have given me more love and hope and strength than they will ever know. They have also convinced me that every person has that spirit within that yearns for mercy and justice. The love for justice that is in us is not only the best part of our being but it is also the most true to our nature. The spirit of love may be thickly covered over by hurt or pride or too much money or too much power, but it is still there, yearning to be released, ready to serve the neighbor who is in need. When we respond to that yearning we release an energy for full life that is powerful and new. Life begins to make sense, to have meaning and purpose. The good that is possible comes into view and the death that is all around us loses its power to destroy. Wholeness happens because we are expressing with our body what is most true to God's nature and to our own.

It is supposed to be a very bad time in our country. There is no doubting that apathy and cynicism and boredom are around us like storm clouds. But nothing fundamental has changed. People who have lost their hunger for justice are not ultimately powerful. They are like sick people who have lost their appetite for what is truly nourishing. Such sick people should not frighten or discourage us. They should be prayed for along with the sick people who are in the hospital.

Nothing fundamental has changed! The spirit of love is still present in every person, waiting to be put to work for justice. We in the farm workers' movement see it every day in every city of the country. As we tell our story and do our work, people respond and join the boycott of grapes, head lettuce, and Gallo wines. They not only make a personal boycott pledge but they tell their friends, they join us on picket lines, they contribute money and energy and love, they write stories and make leaflets, and in thousands of other ways they add their spirits and their energy to ours. The sacrifices of the farm workers and the self-giving of the boycott supporters combine to make an unstoppable, nonviolent force for justice. These beautiful people who love justice and who are willing to put that love into practice are the reason why we will win back the grape contracts and go on to build a strong democratic union for all farm workers in our country.

Jesus is a disturbing friend to the poor. He puts into practice what it means to sacrifice for others. His words are powerful because his life is an example of what it means to hunger and thirst for righteousness. He challenges us to be different than we are, he leads us away from death and in the direction of life, and he promises us that we will discover the blessings of God if we join him in his work among the poor, the sick, the lonely, the powerless.

An Assortment of Responses

Aside from his speeches, Chavez kept a busy schedule responding to an endless array of letters. The six letters included, all from 1970, are representative in style and tone.

May 15, 1970

SP4 Ralph Gonzalez Velez
HQ Det, 31st Medical Group
APO New York 09175

Dear Brother Velez:

Thank you for your beautiful letter. I am glad for you that you have found pride in your heritage and your people, and also that you are looking and working toward a future in which you can help your brothers.

Our movement, la huelga de los trabajodous compesinos, is not a CHICANO movement, and certainly not <u>the</u> Chicano movement. We are struggling and working for the freedom and dignity of all farmworkers, Mexican, Filipino, Black, Anglo, and <u>all</u> others. Many people see only the Mexicans in our struggle, and recognize our fight as a Chicano movement, but this is not the true picture of what we are doing.

There is much happening among the Chicanos in this country. Much of it is good, and I am glad that they are beginning to come together and work united for justice.

You are very welcome to join us in Delano when you return. Please let us know when you will be coming.

I am sending some materials on the strike and the boycott. I hope that they will be helpful to you.

Viva la huelga! Viva La Causa!

Cesar E. Chavez
CEC/lc

September 16, 1970

Miss Joan Bonnar
1305 W. Rudy Avenue
Porterville, California 93427

Dear Miss Bonnar:

I want to thank you for your kind letter. I feel fine now so don't worry about me—just keep me in your prayer, me and the other brave people working with me.

I know a fast is very hard, but believe me I feel so much better after I have been on one. I have the help of a very good personal friend and Doctor who watches over me and I let him do the worrying for me. I listen to him so I really not too concerned about my health as the other people.

Give my regards to all of your family. I request that all of you keep us in your prayers and be ready to assist us in our struggle should this become necessary.

Your friend,

Cesar Chavez
CEC/lc

October 3, 1970

Charles W. Fish
375 Orchard Ave.
Hayward, Calif. 94544

Dear Mr. Fish:

Thank you very much for your letter offering your help to our union. We are always interested in people who believe in our cause and are willing to help correct the injustices in agriculture.

You should know however that our work style is accelerated, particularly the sign with the table grape growers. We have requests from farm workers all over California requesting our assistance.

It is not uncommon for us to work 14 to 16 hours days. Nor do we have days off we work every day. Also we do not offer salaries, all the people on our staff are volunteer. They work for substance and $5.00 a week.

Please let us hear from you.

Sincerely,

Cesar E. Chavez

October 3, 1970

Mr. Charles Huber
Space Data Agencies
3560 W. Bayshore Road
Palo Alto, Calif. 94303

Dear Mr. Huber:

I wish to thank you for the assistance you have given to the Union and especially to commend you for the work you have done in completing the commemorative stamps. They are beautiful and inspiring. We can rely on them quite heavily in our efforts to raise a stronger defense fund.

I am sure by this time you are aware of the new boycott declared against all scab lettuce. Please assist us in any way that you believe can futher a successful and non-violent conclusion of this strike.

With warmest regards,

Cesar E. Chavez
Director

October 3, 1970

Mr. William Arbogast
788 Loma Verda Avenue
Palo Alto, Calif. 94303

Dear Brother Arbogast:

Daneen and Ruben Montoya have told me of the detailed work, the time you contributed and your enthusiasm in assisting them in the completion of the new poster. The poster is beautiful as are the commemorative stamps. They will prove to be real fund raisers, funds that are desperately needed to finance our new lettuce boycott.

We would appreciate any help you can give us in future projects. If you have ideas for fund raising please contact them. We are extremely grateful for your interest and support.

Thank you once again.

Sincerely,

Cesar E. Chavez
Director

CEC/lt

November 7, 1970

Director
Social Security Administration
2619 F
Bakersfield, Ca. 93301

Dear Sir:

We have been finding a surprisingly large number of people who are working without Social Security numbers. In the Union our membership records; our union health plan; and our seniority system are all based on the workers' Social Security numbers. If people are working without valid Social Security cards it makes it extremely difficult for us to insure that they receive all the benefits that they are entitled to. Of course, it also means that they are not getting their Social Security benefits.

I am sure that you realize the importance of this matter. For that reason I would appreciate it if you could send an agent to Delano at the earliest possible convenience to discuss what we can do about this problem.

Thank you for your time and consideration. I hope to hear from you soon.

Sincerely,

Cesar E. Chavez
Director UFWOC, AFL-CIO

CEC:nk
l c/c

Forty Acres

This selection is Chavez's introduction—signed on October 12, 1970, Columbus Day—to Mark Day's book Forty Acres, *which told the story of the UFWA's early struggle for workers' rights.*

A great deal of change has taken place among farm workers since our struggle began in 1965. Before the strike started, we had to work ten days in order to get ten people together for a meeting. Now we can get a thousand people to a meeting in only a few hours. The awareness of the people has been magnified a thousand times over. People have lost their fear. And, because there has been a concrete success in Delano, workers throughout the country are making fantastic demands on our time, organizers, and resources. If we had the resources, we could be organizing simultaneously all over the southwestern United States.

I have always believed that, in order for any movement to be lasting, it must be built on the people. They must be the ones involved in forming it, and they must be the ones that ultimately control it. It is harder that way, but the benefits are more meaningful and lasting when won in this fashion. It is necessary to build a power base. Money by itself does not get the job done. This is why poverty programs have so much difficulty. Although many nice things are said and many wheels are spinning, very little real social change takes place. To try to change conditions without power is like trying to move a car without gasoline. If the workers are going to do anything, they need their own power. They need to involve themselves in meaningful ways. Once they achieve a victory, they can make use of their power to negotiate and change things for the better.

I have often been asked what kind of a union I am trying to build and what type of society I want to see in the future. It seems to me that, once the union members are taken care of in terms of better wages and working conditions, the union must involve itself in the major issues of the times. The problem often arises that a group gets too involved in its own successes and doesn't have time for anything else. It is my hope that we keep ourselves focused on our ideals. It is much easier to profess something by words and not by deeds. Our job, then, is to educate our members so that they will be conscious of the needs of others less fortunate than themselves. The scope of the worker's interest must motivate him to reach out and help others. If we can get across the idea of participating in other causes, then we have real education.

As for the nation as a whole, it doesn't matter to me how our government is structured or what type of political party one may have. The real change comes about when men really want it. In a small way we try to change ourselves and we try to change those with whom we come into contact. You can't organize the masses unless you organize individuals. I like to think of our group as a "doer" type union. We place a great deal of emphasis on doing things and very little on theorizing or writing about them.

I think that our philosophy of cooperation with all groups has helped us a great deal. Our people have developed the ability to respect everyone with whom they come into contact: a wealthy church group or a poor Puerto Rican group in New York City. We try to respect their beliefs and ideals. We try to get them to help us on their own terms. We attempt to show them that by assisting us they are doing something to solve their own problems. A lot has to do with respecting other groups. The best thing we have going for us is having all kinds of people help us in a variety of ways.

For example, we tell people, "If you don't eat lettuce today, you are really helping us." This is the key to successful organizing: letting people who want to help know what they can do. Many movements do not reach this stage. Everything we do must be clearly defined.

During the course of our struggle, we have come to realize that the poor and disadvantaged will not make the gains they need only by political action. We must do more than merely involve ourselves in politics. A grape grower in Delano has one vote. We have a thousand votes to his one vote. But the grower can pick up a telephone, call Washington, and make himself heard. He has more power than we do. We have begun to ask *why*. Obviously, he has more power because he has the economic power. If we had economic power, our thousand votes would count a thousand times more than any individual's vote.

Economic development is a *must* for our membership. Why can't farm workers have a bank? Their wages will still be low for many years to come. If we can retain our increases by buying cooperatively, I think we will be in good shape. We must also get away from the "superconsumerism" atmosphere that surrounds us. We are virtually forced to buy everything that glitters and shines.

Meanwhile, I am not so alienated as others about the absence of political leadership here in the United States. We felt the loss of John and Robert Kennedy very keenly. But, despite this present bad season, I am confident that leadership will appear that is responsive to the needs of the people. Bad times bring good times!

I am often asked if our youth, especially the young Mexican Americans, will choose the way of violence to make the necessary changes in our society. I don't think that violence will be a way of life for any significant number of people. Although many may espouse the rhetoric of violence, few will physically commit violence. Meanwhile, we must be vitally concerned about educating people to the significance of peace and nonviolence as positive forces in our society. But our concern must not be frozen on a highly sophisticated level. We are concerned with peace, because violence (and war is the worst type of violence) has no place in our society or in our world, and it must be eradicated. Next to union contracts, we must focus our attention to bring about the necessary changes in our society through nonviolent means. We must train effective organizers for this purpose.

We must acquaint people with peace—not because capitalism is better or communism is better, but because, as men, we are better. As men we don't want to kill anyone, and we don't want to be killed ourselves. We must reach everyone so that this message can go out. If we do this correctly, our people will rise above mere material interests and goals. They will become involved in cultural matters. And we need a cultural revolution among ourselves—not only in art but also in the realm of the spirit. As poor people and immigrants, all of us have brought to this country some very important things of the spirit. But too often they are choked, they are not allowed to flourish in our society.

People are not going to turn back now. The poor are on the

march: black, brown, red, everyone, whites included. We are now in the midst of the biggest revolution this country has ever known. It really doesn't matter, in the final analysis, how powerful we are, how many boycotts we win, how many growers we sign up, or how much political clout we possess, if in the process we forget whom we are serving. We must never forget that the human element is the most important thing we have—if we get away from this, we are certain to fail.

This book, by Father Mark Day, tells of our struggle. It is unique, inasmuch as it was written by an insider, and it is my hope that it will attract more followers to our cause.

Twenty Days in Jail

After going to jail for civil disobedience, Chavez spoke to El Malcriado about the diversity he saw in jail and about the tragedy of poverty leading people to lives of crime. He commended those who held the picket line while he was detained. The exchange was published in December 1970.

EL MALCRIADO: How do you feel after going to jail for civil disobedience?

CESAR: Well, it was partially civil disobedience. It wasn't a real classic case of civil disobedience. I was sentenced to an indefinite period. So I couldn't look forward to a year or two; I didn't know what was going to happen. Really what the judge was saying is that it is up to me to get out of jail if I called off the boycott. That put the responsibility on me to say: No, I'll never call it off. It wasn't the classic civil disobedience case but it was a very good case. It was hard but now that it's over, I feel elated.

EL MALCRIADO: What was your relationship with the other inmates?

CESAR: I made a lot of friends, inside with the inmates, did a little organizing and spread the word around quite a bit. I wasn't too successful in convincing anybody about non-violence inside, but they are all with us. This includes blacks, whites and chicanos. The saddest thing is that the people who are in jail by and large are poor people. Only poor people go to jail and stay there. Also men who don't have anyone on the outside who really cares for them. Or who have someone on the outside who cannot really help them. It's very, very sad. Mostly young people. The routine . . . they put them in jail, they book them. Then they bring them into court and have the hearing and bring them back. It's a completely different world. I couldn't help feeling sorry for them. At least I had something on the outside going for me and I had the conviction of the cause. But they don't have any of those things. I learned that there is a very serious problem on the whole question of parole. Parole, I think, is a damaging, unconstitutional and damning thing for people. It gets a guy, puts him on parole, and they'll never let him go.

EL MALCRIADO: Did those on the vigil keep you company?

CESAR: Yeah, I never felt alone. For one thing, at night I could hear their singing. I heard the mañanitas. I thought, "This is the first time they give me mañanitas." Well, they were for the Virgin and the Chicanos were all over the jail. Four-thirty in the morning gritando, gritos de La Raza. See the determination? The growers said they were going to do the same thing. They lasted a day. But the people were really beautiful. The visitors were a tremendous support. I talked to about 150 the 1st Saturday and about 300 the 2nd Saturday. A lot were women. It gives you a tremendous feeling. I was very happy that Coretta King, Ethel Kennedy and Bishop Flores came. They did a lot of good for me spiritually and an awful lot of good to the people.

EL MALCRIADO: What did you think of our opposition's violence during Ethel Kennedy's visit?

CESAR: It's a clear example exactly how violence, whoever does it, really hurts their cause. Those guys really lost points. The day after it was on TV, how bad the guys were. A lady came to the vigil in a Cadillac and gave $25. They wanted to take her name and address and she said no, I trust you: I'm giving you $25 because I think I understand one thing—I want to become an American again. I can't give you my name because my son is a grower. You see, that kind of spirit, that kind of discipline, nobody can reject. You can't beat it.

EL MALCRIADO: During the confinement, how did you feel physically and mentally?

CESAR: Physically very well. Psychologically I was prepared. Spiritually I knew I was going to jail. So I just made up my mind that I was going to go and not be suppressed. I said that they could have my body here but my spirit's going to be free. It took me a couple of days to get used to the routine. You see, all of a sudden I'm in jail—I'm confronted with just an upside down of my life schedule. On the outside I'm going 16 hours a day every day. I had to schedule my time inside so I would use it wisely and make the best out of my stay. I just settled down and said I got to work myself out of it, and I did. In fact the almost three weeks in jail did not seem like a long time. I lost about 15 pounds, eating about a quarter of what I would usually eat.

EL MALCRIADO: What are your thoughts about possibly going back to jail?

CESAR: I don't want to go back, but if I have to I will. To commit civil disobedience I wouldn't have had a hearing. I would just tell the judge I'm guilty, give me the maximum time. Although I wanted to do that, I had to consider the union. If it had been me personally, I would have pleaded guilty and asked for the maximum time.

EL MALCRIADO: What is in store for our future?

CESAR: Back to the grind.

Nothing Has Changed

By explaining what La Causa *was early in its history, Chavez communicates its relation to other parts of* El Movimiento *of the sixties. In this interview, Chavez outlines the early goals of* La Causa, *goals that were eventually surpassed. This piece was reprinted in* 1971 *in* Aztlán: An Anthology of Mexican-American Literature.

MOVEMENT: Last year you said that NFWA was half-way between a movement and a union. Now there seems to have been a change in the NFWA from a year ago as it moved from agitation to organization.

CHAVEZ: I don't agree with you. It's a case of carrying on 40 different strikes. We haven't changed. I think the outside world has changed, because we're not a new thing. It's happened to civil rights. It happens to everybody. Our help is not coming from the same place it was coming from before.

MOVEMENT: One of the reasons people give—students, especially—as an argument for not working with the strike anymore is the merger of the union with the AFL-CIO. People felt that the union would go bureaucratic and control would slip from Delano into the hands of George Meany. Would you speak to this issue?

CHAVEZ: We were as much pained as they were. We were pained for different reasons. We were pained that all of these forces—I'm talking about the students and others who felt this way—had such little faith in people. These same people are guilty of idolizing the poor. This is not right because it isn't the truth. I remember some of the fellows that helped us in the beginning had a very strange picture of poor people, in this case the farm workers. Like farm workers are all saints, you know.

MOVEMENT: What effects does that have?

CHAVEZ: A bad effect on people. You can't help people if you feel sorry for them. You have to be practical. This type of feeling doesn't carry you for more than what it carried those people who were helping us. After a little while it becomes old, and there is no real basis for doing things that you're doing. There's got to be more.

The forces that have been so helpful to the civil rights movement and to us have moved on. The movement doesn't stay still. It's like a cyclone: it swoops.

MOVEMENT: You're talking about something that would be a political force, not a political party?

CHAVEZ: A political force, but not a party. There has to be discipline in a party.

It's not bad what the two parties do, because they are the pros. They are in power and the only criticism we can make is of ourselves for not being able to get that much power to counteract what they are doing.

MOVEMENT: It's like criticizing them for being what they are.

CHAVEZ: But that's not going to change anything. If we criticize ourselves, then that begins to change things.

I think groups that deal in power become impatient with groups who are strangers to power. I think even in individuals you can see this. A good example is Malcolm X. (I am reading his autobiography now.)

When he talks about Uncle Toms, he puts it clearly. He's saying that these guys will go to work for the devil white man. He's saying a lot more (he doesn't make it clear but I'm sure this is his thinking), that the Negro thinks that if he gets ahead he is going to be getting his people ahead. Malcolm X knew about power although he didn't put it in those words.

MOVEMENT: Malcolm X had a tremendous effect on black organizers.

CHAVEZ: He knew what he was doing. They understood him, and they didn't understand the others. But he had a good base; he came right from the gutter so he wasn't compromised. The guys who don't come from the gutter have to compromise because they're going to school, they're getting a job, they're working for the government, all these little compromises which, by the time you get to be a leader, have got your hands tied up.

You organize for power so that you can get something. You organize so that you can build power to do something with it, and so, when you look back, you've got to see some people out there doing something. What I'm trying to say is you can't organize by just speaking. The civil rights movement's biggest drawback is that they don't have a group that pays its own way. They don't have a membership group. This is the kind of power that is needed.

Malcolm X was an organizer, but Stokely (Carmichael) is entirely different. I don't see any building.

The approach that Malcolm X used was the house meeting. He was doing those things that we know pay: being patient and just accumulating, committing people and so forth. He's gone, but his spirit continues.

MOVEMENT: Is anything missing?

CHAVEZ: People. You don't have people working on it. I mean, who are you organizing? You have to have involvement. It's not a one-man show. There's got to be people involved. Once you have people, then there's power to do things. But money won't do it alone. The moment money is taken away from them, they fall.

MOVEMENT: Because they're depending on money from the outside?

CHAVEZ: As long as you have people, you'll have money, and if the money stops, that means you've lost the people. So there's no reason to continue anyway.

MOVEMENT: Can you see organizing farm workers into one big union?

CHAVEZ: That would be a miracle.

At Riverside Church

Published in Journal of Current Social Issues, *Spring 1971, the following interview took place at a time of negotiation during the grape and lettuce strikes. Chavez was in the process of building a large national union for farmworkers, a task that seemed impossible when he began.*

QUESTION: Mr. Chavez, would you say a little bit about the background of the farm workers movement?

CHAVEZ: In 1962 when we started organizing farm workers in Delano, we really were organizing workers all over the state, particularly in those areas where there are many workers. In 1967 we got the first farm workers' contract in the Salinas Valley with a grower who is involved in growing wine grapes. The majority of the workers in Salinas are migratory workers that come across the border at Tijuana and Mexicali and San Luis. So our organization really has two bases—one in Salinas when the workers are there, and it remains there with the lesser number who remain during the winter months; and another base for workers as they go back south and cross the border. We follow them with the organization and we work right at the border.

In the eight years from 1962 until 1970 when the strike started, we went to Salinas (I personally went there no less than five times) to try to keep workers from striking. I asked them to give us enough time to get through with the grape boycott and strike, and then we would take up their cause.

The lettuce workers have grown to be much more militant and more dedicated—not that the grape workers weren't—but they are even more so. There has been more organization, really more basic organization, among the lettuce and the vegetable workers than there was among the grape workers.

QUESTION: Under what type of ordinance was Dow Chemical granted an injunction and exactly what is the interest of that company in lettuce farming?

CHAVEZ: They are using the California Jurisdictional Dispute Act to get an injunction because there is another union involved—the Teamsters Union. They are saying that it's not a strike against the employers but rather a fight among unions—which is not true.

This is the basis, then, for the injunction on the striking and picketing and the boycott. Dow Chemical claims not to be involved. They say that they are not guilty, that they have nothing to do with the lettuce. But the fact is that Dow Chemical owns about 17,000 acres that are farmed by Bud Antle. The fact is that Dow Chemical has a very close business relationship—all the pesticides, the fertilizers and the herbicides that are used by the Bud Antle Company, as well as the polyethelenes used to wrap lettuce, come from Dow Chemical. Dow Chemical has also broken a rule they have for their directors not to belong to outside corporations. In this case, one of Dow Chemical's directors occupies one of five seats in the Bud Antle Company. We're saying that Bud Antle is really a subsidiary of Dow Chemical—a silent subsidiary, but that is enough.

QUESTION: Would you please clarify the nature of the relationship between the Teamsters and the United Farm Workers Union?

CHAVEZ: We have a signed agreement with the Teamsters. It was signed at the beginning of the conflict in Salinas and was really a renewal of a pact that we had signed with them in 1967. It is a mutual assistance pact, and a jurisdictional pact. It recognizes the right of the Farm Workers Union to organize farm workers; it recognizes the right of the Teamsters Union to organize the truck drivers and the processing end of the industry—the canneries and the packing sheds, etc.

QUESTION: Is there a fund to which contributions can be made in order to support the strike?

CHAVEZ: We are the only union in the United States today that does not have a strike fund. We have never had one, and I think the way things are going we will never have one. So all of the striking that is done is done on the basis of extreme sacrifice to the workers. We have an operating fund in which we put the money donated to the union from throughout the country and the world. Out of this fund, we pay the living expenses—the five dollars a week, room and board, gas and telephone, for all of the people working in the movement. There are about 600 of us now. If you would like to donate, we'd be very happy if you contributed to our existing operating fund. All you have to do is send your donation to me in Delano, California. It's a small town and they know who we are.

QUESTION: What can people do in order to support the United Farm Workers besides making monetary contributions?

CHAVEZ: I have often said that the boycott is the most powerful, the most potent weapon of non-violence. The longer we live and the more evidence we find, the more convinced we are that *in fact* it is a tremendous weapon to bring about dignity and justice, in this case for workers. You see, the whole basis of non-violence is having *numbers* of people involved. And it is very difficult to get people involved unless what we ask people to do is very simple, very concrete and very painless. The reason the grape boycott was so effective was because there were literally millions of people in the United States and in Canada and other parts of the world who were doing something very painless. That was simply not eating grapes and, even more important, one was watching the other! You know, a friend stopping in to visit would open the refrigerator before even saying hello, checking to see if grapes were there. Now, if we can do the same thing with iceberg lettuce, I think we will be in good shape. I think that the most important thing is to begin to get our markets and supermarkets to demand the union label lettuce. It is available, and it has the same label that we have on the grapes—the black Aztec eagle. If you then begin to talk to all of your friends and neighbors, we'll be successful. But you see, all these things take time. Now, if we had a lot of money, we could run a great big campaign throughout the country, and it could be done almost overnight. But since we don't have that, the best way of accomplishing this is like we are doing it now—one to one. If you stop eating iceberg lettuce that does not have the union label, and ask your supermarket managers to show you that the lettuce you buy really is union lettuce, then I think we can go a long way.

QUESTION: You spoke of the increased militancy among the lettuce pickers. Does this have any connection with the bitter and violent struggles of the past in Salinas Valley?

CHAVEZ: The judge who had the injunction ending and banning all picketing and striking was the district attorney who prosecuted—and persecuted—the strikers back in the thirties. So you can see what we are up against. But I think there is more. The reason that the lettuce and vegetable workers are more militant—I don't necessarily mean violent but more militant—is because it is possible now to have a union. The example has been set by the grape workers; so that at every campaign we go to there are more demands and more self-assertion on the part of the workers. Probably it is due to that and also, undoubtedly, to the fact that among the older workers, every single one went through that horrible union-busting operation back in the thirties.

QUESTION: The effectiveness of the grape boycott was dulled somewhat by the heavily increased purchasing of grapes by the Pentagon for consumption by the Army. Were efforts made to halt this? And has similar action been taken by the Pentagon during the lettuce boycott?

CHAVEZ: I am glad that you raised that question because I was forgetting to mention a very important element in the struggle with Bud Antle. The biggest buyer from Bud Antle and Dow Chemical is the U. S. Army. We have the same pattern that we had with the grapes. You see, Dow Chemical and the U. S. Army have had quite a friendship, I understand, for years. They are just continuing that into the salad business! However bad it is, it is probably a lot better than the other things they've been involved in.

In the case of the Army and the armed forces and the increased purchasing of grapes, we just went and told the whole world about it, and also asked our friends to contact their Congressmen and their Senators. Last year we were on the road for a little over 90 days, visiting something like 90 cities in the United States and Canada. Everywhere I spoke, I asked people to get hold of their Congressmen and make a complaint. And you know, it worked! And I think we can make it work again. If nothing else, it will begin to raise this question of the U. S. Army buying all of its lettuce from Bud Antle. And it will also raise another question. As far as we know, they are not bidding on that lettuce. That means they are using your tax dollar unwisely—not that the Army does not use it unwisely on other things. What happens is this: When we begin to see the employers trying to use their natural friends to beat the boycott, even though it is difficult for us to combat this tactic, it is the best gauge we have that things are going our way.

QUESTION: Mr. Chavez, in my town, Riverhead, New York, there have been organizing problems in a potato-processing plant due to the actions of crew chiefs. Would you please comment on this?

CHAVEZ: The problem of the labor contractor, or what you referred to as the crew chief, is a severe problem in organizing because the growers have these men control the jobs. And if they control the jobs, then they also control the lives of those people who work under them. One of the great arms that the growers have had in keeping us from organizing workers is by using fear—not directly by the grower, but through the labor contractor crew chief—the fear of unemployment on those workers who would otherwise want to be members of the union. The system is even more vicious on the East Coast than it is on the West Coast. The sooner we get through with the struggles in California, the faster we will be coming here. When we do that, we are going to have to design some very specific approaches to overcome that very, very difficult problem. It's like having a thousand hiring halls on two legs, you know, and recruiting workers not for the benefit of everyone but for the exclusive benefit of one individual. It's a very damaging, difficult problem to overcome.

QUESTION: Do you think that the lettuce pickers in California are less vulnerable to mechanization, that is automation in the harvesting of crops, than Southern harvesters?

CHAVEZ: They are not less vulnerable to mechanization. In fact, they are very vulnerable to mechanization. Permit me to offer a couple of clarifications. One, the reason that more mechanization is not now active in the fields has nothing to do with the employers' concern for their employees, or the matter of whether or not there are unions in the fields. The simple fact is that they have not come up with the machines to do that job yet. Now, some crops are being mechanized and some will be mechanized completely, but in the majority of these crops the final arbiter—the one who is going to make the final decision—is going to be the American consumer.

Let me explain it this way. When you go to the supermarket, even though you may not *know,* if you were to buy a tomato picked by machine or a tomato picked by hand, nine times out of ten you will choose and buy the tomato picked by hand.

However advanced the machines are, they need a little help from nature. Here's what they do. For instance, in order to get the machines to successfully pick the tomato, the growers have had to go back and come up with different strengths to make the tomato harder. This gives the tomato a harder skin, therefore less water, therefore less flavor. If it weren't for the color, in many cases, you wouldn't be able to tell if you were eating tomato or alfalfa. So the consumer is going to make those decisions!

We are told that they are going to automate strawberries. We know what is going to happen. They are going to have to make them very hard, and I am sure they are going to taste like potatoes—raw potatoes!

But there is a danger that machines are coming in, and we don't know quite how to wrestle with this problem. We do know certain things. We do know that to oppose mechanization is not the right thing to do.

Let me give you a little story to make my point. Right after the Second World War and into the early fifties, there was a story that the General Motors officials conducted a tour for Walter Reuther to see the inventions and the automation taking place on the assembly lines. They started at one end of the line and worked themselves all the way to the very last machine. At every step, machines were displacing one man, or five and six and, in some cases totally. In others, partially. When they got to the very end, one of the General Motors officials asked Walter Reuther, "Well, Mr. Reuther, what do you think of our great inventions?" And he said, "You know, it's really amazing. Terrific! These machines do almost everything except one thing—they won't buy cars."

And so *those* machines won't eat strawberries and they won't eat tomatoes and they won't drink wine. You know, there is more automation in the processing end of it than there is in the fields. Once you get off the fields and into the plants, then you have control over it.

We're not giving up the fight, but we're saying very simply that technology should work for the men, for the worker as well as for the employer. We're saying that somehow there has to be an adjustment, and that the fruits of technology should work equally for workers and for employers. Roughly speaking, we say we would like 50 percent of the profits saved, because the machines should go right back to the workers somehow. But even more than that, we are saying that there ought to be some way, and we've got to find the way, not to neglect those men and women who have made it possible for the employers to have the machines because they worked with their hands while the machines were being developed. We don't have the answers. We've got to seek the answers from the American public.

The employer and the union and the public have a responsibility to work together in solving this problem. It hasn't been successfully solved anywhere that I know of.

There are some things that can be said for mechanization. One of the things is that we would like to see the profits being made—more food being raised at lesser cost—somehow to feed some of the hungry people in the world. If it means losing a few jobs to do that, I'm for it.

At Exposition Park

On May 2, 1971, in the midst of anti–Vietnam War protests, Chavez spoke with sympathy toward a group called Vietnam Veterans Against the War while relating their strife to the greater struggle against violence in American society.

Thank you for inviting me to participate in this meeting. It is hard for me because we in the farm workers movement have been so absorbed in our own struggle that we have not participated actively in the battle against the war.

In thinking about the memorial service I keep thinking about the women in Washington, D.C., who participated in the veterans' protest against the war. The *L.A. Times* reported it as follows:

Anna Pine of Trenton, NJ, wanted to discard her dead son Fred's Air Medal & Bronze Star and Purple Heart and a half-dozen other awards for heroism. But she had already turned away crying when the first former soldier announced, hands trembling, "And so we cast away these symbols of dishonor, shame and inhumanity."

"My son would be here," Mrs. Pine said. "He would throw these things away. But where do I throw them," she wondered, peering through tears about the crowd that had edged her away from the veterans. An hour passed, the crowd dispersed, Mrs. Pine approached the fence. Digging into a big plastic bag, she grabbed a handful of medals and threw them against the statue.

I have eight children. It is almost impossible to imagine the pain of seeing your own child die for a cause that neither of you believe in—especially when there are so many needs in the world and so many specific ways to work for change.

What causes our children to take up guns to fight their brothers in lands far away?

In our case thousands and thousands of poor, brown, and black farm workers go off to war to kill other poor farm workers in

Southeast Asia. Why does it happen? Perhaps they are afraid or perhaps they have come to believe that in order to be fully men, to gain respect from other men and to have their way in the world, they must take up the gun and use brute force against other men.

They have had plenty of examples: In Delano and Salinas and Coachella all the growers carry gun racks and guns in their trucks. The police all carry guns and use them to get their way. The security guards (rent-a-cops) carry guns and nightsticks. The stores sell guns of all shapes and sizes.

It would be easy to put all the blame on the generals and the police and the growers and the other bosses. Or on violence in TV or the movies or war toys.

But we are also responsible. Some husbands prove to their children that might makes right by the way they beat on their own wives. Most of us honor violence in one way or another, in sports if not at home. We insist on our own way, grab for security, and trample on other people in the process.

But we are responsible in another, more basic way. We have not shown our children how to sacrifice for justice. Say all that you will about the army, but in time of crises the army and the navy demand hard work, discipline, and sacrifice. And so too often our sons go off to war grasping for their manhood at the end of a gun and trained to work and to sacrifice for war.

For the poor it is a terrible irony that they should rise out of their misery to do battle against other poor people when the same sacrifices could be turned against the causes of their poverty. But what have we done to demonstrate another way? Talk is cheap and our young people know it best of all. It is the way we organize and use our lives every day that tells what we believe in.

Farm workers are at last struggling out of their poverty and powerlessness. They are saying no to an agricultural system that has condemned them to a life of economic slavery.

At the same time they are making a new way of life for themselves and their children. They are turning their sacrifices and their suffering into a powerful campaign for dignity and for justice.

Their nonviolent struggle is not soft or easy. It requires hard work and discipline more than anything else. It means giving up on economic security. It requires patience and determination. Farm workers are working to build a nonviolent army trained and ready to sacrifice in order to change conditions for all of our brothers in the fields.

Our opponents are at work every day to crush us or to get us off target or to outmaneuver us with the American public. There is no way to defeat them unless we also are at work every day—week after week, month after month, and year after year if necessary, outlasting the opposition and defeating them with time if necessary.

That is what it takes to bring change in America today. Nothing less than organized, disciplined, nonviolent action that goes on every day will challenge the power of the corporations and the generals.

The problem is that people have to decide to do it. Individuals have to decide to give their lives over to the struggle for specific and meaningful social change. And as they do that others will join them, and the young will join, too.

If we provide alternatives for our young out of the way we use the energies and resources of our own lives, perhaps fewer and fewer of them will seek their manhood in affluence and war. Perhaps we can bring the day when children will learn from their earliest days that being fully man and fully woman means to give one's life to the liberation of the brother who suffers. It is up to each one of us. It won't happen unless we decide to use our own lives to show the way.

On Money

Addressing a group of church members in La Paz, California, on October 4, 1971, Chavez emphasized the power of the Church in organizing groups for causes. He shows here that everyone, even the poorest community member, can be a part of something larger than him- or herself.

When we are really honest with ourselves we must admit that our lives are all that really belong to us. So it is how we use our lives that determines what kind of men we are. It is my deepest belief that only by giving our lives do we find life. I am convinced that the truest act of courage, the strongest act of manliness is to sacrifice ourselves for others in a totally nonviolent struggle for justice. To be a man is to suffer for others. God help us to be men!

What I'm going to say may not make much sense to you. On the other hand, it may make an awful lot of sense. This depends on where you are in terms of organizing and what your ideas are about that elusive and difficult task of getting people together—to act together and to produce something.

Labor unions today have a heck of a time organizing workers. The church has a heck of a time organizing people. The government has a heck of a time organizing people. The Republican Party has a very difficult problem. So does the Democrat Party. So does almost any institution have a heck of a time organizing people. Why is it difficult? First of all, if these institutions hadn't been successful, they wouldn't exist. There were churches that were successful. There were unions that were successful. There were government departments that were successful. Someone had the right idea. But that's in the past. Talking about those successes is like getting up and telling workers about the great and joyous campaigns in the thirties to organize workers. And they say, "So what? What about us today?"

Organizing is difficult because in our capitalist society we believe the only way things get done is with money. Let's examine this assumption by using the farm worker struggle as an example. Since about 1898, there have been many efforts to organize farm workers in California and other states. Almost invariably, at the end of each struggle someone would report, "The workers weren't ready for it. They didn't want the union. They didn't do their share to get organized." But every report of organizing attempts also included a more honest statement: "We had to stop the organizing drive, or we had to temporarily disband, because we ran out of money." It's a shame.

There isn't enough money to organize poor people. There never is enough money to organize anyone. If you put it on the basis of money, you're not going to succeed. So when we started organizing our union, we knew we had to depend on something other than money. As soon as we announced that we were leaving the Community Service Organization (CSO), the group that I worked with so many years, to organize field workers, there were people who wanted to give us money. In fact one lady offered us $50,000 to organize workers. When I said no, she was very hurt. I told her, "If I take the money now, that would be the worst thing I could do. I don't want the money. Some other time I will, but not now." Fifty thousand dollars wasn't enough. The AFL-CIO had just spent a million and a half dollars and they failed. So why did we think we could do it with $50,000?

We started with two principles: First, since there wasn't any money and the job had to be done, there would have to be a lot of sacrificing. Second, no matter how poor the people, they had a responsibility to help the union. If they had $2.00 for food, they had to give $1.00 to the union. Otherwise, they would never get out of the trap of poverty. They would never have a union because they couldn't afford to sacrifice a little bit more on top of their misery. The statement "They're so poor they can't afford to contribute to the group" is a great cop-out. You don't organize people by being afraid of them—you never have; you never will. You can be afraid of them in a variety of ways. But one of the main ways is to patronize them. You know the attitude: Blacks or browns or farm workers are so poor that they can't afford to have their own group. They hardly have enough money to eat. This makes it very easy for the organizer. He can always rationalize, "I haven't failed. They can't come up with the money, so we were not able to organize them."

We decided that workers wanted to be organized and could be organized. So the responsibility had to be upon ourselves, the organizers. Organizing is one place where you can easily get away with a failure. If you send a man to dig a ditch three feet by ten feet, you'll know if he did it or not. Or if you get someone to write a letter, you'll know if he wrote it. In most areas of endeavor, you can see the results. In organizing, it's different. You can see results years later, but you can't see them right away. That's why we have so many failures. So many organizers that should never be organizers go in and muddy the waters. Then good organizers have to come in, and it's twice as hard for them to organize.

We knew we didn't have the money. We knew farm workers could be organized and we were going to do it. We weren't going to accept failure. But we were going to make sure that workers contributed to the doing of this organizing job. That has never been done in the history of this country.

We started out by telling workers, "We are trying to organize a union. We don't have money, but if you work together it can be done." Ninety-five percent of the workers we talked to were very kind. They smiled at us. Five percent asked us questions, and maybe one percent had the spirit and really wanted to do something.

We didn't have any money for gas and food. Many days we left the house with no money at all. Sometimes we had enough gas to get there but not enough to come back. We were determined to go to the workers. In fact, at the very beginning of the organizing drive, we looked for the worst homes in the barrios where there were a lot of dogs and kids outside. And we went in and asked for a handout. Inevitably, they gave us food. Then they made a collection and gave us money for gas. They opened their homes and gave us their hearts. And today they are the nucleus of the union's leadership. We forced ourselves to do this. We kept telling ourselves, "If these workers don't get organized, if we fail, it's our fault not theirs."

Then the question came up, how would we survive? My wife was working in the fields. We used to take the whole family out on Sundays and earn a few dollars to be able to survive the following week. We knew we couldn't continue that way. And we knew that the money had to come not from the outside but from the workers. And the only way to get the money was to have people pay dues.

So we began the drive to get workers to pay dues so we could live, so we could just survive. We were very frank, very open. At a farm worker's convention, we told them we had nothing to give them except the dream that it might happen. But we couldn't continue unless they were willing to make a sacrifice. At that meeting everyone wanted to pay $5.00 or $8.00 a month. We balked and said "No, no. Just $3.50. That's all we need." There were about 280 people there, and 212 signed up and paid the $3.50 in the first month.

Ninety days from that day, there were twelve people paying $3.50. By that time we had a small community. There were six of us, four of us working full-time. There were a lot of questions being asked. Some said, "They're very poor and can't afford it. That's why they're not paying." And a few of us said, "We're poor, too. We're poorer than they are, and we can afford to sacrifice our families and our time. They have to pay."

I remember many incidents when I went to collect dues. Let me tell you just one. I'd been working twelve years with the mentality that people were very poor and shouldn't be forced to pay dues. Keep that in mind because that comes in handy in understanding what you go through when you're not really convinced that this is the way it should be.

I went to a worker's home in McFarland, seven miles south of Delano. It was in the evening. It was raining and it was winter. And there was no work. I knew it. And everyone knew it. As I knocked on the door, the guy in the little two-room house was going to the store with a $5.00 bill to get groceries. And there I was. He owed $7.00 because he was one full month behind plus the current one. So I'd come for $7.00. But all he had was $5.00. I had to make a decision. Should I take $3.50 or shouldn't I? It was very difficult. Up to this time I had been saying, "They should be paying. And if they don't pay they'll never have a union." Three-fifty worth of food wasn't really going to change his life one way or the other that much. So I told him, "You have to pay at least $3.50 right now or I'll have to put you out of the union." He gave me the

$5.00. We went to the store and changed the $5.00 bill. I got the $3.50 and gave him the $1.50. I stayed with him. He bought $1.50 worth of groceries and went home.

That experience hurt me, but it also strengthened my determination. If this man was willing to give me $3.50 on a dream, when we were really taking the money out of his own food, then why shouldn't we be able to have a union, however difficult. There had never been a successful union for farm workers. Every unionizing attempt had been defeated. People were killed. They ran into every obstacle you can think of. The whole agricultural industry along with government and business joined forces to break the unions and keep them from organizing. But with the kind of faith this farm worker had, why couldn't we have a union?

So we set out to develop exactly that kind of faith. And by the time the strike came, we had that kind of resolution among members. Only a small percentage of the workers were paying dues. But it was ingrained in them that they were going to have a union come hell or high water. That's the kind of spirit that kept us going and infected other farm workers—this little core of people who were willing to stop talking and sacrifice to get it done.

That was seven or eight years ago. We had different problems in the union then than we have today. But the kind of problems we had then were problems like not having enough money to pay rent. We told the workers, "If you're buying a house, leave it. Better get a smaller house where you pay little rent because we can't pay much rent." It was a lot of sacrifice and they did it. And we won the strike.

A few months ago, a local union from San Francisco came to ask us to help organize people from a couple of factories that are moving from the Bay Area to the San Joaquin Valley and running away from their contracts—runaway shops. They offered us money. We told them we didn't need money. All we needed was a telephone and a little money for gas and for food to eat on the picket line. We got that. But we said we needed someone from their union to direct us because we couldn't direct the drive. We wouldn't want to commit mistakes. It wouldn't be fair for us to do all the work for their union. But we told them we'd do everything if they provided the director. You know what? We assigned ten people to that drive. How much does it cost to be on the picket line? The way we eat? Nothing, you know. We've come from the struggle. And how much gas? A dollar and a half per car each day. Four cars at a dollar and a half a day. You know what? They couldn't put an organizer in the field for that job. You know why? Because they didn't have the money. It's too expensive to do it. It's too damned expensive for a guy earning about $22,000 a year including fringes. We told them, "Look. Bring him anyway—not knowing, you know. We'll get him a place to sleep with the workers. And we'll find a home that will feed him." And they said, "Our organizers won't do that. They have to have a motel and all those things." I said, "You won't have a union then." And they said, "That's right." In that union those two or three plants represented about 25 percent of their membership. They won't increase their membership anymore. They can't organize because they depend on money.

When we had that big fight with the Teamsters in Delano, we beat them with the numbers game. Every time they brought in an organizer, I think they get $35,000 a year in some cases, we got ten workers and told them, "Your job is to keep that guy from gaining any ground with the workers." The Teamsters brought in a lot of organizers but after a while it was too expensive. All we needed was just enough to eat and a little gas. We don't have to worry about money. That's how things get done.

The corporations do it differently. They pay very good wages. Then if their top people don't produce, they have carcasses all over the place. If they don't produce in a month, they say, "Look Brother, you're not cutting it. We're paying you a lot of money because we want results." The other way is not to pay anything. If you try to be in between, you're not going to get anything done. I'm convinced that's how these things work. In unions and in churches and in groups that are made up principally of people, you don't fire people for nonperformance like they do in the big corporations. However, we know you have guys who are not that effective, guys who won't do the work. They don't get fired. If you get a job in the church or in the unions you're in for life, brother, whether you can cut it or not. Very, very seldom does someone get fired. That's true even in our union. When a strike is called, everybody comes in to work. Then after a while we begin to see that some guys aren't cutting it. We actually haven't hurt the growers that much by taking them out on strike. And we have a very difficult time trying to get them to understand if they're going to organize workers, they've got to work.

Money is not going to organize the disadvantaged, the powerless, or the poor. We need other weapons. That's why the War on Poverty is such a miserable failure. You put out a big pot of money, and all you do is fight over it. Then you run out of money and you run out of troops. It's just like those revolutions. If you haven't got the money, you haven't got the troops.

We didn't worry about money at the beginning. Now we're beginning to feel a little of that coming. And I'm very worried. For instance, we gave a $5.00 weekly allowance and we still do, though it's more than that when you consider rent and food. But now, some don't think $5.00 is enough. They'd like to get $10.00. Maybe they should get $10.00. But there has to be some point where you say, "If you want to make money, go back to the fields." When we started the strike, workers were getting 95 cents an hour. Now people packing grapes during harvest, at piece rate, average $3.00 and $3.50 an hour plus some fringe benefits. Those are very good wages. In lettuce, the piece rate wages went up almost 300 percent in the first contract. So we tell the workers, "If you want to make that kind of money, go back. That's where the money's going to be. Not here."

We'll organize workers in this movement as long as we're willing to sacrifice. The moment we stop sacrificing, we stop organizing. I guarantee that. There are workers in Florida, in Texas, in New York, and in the southern states who are going to be very difficult to organize. But they have to be organized. We have to help our brothers in other countries, too. We got a letter from Guatemala a couple of days ago. People there are having a devil of a time organizing because the government is very repressive. Since their struggle is against American companies, they feel we could boycott them here to get them organized there. And I know that's true. But we're not going to do it by paying wages. We can't. When we first started talking about a boycott, everyone told us, "You'll never do it. Boycotts never work." Every single union told Jim Drake, the first organizer of the boycott, "It can't be done. We've tried it and we are a bigger union. And we have a lot of money." We told ourselves that's one more reason why we should try it. So we put a lot of manpower into cities around the country. At one time we had about five hundred full-time people on the boycott not counting a tremendous number of supporters. You know why we were helped? Because they knew our guys weren't getting paid. So they didn't mind doing the same. But you do mind helping if you know that the other guys are getting a big fat salary.

When you sacrifice, you force others to sacrifice. It's an extremely powerful weapon. When somebody stops eating for a week or ten days, people come and want to be part of that experience. Someone goes to jail and people want to help him. You don't buy that with money. That doesn't have any price in terms of dollars.

Those who are willing to sacrifice and be of service have very little difficulty with people. They know what they are all about. People can't help but want to be near them—to help them and work with them. That's what love is all about. It starts with you and radiates out. You can't phony it. It just doesn't go. When you work and sacrifice more than anyone else around you, you put others on the spot and they have to do at least a bit more than they've been doing. And that's what puts it together.

These observations tie in directly with the whole question of organizing. Why do we have leaders? We put some people out in the fields and all of a sudden they hit, they click. Everyone's happy with them, and they begin to move mountains. With other people there are problems and heartaches. They just don't go. When we look and see what's happening, almost invariably the differences are along the lines of willingness to sacrifice and work long hours.

We didn't start out knowing these things. We have discovered them. During those six years of strike and boycott it never seemed like that much of a struggle. We accepted it as a fact. Now that we're over that big hurdle, we look back and say, "My God. People really sacrificed. And the things that I asked them to do! Did I really ask them to do that much?" I asked them to do it to the maximum, and they did it.

Question: What's your dream for the farm workers' union?

Answer: My dream is that farm workers will someday have enough power to take care of themselves, and if they gain that, that they don't become selfish . . . that the movement doesn't go to hell, in other words. And that's difficult. We're already beginning to see a few danger signs.

Only when we have a union that isn't selfish can we help other people. The first step in building a union is to help yourself. You sacrifice for ten years to have a union. You get better wages. So what? It's nice. But the real trick is to have a union, to have that power, and to selflessly help brothers completely unconnected with you. In order to get there, the movement has to be guided by some kind of philosophy. Everything comes back to how you deal with money.

Let me extend my dream. If the workers in California get organized, they can assist the organizing of people in Florida. The people in California and Florida together can assist the organizing of other workers. With a boycott they can help organize farm workers around the world. My God! There just aren't any other unions for farm workers in the rest of the world. One of the greatest miscarriages of justice is that the people who provide food for the world don't have enough food for themselves. It's horrible. I just can't understand it. Take the Philippines for instance. There are no unions there. They import people to work just like we do here. And they move them from island to island, from province to province. In West Germany, they bring in farm workers from Spain and Portugal. In Mexico, they can't get Mexicans to work in the hemp so they import workers from Guatemala and treat them like braceros. They're exploited just as the Mexicans are in this country. The damn exploitation of farm workers is consistent.

Imagine what could happen with one selfless act on our part. We could take on the Philippine sugar industry and knock the hell out of them with a boycott. It could bring a union to Filipino farm workers. Then we'd say to them, "Take care of yourselves first. Organize your union. And when that's done, we want you to help Malaysia or the rest of Asia." Same thing with Latin America. That's the dream. Frankly, we're not going to do that now. We have so many problems ourselves. More people are out to destroy us than ever before. The right wing is spending hundreds of thousands of dollars to get us.

And we have other problems. When we started the movement, no one questioned the $5.00 per week. Now some people who have worked and sacrificed for a long time want a little more security. No one can blame them. But we are still in a giant struggle, and workers in Florida and Texas are still going hungry. How can we be making money! I'm just talking about the staff now. With the workers? That's a tough one! To reverse that trend is going to be very difficult. It's going to take a long time.

We'll have many fights with them, many arguments. We may not be here if we argue too strongly. Look for a minute at how difficult it is: We start telling workers, "Now look. You've got a lot of money. You shouldn't get more money." Then they say, "Why not? The employers are making more profit." And what do we answer? "We're going to get less money so the employers can make more money so we can help our brothers?" It's a *very difficult* question. . . . The workers get strong. I don't know if that's going to change the employers. I don't think so. But it doesn't have to start with the workers. If the staff and the leadership of the union stick to the style of sacrifice and service, then the workers who are in leadership positions may begin to get the idea of self-sacrifice. Then we will really have something. Like everything else it has to begin in your own life and in those people who have given their lives to build the union. But it is hard, and we have a long way to go.

Why Delano

Chavez's eventual success in Delano was not an accident. In Why Delano, *he explains the strategic planning that led to such a monumental victory for the NFWA. This piece appeared in 1972 in* Aztlán: An Anthology of Mexican-American Literature.

In community organizing you need a continuous program that meets the needs of the people in the organization. I have seen many groups attempt community organization and many have failed. The biggest reason for this is that there is a big emphasis on meetings and discussion and writing up programs and not on working with the people. Many organizers get lost in the shuffle of going to meetings, and somehow those who are being organized are lost. Too often we see as a remedy to this, people suggesting that you should have a survey or a study made.

Anyone who has done any community organizing would agree with me that you can't have a program until you have the people organized. I don't mean you have to wait until you're fully organized, but how can you write a program without the participation of those you are trying to organize?

Another problem is respectability. If a minority group does "nice" things, like taking a petition to the Mayor, or having tea parties with the PTA, it's going to become respectable. And once you become a respectable group, you're not going to fight anymore. I've had a lot of experience in that. So if your group is going to City Hall or the Police Department and fight with the Police Chief, and someone on your Executive Board is friends with him, you're going to think twice before attacking him.

If an organizer comes looking for appreciation he might as well stay home. He's not going to get any, especially out of a group that's never been organized or had any power before.

A lot of people have asked me—why Delano, and the answer is simple. I had no money. My wife's family lived there, and I have a brother. And I thought if things go very bad we can always go and have a meal there. Any place in the Valley would have made no difference.

I had some ideas on what should be done. No great plans; just that it would take an awful lot of work and also that it was a gamble. If I can't organize them to a point where they can carry on their own group then I'm finished, I can't do it, I'd move on and do something else.

I went around for about 11 months, and I went to about 87 communities and labor camps and in each place I'd find a few people who were committed to doing something; something had happened in their lives and they were ready for it. So we went around to the town, played the percentages, and came off with a group.

We had a convention here in Fresno, the first membership meeting, to set up a union—about 230 people from as many as 65 places. We knew the hardest thing would be to put across a program that would make them want to pay the $3.50 (monthly dues), because we were dependent on that. I felt that organizing couldn't be done on outside money.

We had signed up about 1100 people. The first month 211 payed. At the end of three months we had 10 people paying. Talk about being scared! But we went back and kept at it. By this time Dolores (Huerta) was helping me up in the Northern part of the Valley, and I was getting help from Gilbert Pedilla, both of whom are Vice-Presidents now. Gradually the membership was increasing. At the end of six months we were up to about 200 members. Instead of going all over the Valley as I did at first, I started staying in one place long enough for them to get in touch with me if they wanted to. We put a lot of emphasis on the people getting members.

We had hundreds of house meetings. Sometimes 2 or 3 would come, sometimes none. Sometimes even the family that called the house meeting would not be there.

I wasn't trying to prove anything to anyone who had given money. If I'd been under a board or a grant I don't think it would have worked. In the first place, I had to get the dues in order to eat. I suspect some of the members were paying dues because they felt sorry for me.

At the beginning of the strike we had $85 in the treasury.

To Be a Man Is to Suffer for Others

Following the example of Mahatma Gandhi, one of his role mod-
els in nonviolent action, Cesar Chavez undertook a fast as a part of
the Delano Grape Boycott. The fast was highly controversial for
the staff of the United Farm Workers union, but it was a personal
choice for Chavez. This speech, delivered at the end of his fast,
demonstrates his commitment to community and justice even in a
state of physical weakness. The speech was published in 1972 in
Aztlán: An Anthology of Mexican-American Literature.

We are gathered here today not so much to observe the end of the
fast but because we are a family bound together in a common
struggle for justice. We are a union family celebrating our unity
and the nonviolent nature of our movement. Perhaps in the future we will come together at other times and places to break
bread and to renew our courage and to celebrate important victories.

The fast has had different meanings for different people. Some
of you may still wonder about its meaning and importance. It was
not intended as a pressure against any growers. For that reason we
have suspended negotiations and arbitration proceedings and relaxed the militant picketing and boycotting of the strike during
this period. I undertook this fast because my heart was filled with
grief and pain for the sufferings of farm workers. The fast was first
for me and then for all of us in this union. It was a fast for nonviolence and a call to sacrifice.

Our struggle is not easy. Those who oppose our cause are rich
and powerful and they have many allies in high places. We are
poor. Our allies are few. But we have something the rich do not
own. We have our own bodies and spirits and the justice of our
cause as our weapons.

When we are really honest with ourselves we must admit that
our lives are all that really belong to us. So, it is how we use our

lives that determines what kind of men we are. It is my belief that only by giving our lives do we find life. I am convinced that the truest act of courage, the strongest act of manliness is to sacrifice ourselves for others in a totally nonviolent struggle for justice.

To be a man is to suffer for others. God help us to be men!

Do We Exist?

This letter, written on May 15, 1972, is a response to the obstacles faced by farmworkers in Arizona. The state's growers had put pressure on politicians to pass a law making it illegal for labor to organize and boycott producers. However, Chavez looked at the larger picture. "What is it that causes sane men to act so hastily and cruelly?" he asked.

Dear Brothers and Sisters:

Our people have been poor for more years than we can remember. We have made only a small amount of progress these past ten years of work and struggle. Our women and children still die too often and too young. There is too much hunger and disease among us. Not even 5 percent of America's migrant farm workers are protected by union contracts. Yet there is a great fear of our union—a fear that I do not fully understand, but that I know is present with most growers and especially among the lettuce growers in the current resistance to the rights of their workers. Growers through the Farm Bureau are seeking to bring the whole machinery of government against us. Why are they so afraid of a union for migrant farm workers? Is it so much to ask that the poorest people of the land have a measure of justice?

In Arizona, a major lettuce producing state, the growers and the politicians have just passed a law that destroys the right of farm workers to have a union. Farm workers under this law cannot engage in consumer boycotts. Supporters of our union could be arrested for telling their friends not to buy lettuce. Farm workers are put in the humiliating position of having to go to a special Agricultural Labor Relations Board (appointed by Republican Governor Jack Williams) for a government conducted election to determine their right to strike. The law provides that seasonal and migrant workers would never have a chance to vote. Growers can not only frustrate an election for 2–3 months; they can actually avoid elections by a minor change in hiring practices. Even if workers should vote for the union, an employer can seek a decertification election after only a 3 month waiting period. The bill is discriminatory. It is aimed only at farm workers who are mostly black, brown and Indian. No other labor force is asked to live with these repressive measures. This is what the Farm Bureau means when they advocate "free elections" and "responsible legislation."

Farm Workers in Arizona tried to tell their legislators about the unfairness of this law. They collected letters and petitions and brought them to their representatives. They were met with cold indifference. They were patient but could not get appointments. In many cases, their letters were thrown into trash cans in front of their eyes. After the bill passed, it was brought to the governor by the Highway Patrol. He signed it immediately. The next day the governor was asked by a reporter to comment on the farm workers who wanted to meet with him. He responded: "As far as I'm concerned, these people do not exist."

What is it that causes sane men to act so hastily and so cruelly? It cannot be that we are so powerful. In the context of the great corporations, we are like a mosquito on an elephant's back.

This attack on our union in Arizona and in every major state is also an attack on the spirit of justice in America. Why shouldn't farm workers finally have a chance to hold their heads high in their own organization? Why shouldn't there be food on the tables of the families who work so hard to harvest that food? Why shouldn't poor people be allowed to struggle nonviolently for justice? The answers seem so obvious but the Farm Bureau, the lettuce growers and the politicians are deaf to our pleas.

My major concern is not this particular Arizona law. The fast is not out of anger against the growers. My concern is the spirit of fear that lies behind such laws in the hearts of growers and legislators across the country. Somehow these powerful men and women must be helped to realize that there is nothing to fear from treating their workers as fellow human beings. We do not seek to destroy the growers. We only wish an opportunity to organize our union and to work nonviolently to bring a new day of hope and justice to the farm workers of our country. It is long overdue and surely it is not too much to ask. Justice for farm workers is our only goal; it is the goal of our nonviolent lettuce boycott. Will you help us by making a committment not to eat or buy lettuce. This is a small sacrifice that can bring a great change for migrant farm workers. I ask for your prayers and your continued help in our struggle.

Your Brother,
Cesar E. Chavez

Regaining the Strength

Written on June 4, 1972. After the success of the Delano Grape Boycott, Chavez began to work with a more diversified group of farmworkers, including lettuce workers, for whom he fasted in 1972. The Mass during which Chavez broke his fast took place in Phoenix, Arizona.

I want to thank you for coming today. Some of you have been to the Santa Rita Center many times. Some have made beautiful offerings at the Mass. I have received letters and telegrams and lettuce boycott pledges from all over the world. All of these expressions of your love and your support for the farm workers' struggle have strengthened my spirits and I am grateful. I want especially to honor the farm workers who have risked so much to go on strike for their rights. Your sacrifices will not be in vain!

I am weak in my body but I feel very strong in my spirit. I am happy to end the fast because it is not an easy thing. But it is also not easy for my family and for many of you who have worried and worked and sacrificed. The fast was meant as a call to sacrifice for justice and a reminder of how much suffering there is among farm workers. In fact, what is a few days without food in comparison to the daily pain of our brothers and sisters who do backbreaking work in the fields under inhumane conditions and without hope of ever breaking their cycle of poverty and misery. What a terrible irony it is that the very people who harvest the food we eat do not have enough food for their own children.

It is possible to become discouraged about the injustice we see everywhere. But God did not promise us that the world would be humane and just. He gives us the gift of life and allows us to choose the way we will use our limited time on this earth. It is an awesome opportunity. We should be thankful for the life we have been given, thankful for the opportunity to do something about the suffering of our fellow man. We *can choose* to use our lives for others to bring about a better and more just world for our children. People who make that choice will know hardship and sacrifice. But if you give yourself totally to the nonviolent struggle for peace and justice, you also find that people will give you their hearts and that you will never go hungry and never be alone. And in giving of yourself you will discover a whole new life full of meaning and love.

Nan Freeman and Sal Santos have given their lives for our movement this past year. They were very young. It hurt us to lose them, and it still hurts us. But the greatest tragedy is not to live and die, as we all must. The greatest tragedy is for a person to live and die without knowing the satisfaction of giving life for others. The greatest tragedy is to be born but not to live for fear of losing a little security or because we are afraid of loving and giving ourselves to other people.

Our opponents in the agricultural industry are very powerful, and farm workers are still weak in money and influence. But we have another kind of power that comes from the justice of our cause. So long as we are willing to sacrifice for that cause, so long as we persist in nonviolence and work to spread the message of our struggle, then millions of people around the world will respond from their hearts, will support our efforts, and in the end we will overcome. It can be done. We know it can be done. God give us the strength and patience to do it without bitterness so that we can win both our friends and opponents to the cause of justice.

Nan Freeman

Delivered in 1972. Nan Freeman was a college student in Florida who volunteered as a part of the UFWA strike picket in Belle Glade. Early in the morning, Freeman and another college student were distributing leaflets about the strike to truck drivers when the trailer of a truck skidded and killed her. Nan Freeman was considered a martyr for the farmworkers' movement, and the tragedy of her death attracted notice to the farmworkers' cause.

On Tuesday, January 25, 1972, Nan Freeman, a young Jewish woman from Boston, gave her life for farm workers. She was eighteen years old when she died.

To some she was a young girl who lost her life in a tragic accident. To us she is a sister who picketed with farm workers in the middle of the night because of her love for justice. She is a young woman who fulfilled the commandments by loving her neighbors, even to the point of sacrificing her own life. To us, Nan Freeman is *Kadosha* in the Hebrew tradition, "a holy person" to be honored and remembered for as long as farm workers struggle for justice.

How can we measure the gift she has given to our cause? Will God give her another life to live? God has given Nan Freeman just one life, and now that life is ended. Think of that, all who cherish our farm workers union: Nan Freeman, our young sister, has poured out her *one life* so that farm workers everywhere might be more free.

There is no way to repay her immeasurable gift. There are no words to thank her for what she's done. Some things we can do: our whole movement is declaring a period of mourning that will correspond to the traditional seven-day period of mourning.

We can remember Nan Freeman. We can honor her life and express our thoughts to her family. We can give more of ourselves just because she has given everything. We must work together to build a farm workers' union that is worthy of her love and sacrifice.

Juan de la Cruz

Delivered in Arvin, California, on August 21, 1973. Juan de la Cruz was a farmworker marching in a picket line in Arvin, California, in August 1973, when he was shot. After his death, Chavez called off the strike against the DiGiorgio Corporation.

We are here to honor the life of Juan de la Cruz. On behalf of his family, we speak to all those who mourn here and throughout the country. Juan de la Cruz was a simple and a good man. He is gone and we miss him, and yet he is alive in our respect and love for his life. He was a humble farm worker and yet in his dying thousands of people have come to pay honor to his life. What is it about the life of our brother, Juan, that produces such a response in us?

Last night as we walked in a candlelight procession through Arvin, I was thinking about the earliest days of our union. I remember with strong feelings the families who joined our movement and paid dues long before there was any hope of winning contracts. Sometimes, fathers and mothers would take money out of their meager food budgets just because they believed that farm workers could and must build their own union. I remember thinking then that with spirit like that we had to win. No force on earth could stop us.

Juan de la Cruz is part of that spirit. He joined the union in its earliest days. He could have held back. He could have waited to see which side was going to win. Instead he threw himself into our struggle with the DiGiorgio Corporation. He picketed. He worked on the boycott. He went to jail. He did not hold back. He gave himself completely so that all farm workers might someday be free.

It is hard to turn your back on such a person. His example of service and sacrifice reaches the spirit of each one of us. His life and his deeds of love pull on our best instincts and cause us to want to give something of ourselves.

Juan has not only given himself in life, but he has now given his only life on this earth for us, for his children, and for all farm workers who suffer and who go hungry in this land of plenty. We are here because his spirit of service and sacrifice has touched and moved our lives. The force that is generated by that spirit of love is more powerful than any force on earth. It cannot be stopped.

We live in the midst of people who hate and fear us. They have worked hard to keep us in our place. They will spend millions more to destroy our union. But we do not have to make ourselves small by hating and fearing them in return. There is enough love and goodwill in our movement to give energy to our struggle and still have plenty left over to break down and change the climate of hate and fear around us.

We are going to win. It is just a matter of time. And when we win there will be a strong and vital service center and hiring hall and field office in the Lamont-Arvin area. It seems only fitting and proper that our union office here be named in honor of Juan de la Cruz.

Juan de la Cruz has not given his life in vain. He will not be forgotten. His spirit will live in each one of us who decides to join the struggle and who gives life and strength to others. Juan is a martyr in a just cause. He will give purpose and memory to his life and death by *what we do*. The more we sacrifice, the harder we work, the more life we give to the spirit of our brother, Juan de la Cruz.

In Coachella

Chavez spoke in Coachella, California, in 1973 to workers in the farming community in an effort to garner support for his union and benefit marginalized farmworkers, telling them what a good union does for its members.

Brothers and sisters in the field—for you are our brothers and sisters of the fields, just as your mothers and fathers were the brothers and sisters of our mothers and fathers. We are the people of the fields, the people who have made the trees and the vines the work of our lives. We know together what the truth is and you know, as we know, that there was never anyone to care about us until the Farm Workers Union came. Only the Farm Workers Union gave us new hope and new dreams for our families and our children. You know that and we know that and nothing can ever change it. Before the Farm Workers Union we had only each other to care for. It was our common problems and our common suffering that gave birth to this union, our own union, the Farm Workers Union. All around us were those who said that it could never be done. Everywhere people said that the growers were too strong for us, that the police would be against us, that the courts would beat us down, and that sooner or later we would fall back into the poverty and despair of our forefathers. But we fooled them. We fooled them because our common suffering and our love for each other and our families kept us together and kept us sacrificing and fighting for the better tomorrow that all of us dream about as we work among the vines.

Stop and think: What do you dream of as you work day after day in the hot sun? You dream of a nicer home for your wife, a good school for your kids, some dignity and rest for the older ones. Those have always been the dreams of the farm workers, but they never started to come true until we built this union. No one can ever erase from your minds or our minds that there was no one who cared, no one who fought for us, no one who helped hold out to us hope for a brighter tomorrow. It was the Farm Workers Union, *your* Farm Workers Union which did it. Never until the Union came did our wages move ahead. Think of it: We are the youngest union in America and yet we have *doubled* our basic wage, and even more!

Never was our health or the health of our families given any consideration until your Farm Workers Union. Remember the days when the vines were our toilets. Remember the indignities that our wives and mothers and daughters experienced. Think back upon it, brothers and sisters. It is a brighter day today in the fields and all of us who look deeply into our hearts know that the difference is entirely because of our union—*the first union that ever cared!*

But more than that we need to remember that there was something which made that *union,* for unions are not pieces of merchandise to be bought at a corner store. Our union was born out of our common suffering, our common hopes for our children, and our common love for each other.

Brothers and sisters, that love is still strong in our hearts. We think it is still strong in your hearts. We all must know that to let outsiders come in and destroy that love we have for each other is to destroy what we can make tomorrow mean for our children and our loved ones.

We came as far as we are today through sticking together. We will go even further tomorrow if we remember that under everything else our strength is our love and respect for each other.

After a Bus Accident

Early one morning in 1973, a bus carrying farmworkers skidded off the road, killing nineteen workers, because of the shoddy condition of the bus. On February 11, 1974, Chavez published this commentary in the Los Angeles Times.

On Monday, Jan. 14, 1974, Pablo Arellanos, 54, started picking up farm workers at 2 a.m. for Jesus Ayala, a labor contractor. By 3 a.m. or 3:30 a.m., Pablo had a busload of people and began his 135-mile trip to High and Mighty Farms lettuce fields near Blythe. Then, after a full day working in the fields himself, Pablo drove the workers back to Mexico at night and cleaned the bus before trying to get some sleep for the next day.

Early Tuesday, he again picked up a crew of farm workers and headed north. On approaching Blythe shortly before sunrise, the bus missed a turn and careened off the road into a drainage ditch. On impact, seats and farm workers were thrown to the front of the bus, crushing Pablo to death and trapping many others who soon drowned in the ditch.

For three days, we visited the families of the dead workers and sought more information about the causes of the accident.

Among the dead, we discovered, were men, women and children. In one family, a father and his three teenage children were killed.

Amid the grief there was great bitterness. The workers were—and still are—bitter because they've been through this kind of tragedy too many times before. The workers learned long ago that growers and labor contractors have too little regard for the value of any individual worker's life.

The trucks and buses are old and unsafe. The fields are carelessly sprayed with poisons. The laws that do exist are not enforced. How long will it be before we take seriously the importance of the workers who harvest the food we eat?

On Saturday, Jan. 19, 2,000 farm workers crowded into the

Calexico National Guard Armory for a funeral mass celebrated in Spanish. Afterward, at the request of the farm workers' families, on behalf of their union, I made the following remarks:

"We are united here in the name of God to pay final tribute to our brothers and sisters who lost their lives in a tragic bus accident. We are here also to show our love and solidarity for the families who have lost so much in the deaths of their loved ones.

"We are united in our sorrow but also in our anger. This tragedy happened because of the greed of the big growers who do not care about the safety of the workers and expose them to grave dangers when they transport them in wheeled coffins to the fields.

"There have been so many accidents—in the fields, on trucks, under machines, in buses—so many accidents involving farm workers.

"People ask if they are deliberate. They are deliberate in the sense that they are the direct result of a farm labor system that treats workers like agricultural implements and not as human beings. These accidents happen because employers and labor contractors treat us as if we were not important human beings.

"But brothers and sisters, the men and women we honor here today are important human beings. They are important because they are from us. We cherish them. We love them. We will miss them.

"They are important because of the love they gave to their husbands, their children, their wives, their parents—all those who were close to them and who needed them.

"They are important because of the work they do. They are not implements to be used and discarded. They are human beings who sweat and sacrifice to bring food to the tables of millions and millions of people throughout the world.

"They are important because God made them, gave them life, and cares for them in life and in death.

"Now that they are gone, how can we keep showing how important they are to us? How can we give meaning to their lives and their sacrifice?

"These terrible accidents must be stopped! It is our obligation— our duty to the memory of those who have died—to see to it that workers are not continually transported in these wheeled coffins, these carriages of death and sorrow. The burden of protecting the lives of farm workers is squarely on our shoulders.

"Let the whole world know that the pain that today fills our hearts with mourning also unifies our spirits and strengthens our determination to defend the rights of every worker.

"Let the labor contractors and the growers know that we will never stop working and struggling until there is an end to the inhuman treatment of all farm workers."

Before the Automobile Workers

As a part of his nationwide tour, Chavez spoke in Los Angeles in June 1974 to automobile workers' union members to thank them for their support and ask for their help in the struggle against the Teamsters Union, which was hindering the fight of the UFWA.

Thank you very much, Brother McDermott, Brother Woodcock, Brother Mazey, and Delegates to this 24th Constitutional Convention:

We want to congratulate all of the officers that were elected here. We want to tell you that we bring greetings to you from the farm workers who are now struggling in the fields in California and Arizona to *bring back a union,* workers who are struggling across the United States and Canada on the boycott, from all of them we bring greetings to you, congratulations on your convention and ask that all good luck remain with you and your union for the time to come.

We have been touring the United States lately and we are amazed that there is still great support for the farm workers' cause.

As we come to the Convention, we remember so many of you have been with us on the picket lines in California in 1968, 1969, and with us throughout this country with the boycott picket lines.

We want to especially thank the many locals, too numerous to count, of your great union which have been assisting us in the boycott, the CAP Council, and all of the men, women, and rank and filers and officers of your great union, for the tremendous support we have gotten throughout the ten years of rough going for our union.

We're asking all of you to boycott grapes, to boycott lettuce, and to boycott the yellow wines. There is a little confusion about which lettuce to boycott, and I would like to tell you that we're boycotting the western iceberg head lettuce. It's a very long name for a small lettuce. The western iceberg head lettuce is the only lettuce that looks like lettuce so there's no confusion; it's a round head lettuce. If it does not bear the emblem of the Black Thunderbird, the union label of our union, you should not eat it.

And on grapes, the same thing. There is only one grape grower with a contract in this union, and those grapes are marked with the union label. If you don't see the union label, don't buy the grapes.

And on the wine, the Gallo wine, you know, that is the biggest wine company in the world. And they put out at least twenty labels. In some cases, the word Gallo does not appear on the label.

There are two ways to find out if you're drinking Gallo wine. If you don't see the name Gallo on the label, you will read on the small print the words "Modesto, California." And if it says "Modesto, California," that's Gallo wine. And another way to find out if you're drinking Gallo wine is drink the stuff, and if you get sick, that's also Gallo wine.

As you may know, among the labels that are made by Gallo is the one called Ripple, and there's a button out and it's very popular these days. The buttons say simply, "Nixon Drinks Ripple."

As we travel throughout the country, we're asked constantly whether the farm workers are going to survive. I want to tell you that the farm workers are well and alive in California; they're striking and they're doing what they must do as workers to defend their interests.

Today in Monterey, California, the president of the Teamsters Union, Frank Fitzsimmons, was there at 11 o'clock to issue a charter to *their* farm workers in California.

We called a special work stoppage today of all the Teamster companies or workers of growers under a Teamster contract, and right this moment 90 percent of those workers that are in the Teamsters Union are not working because they're with us demonstrating against Fitzsimmons.

The farm workers know what it is to have a democratic union. They're not going to settle for anything less than the type of union that they want and the union they feel represents them.

We don't know anything about driving trucks or trucking. We don't know anything about organizing growers, but we know a few things about organizing farm workers.

You see, it is very plain and clear. If the farm workers are given the right to determine by their own free will which union they want, if they could get an election to let everybody know which union they want, we tell you, brothers and sisters, that the farm workers would vote 90 to 95 percent for this union as the farm workers' union.

I was in Coachella, a scene of great struggle for our union not long ago, and the picket lines in our union, as you know, are family affairs. The mother comes out and the father and the kids and the grandfather and the first and third and fourth and fifth cousins, they all come to the picket lines to help one another.

I was there not long ago when a group of the kids—ages eight, ten, twelve years old—in the picket line tell a little story that they wanted to tell me and they told me the story.

It's about three men who are traveling out in the countryside in an automobile, and the car breaks down and they realize that they're going to have a difficult time making it back to the city, so they go to the nearest farmhouse and ask the farmer if he could put them up for the night, and the farmer said that he could put them up for the night.

I have to tell you that one was an Indian, a Hindu from India; the other one was a Rabbi; and the third one was an unnamed Teamster official. And so after they got to the house and had a good supper, the farmer told them that he had space for two of them in the house and that the third one would have to stay in the barn because he did not have enough space for them in the house. And after they ate, the Hindu said that he would go to the barn because he had never slept in an American barn. He went to the barn and after a while the people turned out the light, and they were ready to go to sleep when there was a knock on the door. And when the door was opened, the Hindu was in the door, and he said that he couldn't sleep in the barn because there was a cow there and because of his religion he couldn't stay there.

The good Rabbi said that he would go to the barn. So the Rabbi went to the barn, and the people closed the door and turned out the lights and were getting ready to go to sleep again when there was another knock on the door.

The door was opened and the Rabbi was at the front door saying that he couldn't stay in the barn because there were pigs in the barn.

And so the Teamster said that he would go to the barn. And so he went to the barn, and the people turned out the light and were just getting ready to go to sleep when there was a commotion at the front door. The people opened up the front door and the cow and the pig were at the front door.

Brothers and sisters, the idea and the struggle to organize workers is not new. Since 1880, there have been writings of strikes in California of workers trying to get a union together for themselves. We have the American Indian. When you read your history books that there was a revolution and that there was an uprising, there was no uprising. The workers were striking to get a union.

Then came the Chinese who were brought here to build a railroad, and when the railroads were ended they went to work in the fields. And they had strange ideas that they wanted to have a union, and the growers then went to Japan and imported thousands of Japanese to come and replace the Chinese. The Japanese came to California and they had worse ideas. Not only did they want a union, but they also wanted to own the land.

And then the Hindus came and the Filipinos and the blacks and the Oakies and the Mexicans, and every single group of workers tried to organize a union and in every single instance they were beaten back.

The socialists, the Communists, the CIO, the AFL, the AFL-CIO, every single attempt to organize workers has been pushed back and destroyed. And then, finally, in 1962, our union made its appearance. And we're the first union in the history of agriculture, and thanks to you and to many people across the country we were able to get contracts and establish a union.

The growers found out soon enough that they, by themselves and the tricks they had, were no longer going to work to destroy the union, and they sought and found different alternatives to destroy our union. And so it's ironic that in this same hall, in December of 1972, Charles Colson—I'm sure you know who he is—Charles Colson was the intermediary to get Frank Fitzsimmons from the Teamsters Union at a National Farm Bureau Convention here in this hall—this is where the plot was hatched so that they could go and take our contracts from us the following spring of 1973.

Brothers and sisters, we know that it's very strange that when those contracts were gotten in 1970 for three years, that in

Coachella last year, in April of last year, we had as an example thirty-four contracts in other valleys.

On April 15 at midnight, we had thirty-four contracts. The next morning we had two contracts, and the Teamsters had thirty-two contracts. How could it be when there were no elections held? How could it be when the workers didn't know what had happened? How could it be when we were in negotiations with the growers? How could it be when we had been struggling with those workers for about ten years? We were an incumbent union; we had a contract with the growers. That's the way the contracts were taken away from us.

We don't know about the Teamsters Union in other places in industry. We know about the Teamsters Union and the Teamster workers, the Teamster people who work in agriculture. And we got to conclude from what we have seen that the Teamsters in agriculture is nothing but a company union. It's a tool doing the dirty work of the employers to destroy unions and of workers to think union.

Brothers and sisters, we went back in April of 1973 and told the growers and the Teamsters, when did you have elections? Let's have elections, and let the workers decide. If the workers decide that they don't want anything to do with the Farm Workers Union, we'll pack up and leave. We'll call the strike off and we won't have a boycott and you can have the workers. But if we win the election, we want the Teamsters to leave, and we want the growers to negotiate with our union.

And we were told then that it's too late to have elections. We went back this April, a year later, and we again challenged them for an election and we made a ridiculous proposition to them. We said, you won't give us an election; obviously, you're afraid you'll lose. That's why you won't give us an election.

Let me make a ridiculous proposition. We proposed a deal to the growers in Coachella and the Teamsters; we said, "Let the strikebreakers go, and let them decide for everybody which union they want." And they wouldn't take us on.

You know why? Because not even the people working in the fields are against this union. And everybody knows this.

The only way that this conflict can end is either to have elections to let the people decide or to make the strike and the boycott so powerful that the growers will not be able to sell their grapes and their lettuce and their wines until they come to us and they negotiate with us and we get a contract.

We did not only lose contracts; we lost some cherished things that we had fought so long to get: the whole idea of the labor contractor, the hiring boss, the whole idea of the man who had been exploiting workers is the third party, the crew chief—we had got rid of him, and we established hiring halls in his place. We lost that. The workers don't have that now. They're back to their old tricks of letting the labor contractors hire the workers and fire the workers.

We lost the great fight that we had put on for control of pesticides; simple conveniences for workers, like toilets in the fields. You don't find a toilet in those grape fields and lettuce fields today since our union was kicked out. The idea of having ice-cold potable water with individual drinking cups for the individuals is gone. These are the things that went out with those contracts.

But also, we don't mourn. We know that if we have to fight again to establish our union to fight with the workers to have a truly democratic union, a union that belongs to the workers, we will do it again, because if it must be done, we will do it.

We know that the workers are committed to the struggle. We know that they're willing to sacrifice. We know that they have determination. But we also know that this determination comes because of unions like the UAW who are still with us for so many years. You give us the encouragement to continue struggling. We know that come hell or high water, the Farm Workers of America are going to have a free union; they're going to have a democratic union, and they're going to have their own union. They're going to be able to determine like you do and all the workers in America which union they want. That we guarantee you.

Because, brothers and sisters, once the workers have tasted a little freedom, once the workers have seen what the union can do for them, once the workers are able to compare two unions, once the workers have struggled for so many years, then they're able to make this miracle come true. Once the workers know and have felt what it is to be free and know what it is to sit across the table from an employer, once workers know they cannot be fired at the whim of the employer—these things make an impression on the workers. And because of this, workers are willing to sacrifice and fight as long as it takes to bring back that kind of life that they had for three precious years. We have had a whole series of obstacles.

There are two Californias; there is rural California and there is also urban California. And in rural California . . . I want to let you know that the judges in those places, with few exceptions, are owned by the growers.

We have some of the most ridiculous injunctions against us. We're now striking in ten different places in California. Not only in grapes and lettuce; there are some strawberry strikes, cantaloupe strikes in every single place. We have the same injunctions because, you won't believe this, a group of district attorneys from various counties got together and got a grant from the federal government to get together and standardize an injunction. And now they have a standard injunction. Every time we have a strike, they just throw it in the hopper, and they come up with a restraining order against us, which means that in places where we have two, three, four hundred people striking we are reduced to five or six people in the picket lines. That means that we can't use the bullhorn. That means that we get tremendous harassment; that means that like last year we had almost five thousand people arrested for breaking the injunction, which means that they're free then to go to Mexico and import numbers of illegals to come and break the strike, which means that there are now people in California who make a business—it's a flourishing business—to run this private police force and this private patrol. A flourishing business to be in is the business of a professional strikebreaker or strikebreaker recruiter. These are the new industries in California because of our struggle. And because of that, the boycott must continue; the boycott must go on to be able to overcome, because we cannot do the organizing in the traditional way that you do it.

Until we get 100 percent of the workers on strike, it really doesn't mean anything, because two days later they will replace all those with people from Mexico. That is what we are up against.

Brothers and sisters, we know that right now in California there are at least sixty to seventy thousand illegals from Mexico breaking strikes and working elsewhere. And we make a petition to all of you; we make a petition that every Congressman and every U.S.

Senator must know what is going on so they can register the proper complaint with the Attorney General of the United States to get him to start enforcing the laws in regard to the wide-open door policy, the invitation to the illegals, to come and break our strikes.

If we were able to remove the illegals from California, at least from the strike fields, we would win the strike overnight. This is another reason why we must continue the struggle of the boycott to be able to win.

The strike last year was a terrible bloody strike, costly. We had almost five thousand people jailed; over two hundred people were beaten up and were sent to the hospital. We had forty-four people shot and wounded, twelve people seriously, and two people were killed.

All on our side.

The gimmick of the county sheriff bringing helicopters in our picket lines and dispersing pickets, calling our picket lines illegal assemblies and either beating us or taking us to jail or forcing us to give up the picketing, blocking the county roads at midnight so we wouldn't go to picket at five o'clock in the morning—all these outrageous acts against the union, and even with all of that we continued to struggle, continued to fight and continued to have hope that we're going to win.

We want to tell you that your help from your union is substantial and we appreciate it.

Brother [Leonard] Woodcock and Brother [Emil] Mazey and the rest of the officers, and all of you: We have been receiving from your union since last April $10,000 a week, and without that money we'd be dead today. And we stand here today to tell you that we appreciate that. We want you to know that.

We want you to know that as the union won at Farah, we'll win; as you've beaten the General Motors people, we'll beat the growers in California. But let me tell you that although you don't think you'll be paid back, we want to make a commitment. We're going to pay you back in the following way.

We're going to have our own union. And after we build our union, we're going to be with you side by side, struggling to help other workers build other unions.

We know that we have a commitment to help people as we've

been helped. We'll never lose that. And that's the promise we make you right here today.

What we wouldn't do and give to have a union like the UAW. We had a founding convention last year; we built a constitution, and I will tell you that we borrowed a lot from your constitution. What we wouldn't do to have a union like the UAW. The workers out in the fields know about the union; they know about the labor movement. They know about unions today, and they didn't know ten years ago.

They're not afraid; they want a union.

And these workers will struggle as long as it takes; they'll do whatever has to be done, legally and morally and nonviolently; they'll stay with it until we win. That we know.

Not only in California but in Arizona and throughout the United States, farm workers are now in their own revolution. In the fields of California and Arizona and other states it's like the 1930s for this Union. The workers in Florida, the black workers, the Chicano workers in California, the Filipino workers in California, the white workers in Arizona want a union. And there's no power in this earth . . . once the workers get the spirit and the idea and the great desire.

It's like a great thirst, and that thirst is not going to be abated; that thirst is not going to go away until the workers have a union that they can work with and they can work under and they can support, and it's their union.

And brothers and sisters, it doesn't matter what it takes. How long it takes, what we have to give up in terms of sacrifices—we'll stay with it. We'll stay with it because we know that if we give up the fight today, the farm workers may be organized, but they're going to be organized in a very different union that's not going to represent them. There are just too many forces against the workers having a free union under the other unions. There's no way that it will work.

So we want to close by telling you that there's a great irony here. You know men, women, and children who sacrifice and struggle and work too hard. So many things are asked of them: to travel the length and the width of this country; they're asked to move from place to place; they're asked to travel one thousand miles, two thousand miles without job security, to go to the other side of the country, in the hope of finding a job—and if they do find a job, they're going to be paid a pittance for it; to go on hoping that they'll find a home—most likely they wind up under a tree or under a bridge on a river bank; to go with no money, save enough for the gas to get there, risking all of the things that come from being poor and not having the security of a job and of a union. And they're asked that year in and year out, and they do it. They do it because—you see, brothers and sisters—they're laborers, the crucifying labor of the short handle hoe being bent in two. Stoop labor. Ten hours, twelve hours. They do that and they do it willingly. And you know what they do because of that great sacrifice. They are involved in the planting and the cultivation and the harvesting of the greatest abundance of food known in this society. They bring in so much food to feed you and me and the whole country and enough food to export to other places. The ironic thing and the tragic thing is that after they make this tremendous contribution, they don't have any money or any food left for themselves. And that's ridiculous. Here they produce a tremendous amount of food and there is no food left for themselves and for the children.

We're not going to stop struggling until the day comes when they can at least participate in the fruits of their labors, have enough money and enough food to eat for themselves and their families.

Martin Luther King Jr. I

Published in Maryknoll, *in April 1978. The Reverend Martin Luther King Jr. was one of Chavez's great partners and role models in nonviolent protest. Here, he pays a debt of gratitude to King from the United Farm Workers of America.*

In honoring Martin Luther King Jr.'s memory we also acknowledge nonviolence as a truly powerful weapon to achieve equality and liberation—in fact, the only weapon that Christians who struggle for social change can claim as their own.

Dr. King's entire life was an example of power that nonviolence brings to bear in the real world. It is an example that inspired much of the philosophy and strategy of the farm workers' movement. This observance of Dr. King's death gives us the best possible opportunity to recall the principles with which our struggle has grown and matured.

Our conviction is that human life is a very special possession given by God to man and that no one has the right to take it for any reason or for any cause, however just it may be.

We are also convinced that nonviolence is more powerful than violence. Nonviolence supports you if you have a just and moral cause. Nonviolence provides the opportunity to stay on the offensive, and that is of crucial importance to win any contest.

If we resort to violence then one of two things will happen: either the violence will be escalated and there will be many injuries and perhaps deaths on both sides, or there will be total demoralization of the workers.

Nonviolence has exactly the opposite effect. If, for every violent act committed against us, we respond with nonviolence, we attract people's support. We can gather the support of millions who have a conscience and would rather see a nonviolent resolution to problems. We are convinced that when people are faced with a direct appeal from the poor struggling nonviolently against great odds, they will react positively. The American people and people everywhere still yearn for justice. It is to that yearning that we appeal.

But if we are committed to nonviolence only as a strategy or tactic, then if it fails our only alternative is to turn to violence. So we must balance the strategy with a clear understanding of what we are doing. However important the struggle is and however much misery, poverty and exploitation exist, we know that it cannot be more important than one human life. We work on the theory that men and women who are truly concerned about people are nonviolent by nature. These people become violent when the deep concern they have for people is frustrated and when they are faced with seemingly insurmountable odds.

We advocate militant nonviolence as our means of achieving justice for our people, but we are not blind to the feelings of frustration, impatience and anger which seethe inside every farm worker. The burdens of generations of poverty and powerlessness lie heavy in the fields of America. If we fail, there are those who will see violence as the shortcut to change.

It is precisely to overcome these frustrations that we have involved masses of people in their own struggle throughout the movement. Freedom is best experienced through participation and self-determination, and free men and women instinctively prefer democratic change to any other means. Thus, demonstrations and marches, strikes and boycotts are not only weapons against the growers, but our way of avoiding the senseless violence that brings no honor to any class or community. The boycott, as Gandhi taught, is the most nearly perfect instrument of nonviolent change, allowing masses of people to participate actively in a cause.

When victory comes through violence, it is a victory with strings attached. If we beat the growers at the expense of violence, victory would come at the expense of injury and perhaps death. Such a thing would have a tremendous impact on us. We would lose regard for human beings. Then the struggle would become a mechanical thing. When you lose your sense of life and justice, you lose your strength.

The greater the oppression, the more leverage nonviolence holds. Violence does not work in the long run and if it is temporarily successful, it replaces one violent form of power with another just as violent. People suffer from violence. Examine history.

Who gets killed in the case of violent revolution? The poor, the workers. The people of the land are the ones who give their bodies and don't really gain that much for it. We believe it is too big a price to pay for not getting anything. Those who espouse violence exploit people. To call men to arms with many promises, to ask them to give up their lives for a cause and then not produce for them afterwards, is the most vicious type of oppression.

We know that most likely we are not going to do anything else the rest of our lives except build our union. For us there is nowhere else to go. Although we would like to see victory come soon, we are willing to wait. In this sense time is our ally. We learned many years ago that the rich may have money, but the poor have time.

It has been our experience that few men or women ever have the opportunity to know the true satisfaction that comes with giving one's life totally in the nonviolent struggle for justice. Martin Luther King Jr. was one of these unique servants and from him we learned many of the lessons that have guided us. For these lessons and for his sacrifice for the poor and oppressed, Dr. King's memory will be cherished in the hearts of the farm workers forever.

Martin Luther King Jr. II

In this speech, Chavez reminds his listeners that a policy of nonviolence was something radical in the beginning of the struggle of El Movimiento. Its effects may have taken a long time, but it was extremely successful in fighting human rights abuses.

My friends, today we honor a giant among men: today we honor the Reverend Martin Luther King Jr.

Dr. King was a powerful figure of destiny, of courage, of sacrifice, and of vision. Few people in the long history of this nation can rival his accomplishment, his reason, or his selfless dedication to the cause of peace and social justice.

Today we honor a wise teacher, an inspiring leader, and a true visionary, but to truly honor Dr. King we must do more than say words of praise.

We must learn his lessons and put his views into practice, so that we may truly be free at last.

Who was Dr. King?

Many people will tell you of his wonderful qualities and his many accomplishments, but what makes him special to me, the truth many people don't want you to remember, is that Dr. King was a great activist, fighting for radical social change with radical methods.

While other people talked about change, Dr. King used direct action to challenge the system. He welcomed it, and used it wisely. In his famous letter from the Birmingham jail, Dr. King wrote that "The purpose of direct action is to create a situation so crisis-packed that it will inevitably open the door to negotiation."

Dr. King was also radical in his beliefs about violence. He learned how to successfully fight hatred and violence with the unstoppable power of nonviolence. He once stopped an armed mob, saying: "We are not advocating violence. We want to love our enemies. I want you to love our enemies. Be good to them. This is what we live by. We must meet hate with love."

Dr. King knew that he very probably wouldn't survive the struggle that he led so well. But he said, "If I am stopped, the movement will not stop. If I am stopped, our work will not stop. For what we are doing is right. What we are doing is just, and God is with us."

My friends, as we enter a new decade, it should be clear to all of us that there is an unfinished agenda, that we have miles to go before we reach the promised land. The men who rule this country today never learned the lessons of Dr. King, they never learned that nonviolence is the only way to peace and justice.

Our nation continues to wage war upon its neighbors, and upon itself. The powers that be rule over a racist society, filled with hatred and ignorance. Our nation continues to be segregated along racial and economic lines.

The powers that be make themselves richer by exploiting the poor. Our nation continues to allow children to go hungry, and will not even house its own people. The time is now for people, of all races and backgrounds, to sound the trumpets of change. As Dr. King proclaimed, "There comes a time when people get tired of being trampled over by the iron feet of oppression." My friends, the time for action is upon us. The enemies of justice wants you to think of Dr. King as only a civil rights leader, but he had a much broader agent. He was a tireless crusader for the rights of the poor, for an end to the war in Vietnam long before it was popular to take that stand, and for the rights of workers everywhere. Many people find it convenient to forget that Martin was murdered while supporting a desperate strike on that tragic day in Memphis, Tennessee. He died while fighting for the rights of sanitation workers. Dr. King's dedication to the rights of the workers who are so often exploited by the forces of greed has profoundly touched my life and guided my struggle.

During my first fast in 1968, Dr. King reminded me that our struggle was his struggle, too. He sent me a telegram which said "Our seperate struggles are really one. A struggle for freedom, for dignity, and for humanity." I was profoundly moved that someone facing such a tremendous struggle himself would take the time to worry about a struggle taking place on the other side of the continent. Just as Dr. King was a disciple of Ghandi and Christ, we must now be Dr. King's disciples. Dr. King challenged us to work for a greater humanity. I only hope that we are worthy of his challenge. The United Farm Workers are dedicated to carrying on the dream of Reverend Martin Luther King Jr. My friends, I would like to tell you about the struggle of the farm workers who are waging a desperate struggle for our rights, for our children's rights, and for our very lives.

Many decades ago the chemical industry promised the growers that pesticides would bring great wealth and bountiful harvests to the fields. Just recently, the experts are learning what farm workers, and the truly organized farmers have known for years. The prestigious National Academy of Sciences recently concluded an exhaustive five-year study which determined that pesticides do not improve profits and do not produce more crops. What, then, is the effect of pesticides? Pesticides have created a legacy of pain, and misery, and death for farm workers and consumers alike. The crop which poses the greatest danger, and the focus of our struggle, is the table grape crop. These pesticides soak the fields. Drift with the wind, pollute the water, and are eaten by unwitting consumers. These poisons are designed to kill, and pose a very real threat to consumers and farm workers alike. The fields are sprayed with pesticides like Captan, Parathion, Phosdrin, and methyl bromide. These poisons cause cancer, DNA mutation, and horrible birth defects.

The Central Valley of California is one of the wealthiest agricultural regions in the world. In its midst are clusters of children dying from cancer. The children live in communities surrounded by the grape fields that employ their parents. The children come into contact with the poisons when they play outside, when they drink the water, and when they hug their parents returning from the fields. And the children are dying. They are dying slow, painful, cruel deaths in towns called cancer clusters, in cancer clusters like McFarland, where the children's cancer rate is 800 percent above normal. A few months ago, the parents of a brave little girl in the agricultural community of Earlimart came to the United Farm Workers to ask for help. The Ramirez family knew about our protests in nearby McFarland and thought there might be a similar problem in Earlimart. Our union members went door to door in Earlimart, and found that the Ramirez family's worst fears were true:

There are at least four other children suffering from cancer in the little town of Earlimart, a rate 1200 percent above normal. In Earlimart, little Jimmy Caudillo died recently from leukemia at the age of three. Three other young children in Earlimart, in addition to Jimmy and Natalie, are suffering from similar fatal diseases that the experts believe are caused by pesticides. These same pesticides can be found on the grapes you buy in the stores. My friends, the suffering must end. So many children are dying, so many babies are born without limbs and vital organs, so many workers are dying in the fields. We have no choice, we must stop the plague of pesticides.

The growers responsible for this outrage are blinded by greed, by racism, and by power. The same inhumanity displayed at Selma, in Birmingham, in so many of Dr. King's battlegrounds, is displayed every day in the vineyards of California.

The farm labor system in place today is a system of economic slavery! My friends, even those farm workers who do not have to bury their young children are suffering from abuse, neglect, and poverty. Our workers labor for many hours every day under the hot sun, often without safe drinking water or toilet facilities. Our workers are constantly subjected to incredible pressures and intimidation to meet excessive quotas. The women who work in the fields are routinely subjected to sexual harassment and sexual assaults by the grower's thugs. When our workers complain, or try to organize, they are fired, assaulted, and even murdered.

Just as Bull Connor turned the dogs loose on nonviolent marchers in Alabama, the growers turn armed foremen on innocent farm workers in California. The stench of injustice in California should offend every American. Some people, especially those who just don't care, or don't understand, like to think that the government can take care of these problems. The government should, but won't. The growers used their wealth to buy good friends like Governor George Deukmajian, Ronald Reagan, and George Bush. My friends, if we are going to end the suffering, we must use the same people power that vanquished injustice in Montgomery, Selma, and Birmingham. I have seen many boycotts succeed. Dr. King showed us the way with the bus boycott, and with our first boycott we were able to get DDT, Aldrin, and Dieldrin banned in our first contracts with grape growers. Now, even more urgently, we are trying to get deadly pesticides banned.

The growers and their allies have tried to stop us for years with intimidation, with character assassination, with public relations campaigns, with outright lies, and with murder. But those same tactics did not stop Dr. King, and they will not stop us. Once social change begins, it cannot be reversed. You cannot uneducate the person who has learned to read. You cannot humiliate the person who feels pride. And you cannot oppress the people who are not afraid anymore. In our life and death struggle for justice we have turned to the court of last resort: the American people. And the people are ruling in our favor. As a result, grape sales keep falling. We have witnessed truckloads of grapes being dumped because no one would stop to buy them. As demand drops, so do prices and profits. The growers are under tremendous economic pressure.

We are winning, but there is still much hard work ahead of us. I hope that you will join our struggle. The simple act of refusing to buy table grapes laced with pesticides is a powerful statement that the growers understand. Economic pressure is the only language the growers speak, and they are beginning to listen. Please, boycott table grapes. For your safety, for the workers, and for the children, we must act together. My friends, Dr. King realized that the only real wealth comes from helping others. I challenge each and every one of you to be a true disciple of Dr. King, to be truly wealthy.

I challenge you to carry on his work by volunteering to work for a just cause you believe in. Consider joining our movement because the farm workers, and so many other oppressed peoples, depend upon the unselfish dication of its volunteers, people just like you. Thousands of people have worked for our cause and have gone on to achieve success in many different fields. Our nonviolent cause will give you skills that will last a lifetime. When Dr. King sounded the call for justice, the freedom riders answered the call in droves. I am giving you the same opportunity to join the same cause, to free your fellow human beings from the yoke of oppression. I have faith that in this audience there are men and women with the same courage and the same idealism, that put young Martin Luther King Jr. on the path to social change.

I challenge you to join the struggle of the United Farm Workers. And if you don't join our cause, then seek out the many organization seeking peaceful social change.

Seek out the many outstanding leaders who will speak to you this week, and make a difference. If we fail to learn that each and every person can make a difference, then we will have betrayed Dr. King's life's work. The Reverend Martin Luther King Jr. had more than just a dream, he had the love and the faith to act.

Rufino Contreras

Delivered in Calexico, California, on February 14, 1979. Rufino Contreras was a lettuce cutter who was walking the picket line on February 10, 1979, when a company foreman opened fire on the line of UFWA workers. Contreras's death forced the strikers to break the picket for fear of more violence, allowing scabs to go to work without having to cross a picket line. He left behind a wife, son, and daughter.

February 10, 1979, was a day of infamy for farm workers. It was a day without joy. The sun didn't shine. The birds didn't sing. The rain didn't fall.

Why was this such a day of evil? Because on this day greed and injustice struck down our brother Rufino Contreras.

What is the worth of a man? What is the worth of a farm worker? Rufino, his father, and brother together gave the company twenty years of their labor. They were faithful workers who helped build up the wealth of their boss, helped to build up the wealth of his ranch.

What was their reward for their service and their sacrifice? When they petitioned for a more just share of what they themselves produced, when they spoke out against the injustice they endured, the company answered them with bullets; the company sent hired guns to quiet Rufino Contreras.

Capitol and labor together produce the fruit of the land. But what really counts is labor—the human beings who torture their bodies, sacrifice their youth, and numb their spirits to produce this great agricultural wealth, a wealth so vast that it feeds all of America and much of the world. And yet the men, women, and children who are the flesh and blood of this production often do not have enough to feed themselves.

But we are here today to say that true wealth is not measured in money or status or power. It is measured in the legacy that we leave behind for those we love and those we inspire.

In that sense, Rufino is not dead. Wherever farm workers organize, stand up for their rights, and strike for justice, Rufino Contreras is with them.

Rufino lives among us. It is those who have killed him and those who have conspired to kill him that have died, because the love, the compassion, the light in their hearts have been stilled.

Why do we say that Rufino still lives? Because those of us who mourn him today and bring him to his rest rededicate ourselves to the ideals for which he gave his life. Rufino built a union that will someday bring justice to all farm workers.

If Rufino were alive today, what would he tell us? He would tell us, "Don't be afraid. Don't be discouraged." He would tell us, "Don't cry for me, organize!"

This is a day of sorrow but it is also a day of hope. It is a time of sadness because our friend is dead. It is a time of hope because we are certain that Rufino today enjoys the justice in heaven that was denied him on earth.

It is our mission to finish the work Rufino has begun among us, knowing that true justice for ourselves and our opponents is only possible before God, who is the final judge.

What Is Democracy?

This speech, delivered in 1982, allows Chavez to reflect on the pertinence of multiculturalism in the United States. He describes democracy as a system that works only when its citizens are active participants.

After thirty years organizing poor people I have become convinced that the two greatest aspirations of humankind are equality and participation.

These yearnings are indivisible because equality can only be experienced through participation and self-determination. Democracy is not an impassive system. It is sustained by people's involvement. And participation in the democratic process is a key strategy in nonviolent struggle.

Free men and women instinctively prefer democratic change to any other means. It is only the enslaved and shackled—those without hope or faith—who seek violent solutions to their problems.

It is precisely to overcome this frustration and hopelessness that we in the farm workers' movement have involved masses of people in their own struggle. Thus, demonstrations and marches, strikes and boycotts are not only weapons against the growers, but our way of avoiding the senseless violence that brings no honor to any class or community. The boycott, as Gandhi taught, is the most nearly perfect instrument for nonviolent change, allowing masses of people to participate actively in a cause.

Participation in democracy—exercising the power to control our own future—is the best hope for a nonviolent solution to the injustices we face as farm workers, minorities, or poor people. It is also the only hope our nation has of enduring and surviving in a world where the have-nots increasingly vie for ascendency against the traditional forces of wealth and influence now concentrated in Western society.

Yet, instead of recognizing these truths, our country—through its archaic immigration policies and practices—has created an underclass of exploited and ostracized men and women who are excluded from participation, which has been the key to improvement for generations of U.S. immigrants.

Instead of promoting humanity's fundamental aspirations—equality and participation—our immigration policies and the practices of many U.S. employers have endorsed the twin plagues of humanity: exploitation and discrimination. These scourges are most vividly demonstrated in America by cheap wages and wretched working conditions for immigrant workers.

For these workers such exploitation and the poverty it brings destroys their spirits, wastes their potential, and blunts their ideals. It confines them to a daily struggle for survival to simply put bread on the table.

That daily struggle for survival cheats people of the finer things in life: education, religion, and involvement in government and politics. "Primero comer que ser cristiano." You must eat before you are a Christian, goes an old Mexican saying.

America has not yet learned the lesson that in this day and age you cannot have your cake and eat it, too. Some of our basic industries—most of agriculture and segments of the garment and service industries, to name a few—have prospered in recent times by exploiting undocumented immigrants. Employers want their cheap labor and their docile acceptance of miserable working and living conditions.

Yet we as a nation don't want these same immigrants to stake a claim to the promise this country offers to people here and around the world.

When I was a child, I remember that crossing the border illegally was considered a tremendous crime. It used to be. But now many no longer think of it as a crime. People say, "No! I'm going to go the U.S. because I need to work. I need to support my kids. I need a better life."

In this age of television, films, and commercial advertising, when the poor in Third World countries are endlessly reminded of the prosperity that is always beyond their reach, the stigma of crossing borders vanishes. It is no longer a crime in the minds of many people to cross a border to feed their hungry families.

Until we recognize the powerful forces that lure so many immigrants to this land—forces that we often ignite—we can never fashion a policy that will adequately address the acute immigration problems we face.

To be sure, the only long-term solution to the dilemma of illegal immigration is improving the economies of Mexico and other nations from which the immigrants spring.

But what of the people who are here now without papers?

We need to recast our philosophy about immigrants from Third World lands; we must replace the policies that exclude people from participation in our economic and political life because of their race, language, or immigration status with policies that encourage people to participate in society. We need to get people involved.

People are now alienated; among Hispanics, this alienation affects citizens and legal residents as well as undocumented persons. We have all kinds of rules to keep people outside the process. And when you exclude people you deny the yearning for equality and participation that is so key to fulfillment and happiness.

What changes do we have to make?

Some kind of meaningful adjustment in the legal status of undocumented aliens is a critical first step. Whether this adjustment is known as amnesty or called by some other name, no workable proposal for dealing with the question of illegal immigration can succeed without it.

Resolution of their status will enable undocumented workers to rid themselves of the pervasive fear that is so paralyzing; the fear that inhibits them from dealing with their exploitation like other American workers through the process of self-organization and collective bargaining.

At the same time we reckon with the problem of undocumented persons already in the country, we should emphatically reject schemes advanced by some Republican politicians and conservative grower groups to revive the infamous Bracero Program. The politicians now call it by a new name: the "guest worker program." But a fancy title cannot sugar-coat that evil system of replacing domestic farm workers with a new class of slave laborers imported from outside the U.S. to defeat unions and depress wages and working conditions.

Next, we must dramatically reform the U.S. Immigration and Naturalization Service. Perhaps it should be eliminated altogether. In our experience it is the most corrupt, most bigoted agency in our country.

The INS has a long history of dealing with noncitizens; confronting poor human beings who have no legal standing in society. So they feel they can kick them, beat them, demand money from them. They can do almost anything they want because they know these people are not citizens and can't respond.

Today many of the people who work for the INS see all Hispanics as aliens, even though we may be second-, third-, or fourth-generation Americans. In their minds, we're not citizens. It is the worst "gringo" mentality to be found anywhere in the government.

What of society's attitude towards differences in culture and language?

We all know of the so-called "melting pot" theory. It is taught in the schools, preached from the pulpit, and proclaimed by politicians.

This country is not a melting pot anymore. It used to be more of a melting pot when the bulk of the immigrants were white Europeans. But with large numbers of Third World people, particularly Asians, Latin Americans, and Africans, coming to our shores, it is no longer possible or desirable to Anglicise the waves of new immigrants.

We sometimes refer to those who oppose the struggles of minorities and people in the Third World as the "super-Americans." They claim the melting-pot theory still applies. They would like all of us to be melted, poured, and cast . . . and cloned into the all-American boy and girl. So we will all come out looking like Pat Boone and Anita Bryant. They would like all of us to buy their argument that the strength of our country is in its conformity to one ethnic and cultural heritage.

But there are some of us Americans who share a different vision of what our nation is. The strength of America is not in her conformity. We believe the strength of America is in her diversity!

Our country is admired around the world not—as the "New Right" claims—because of her bombers and nuclear arsenal. We are admired for our Bill of Rights and especially for the First

Amendment, which protects diversity. Let us also be admired for our cultural and linguistic pluralism.

For this country to continue to be great we need to include people, but not strip them of their cultural values in the process. I can eat tortillas and still be an American. Our country needs to understand that.

Groups of people will tolerate many things—but don't tamper with their language; don't threaten their religion. And don't meddle with their food or there's going to be a lot of problems. The greatest contribution our government and society can make is to recognize that we are all Americans, yet we are all different.

There has never really been a melting pot. As Continflas says, "Juntos pero no revueltos," together but not together.

We need to establish a federal department of cultural affairs. A department in our government that recognizes we're all one nation but also acknowledges the differences that make us unique and valuable as individuals and as part of the society. Such an agency could handle immigration and citizenship, and be the guardian of the special cultural values each racial, ethnic, or linguistic group has to contribute.

We must also unbridle our citizenship requirements—the laborious and protracted process that often stands as an obstacle to full participation in political life for so many decent and patriotic people whose cultural or linguistic tradition has not yet fallen prey to Anglicization.

A person should not become a citizen automatically. But a man's or woman's character is what should really matter. Not whether he or she speaks English or can survive the bureaucracy. What should count is the fact that he or she has lived here and is paying taxes and is making a contribution to the country. And, of course, the person would have to say, "Yes, I want to live under this system."

We must also change the voter registration laws as they now read. For the large part they are very old and written in a time when everybody went to church on Sunday and took a bath on Tuesday. I would say we should end voter registration. Anyone who is a citizen should have the right to vote.

What I am really talking about—whether it is immigration, citizenship, cultural mores, or voting rights—is making it possible for more people to participatie in the democratic process. If these changes come to pass we will witness a radical reordering—for the better—in our country. For whenever new blood is transfused into our national social and political fabric our nation is enriched and strengthened.

I believe that kind of participation is the real fulfillment of democracy, a realization of humanity's greatest desires. If this country could foster those aspirations, we would not only be true to our best ideals but we would provide an example for the world.

René López

Delivered in Fresno, California, in September 1983. René López was a dairy worker near Fresno, who was part of a group of strikers trying to get UFWA support. He was shot at point-blank range by company-hired men on September 21.

On behalf of all of us here, we extend our deepest sympathies to René's family—his mother, Dolores, his father, Francisco, his brother, Efren, his sister, Lupe, his sister, Rebecca, his sister, Yolanda, his brother, Juan Francisco, and his sisters Iliana [and Grace], and his grandparents, Fernando and Tomas López and Ignacio and Virginia Robles.

Thanks be to God, René's mother, father, brothers, and sisters, whom he loved so much, were able to be with him at his bedside during his final hours. René left them a beautiful heritage of courage, a heritage that, please God, will sustain them, come what may, until they meet him again in paradise.

René López's good deeds are known to all of you and, especially, to the members of his family, good deeds, above all of charity and kindness and human compassion. These deeds go with him and live after him, and for that reason, his funeral this morning is an occasion not for gloom, much less for despair, but rather an opportunity to celebrate, in a spirit of Christian joy, René's life and the goodness and the mercy of God.

The Book of Wisdom tells us: "Length of days is not what makes age honorable, nor number of years the true measure of life. Understanding, this is a man's gray hairs. The virtuous man, though he died before his time, will find rest."

All who knew René López as a personal friend or more immediately as a member of the family can vouch for the fact that he had understanding. By this I mean that he had the gift of faith, the gift of knowing what is truly important in his life.

It was not possible for René to shut his eyes to situations of distress and of poverty which cry out to God, or to keep silent in the face of injustice. *He was that kind of a man.*

René was young, but he was wise beyond his years. He died in the prime of his life, but the number of his years was not the true measure of his life. For this reason, regardless of the number of his days or the length of his years, he will find rest, for grace and mercy awaits the Chosen of the Creator, and protection awaits God's Holy Ones.

René was young, but he had already felt the call to social justice. His mother, Dolores, said that he came home one day with the stub of his union authorization card, showed it to her, and said, "Here is my first union card; now I am important, now I am a man."

But René's first union card was also his last, he will never enjoy the blessings of youth, he will never fulfill all the promises others saw in him, he will never pass on his great love to his own sons and daughters. René has been taken away from us in the prime of his life, before he could share the full measure of his talents and goodness with the world about him. René is gone because he dared to hope and because he dared to live out his hopes.

Rarely do men and women choose to die in the midst of their quest for freedom. They wish to be truly free and to live more fully in this life.

But death comes to us all, and we do not get to choose the time or the circumstances of our dying. The hardest thing of all is to die rightly. René López died rightly; he is a martyr for justice.

René is at peace with God. He has given all that he can give.

But how many more farm workers must fall? How many more tears must be shed? How many more martyrs must there be before we can be free? When will the day come when the joy becomes great and the grief becomes small?

The answer, my brothers and sisters, is in our hands. The answer is in *our* hands.

We who live must now walk an extra mile because René has lived and died for *his* and *our* dreams. We who keep on struggling for justice for farm workers must carry in our hearts *his* sacrifice.

We must try to live as he lived, we must keep alive his hopes, and fulfill, with our own sacrifices, his dreams. We must take René into our hearts and promise that we will never forget his sacrifice.

René's father, Francisco, looking down on his fallen son, said these words: "When he was born, I received him with a kiss, and, now I give him back to God with a kiss."

"Happy are those who died in the Lord: let them rest from their labor for their good deeds go with them."

Amen.

Before the 7th UFWA Constitutional Convention

During Ronald Reagan's administration, the growers won a series of victories against striking farmworkers, spurring Chavez to speak out in September 1984 against the inequities that Reagan's government was supporting.

There is a shadow falling over the land, brothers and sisters, and the dark forces of reaction threaten us now as never before.

The enemies of the poor and the working classes hold power in the White House and the governor's office.

Our enemies seek to impose a new Bracero Program on the farm workers of America; they seek to return to the days before there was a farm workers union, when our people were treated as if they were agricultural implements instead of human beings.

Our enemies seek to hand over millions of dollars in government money to segregated private colleges that close their doors to blacks and other people of color.

Our enemies have given the wealthiest people the biggest tax cuts in American history at the same time they have increased taxes for the poor and working people. They have created a whole new class of millionaires while forcing millions of ordinary people into poverty.

President Reagan is a man with a very special sense of religion. Reagan sees a proper role for government and a proper role for God. It's very simple: Reagan's government helps the rich, and God helps the rest of us.

Our enemies want all of us to carry identification cards issued by the government which only we will be forced to produce to get a job, to apply for unemployment insurance, to keep from being deported by the border patrol.

Our enemies have created the P.I.K. give-away program to give away millions of dollars in cash money to the richest corporate growers in America for not growing crops, while unemployment benefits for farm workers are cut and while food and medical care for the poor are reduced.

Our enemies are refusing to enforce the nation's fair housing laws, which protect black and brown people from discrimination.

Our enemies are refusing to enforce the laws that protect working people on the job from unsafe conditions which cause injuries and take lives.

Our enemies are responsible for the brutal murder of thousands of dark-skinned, Spanish-speaking farm workers through their military support of blood-thirsty dictators in Central America. The men, women, and children who have been slaughtered committed the same crimes we have committed: they wanted a better life for themselves and their families, a life free from hunger and poverty and exploitation.

The same dark forces of reaction which dominate the government in Washington also dominate the government in Sacramento. Governor Deukmejian is a lackey of Ronald Reagan. They collect their money from the same reactionary interests; their decisions are made by the same slick public relations men. They attack working people, minority people, and poor people with the same fervor.

Farm workers are not the only people who have suffered under Deukmejian. But Deukmejian has taken a terrible toll in human suffering among the farm workers of this state.

The law that guarantees our right to organize helped farm workers make progress in overcoming injustice.

At companies where farm workers are protected by union contracts we made progress:

- Against child labor
- Against miserable wages and working conditions
- Against sexual harassment of women workers
- Against favoritism and discrimination in hiring and employment
- Against dangerous pesticides which poison our people

Where we have organized, these injustices soon pass into history.

But under Deukmejian, the law that guarantees our right to organize no longer protects farm workers. It doesn't work anymore! Instead of prosecuting growers who break the law, Deukmejian's men give them aid and comfort. Instead of enforcing the law as it was written against those who break it, Deukmejian invites growers who ignore their farm workers' rights by seeking relief from the governor's appointees.

What does all this mean for you and for other farm workers?

It means that the right to vote in free elections is a sham!

It means that the right to talk freely about the union among your fellow workers on the job is a cruel hoax.

It means the right to be free from threats and intimidation by growers is an empty promise.

It means the right to sit down and negotiate with your employer as equals across the bargaining table—and not as peons in the fields—is a fraud.

It means that 6,300 farm workers who are owed $72 million in back pay because their employers broke the law are still waiting for their checks.

It means that 36,000 farm workers who voted to be represented by the UFW in free elections are still waiting for contracts because their employers won't bargain in good faith.

Are these make-believe threats? Are these exaggerations?

Ask your friends and coworkers who are waiting for the money they are owed from the growers.

Ask your friends and coworkers who are waiting for the growers to bargain in good faith and sign contracts.

Ask your friends and coworkers who've been fired from their jobs because they spoke out for the union.

Ask your friends and coworkers who've been threatened with physical violence because they support the UFW.

Ask the family of René López, the young farm worker from Fresno who was shot to death last year because he supported the union, because he spoke out against injustice, because he exercised his rights under the law.

Farm workers are not the only people who have suffered under Deukmejian. And they are not the only people who are under attack by the dark forces of reaction. Millions of dollars have been spent to place propositions on the November election ballot for the people of California to vote on. The dark forces of reaction have placed Proposition 41 on the ballot. It will reduce the welfare benefits poor people in California receive by 40 percent.

The Republicans want to give poor people—women and children living in poverty—a 40 percent cut in their support money as a Christmas present this December.

There is another proposition on the ballot this November, Proposition 39, the Deukmejian Reapportionment Initiative.

Proposition 39 would redraw the boundary lines for legislative and congressional districts. The existing reapportionment law that sets the current boundary lines was passed by the Democrats in the legislature. It represents a great victory in the long struggle for more political power by Hispanics and other minority people. Deukmejian wants to redraw the boundary lines because he wants to get rid of the friends we have in the Legislature and in Congress—friends who vote to defend the interests of farm workers and other working people. Deukmejian wants to redraw the lines so Mexican people will be split apart into many small communities: so our political strength will not be felt, so we will be forced to vote only for reactionary politicians who back Deukmejian.

The same Deukmejian who is working to deny a better life to farm workers is also working to deny all Hispanics in California the right to full participation in the political process. Deukmejian and the corporate growers who are paying for Proposition 39 want to redraw the lines to send more of our enemies to Sacramento. The Western Growers Association has already given $50,000 to the Deukmejian Reapportionment Initiative. And growers continue to support Proposition 39 with their money and influence.

But brothers and sisters, the dark forces of reaction also want to pass Proposition 39 because they are afraid of us! Deukmejian and the growers have looked into the future and the future is ours!

History and inevitability are on our side. The farm workers and their children—and the Hispanics and their children—are the future in this state. And corporate growers are the past. The monumental growth of Hispanic influence in California means increased population, increased social and economic power, and increased political influence.

Those politicians who ally themselves with corporate growers are in for a big surprise. They want to make their careers in politics; they want to hold power twenty and thirty years from now.

But twenty and thirty years from now—in Modesto, in Salinas, in Fresno, in Bakersfield, in the Imperial Valley, and in many of the great cities of California—those communities will be dominated by farm workers and not by growers, by the children and grandchildren of farm workers, and by the children and grandchildren of growers.

Look at the values we cherish! Look at the things they hold dear! We came from big families; they keep down the size of their families. We take pride in our children. They take pride in the money they make. The growers have money and everything it buys. We have people and numbers. We'll see who triumphs in the end. The day will come when we're the majority when our children are the lawyers and the doctors and the politicians—when we hold political power in this state.

These trends are part of the forces of history that cannot be stopped. No governor and no organization of rich growers can resist them for very long. They are inevitable. Once change begins, it cannot be stopped:

You cannot uneducate the person who has learned to read.

You cannot humiliate the person who feels pride.

You cannot oppress the people who are not afraid anymore.

Our people are on the move. Our day is coming. It may not come this year. It may not come during this decade. But it will come, someday!

And when that day comes, we shall see the fulfillment of that passage from the book of Matthew in the New Testament that "the last shall be first and the first shall be last."

Our duty is clear. We must stand up and defend our rights as free men and women. We must defeat Proposition 39! We must unite with our Hispanic brothers and sisters who don't work in the fields by joining together in this noble crusade.

For twenty-one months we have taken all the abuse and injustice Governor Deukmejian can dish out. He has attacked us where it hurts the most:

He has deprived us of our rights under the law.

He has taken away the ability of many of us to provide for our families.

He has tried to deny us the dignity that can only be ours in a union that we build and control.

Now it is our turn to fight back; it's our turn to strike a blow for all Hispanics in California by defeating Proposition 39.

Proposition 39 was placed on the ballot to destroy the majority coalition of progressive legislators under the leadership of Assembly Speaker Willie Brown and Senate President Pro Tem David Roberti. That majority coalition has preserved farm workers' rights by protecting the Agricultural Labor Relations Act from destruction by the growers. That majority coalition has stood up for the rights of all working people and for the rights of the poor, the sick, the elderly, and the disadvantaged.

Please join with me now in welcoming to this convention the Speaker of the California State Assembly, Willie Brown, and a delegation representing the Democratic members of the California State Assembly.

At the Commonwealth Club
of San Francisco

Chavez spoke on November 9, 1984, many years into the UFWA's struggle, about the terrible conditions farmworkers were still living in, but also acknowledged the victories achieved by the union's work.

Twenty-one years ago last September, on a lonely stretch of railroad track paralleling U.S. Highway 101 near Salinas, thirty-two Bracero farm workers lost their lives in a tragic accident.

The Braceros had been imported from Mexico to work on California farms. They died when their bus, which was converted from a flatbed truck, drove in front of a freight train. Conversion of the bus had not been approved by any government agency. The driver had "tunnel" vision. Most of the bodies lay unidentified for days. *No one, including the grower who employed the workers, even knew their names.*

Today, thousands of farm workers live under savage conditions: beneath trees and amid garbage and human excrement, near tomato fields in San Diego County, tomato fields which use the most modern farm technology. Vicious rats gnaw on them as they sleep. They walk miles to buy food at inflated prices, and they carry in water from irrigation pumps.

Child labor is still common in many farm areas. As much as 30 percent of Northern California's garlic harvesters are under-aged children. Kids as young as six years old have voted in state-conducted union elections since they qualified as workers. Some eight hundred thousand under-aged children work with their families harvesting crops across America.

Babies born to migrant workers suffer 25 percent higher infant mortality than the rest of the population.

Malnutrition among migrant worker children is ten times higher than the national rate.

Farm workers' average life expectancy is still forty-nine years—compared to seventy-three years for the average American.

All my life, I have been driven by one dream, one goal, one vision: To overthrow a farm labor system in this nation which treats farm workers as if they were not important human beings. Farm workers are not agricultural implements; they are not beasts of burden to be used and discarded. That dream was born in my youth. It was nurtured in my early days of organizing. It has flourished. It has been attacked.

I'm not very different from anyone else who has ever tried to accomplish something with his life. My motivation comes from my personal life, from watching what my mother and father went through when I was growing up, from what we experienced as migrant farm workers in California.

That dream, that vision grew from my own experience with racism, with hope, with the desire to be treated fairly and to see my people treated as human beings and not as chattel. It grew from anger and rage—emotions I felt forty years ago when people of my color were denied the right to see a movie or eat at a restaurant in many parts of California. It grew from the frustration and humiliation I felt as a boy who couldn't understand how the growers could abuse and exploit farm workers when there were so many of us and so few of them.

Later, in the fifties, I experienced a different kind of exploitation. In San Jose, in Los Angeles, and in other urban communities, we, the Mexican American people, were dominated by a majority that was Anglo. I began to realize what other minority people had discovered: that the only answer, the only hope was in organizing.

More of us had to become citizens. We had to register to vote. And people like me had to develop the skills it would take to organize, to educate, to help empower the Chicano people.

I spent many years—before we founded the union—learning how to work with people.

We experienced some successes in voter registration in politics in battling racial discrimination—successes in an era when Black Americans were just beginning to assert their civil rights and when political awareness among Hispanics was almost nonexistent. But deep in my heart, I knew I could never be happy unless

I tried organizing the farm workers. I didn't know if I would succeed. But I had to try.

All Hispanics—urban and rural, young and old—are connected to the farm workers' experience. We had all lived through the fields, or our parents had. We shared that common humiliation. How could we progress as a people, even if we lived in the cities, while the farm workers—men and women of our color—were condemned to a life without pride? How could we progress as a people while the farm workers—who symbolized our history in this land—were denied self-respect? How could our people believe that their children could become lawyers and doctors and judges and business people while this shame, this injustice was permitted to continue?

Those who attack our union often say, "It's not really a union. It's something else—a social movement, a civil rights movement. It's something dangerous."

They're half right.

The United Farm Workers is first and foremost a union. A union like any other. A union that either produces for its members on the bread-and-butter issues or doesn't survive.

But the UFW has always been something more than a union, although it's never been dangerous if you believe in the Bill of Rights. The UFW was the beginning! We attacked that historical source of shame and infamy that our people in this country lived with. We attacked that injustice, not by complaining, not by seeking handouts, not by becoming soldiers in the War on Poverty.

We organized!

Farm workers acknowledged we had allowed ourselves to become victims in a democratic society—a society where majority rule and collective bargaining are supposed to be more than academic theories or political rhetoric. And by addressing this historical problem, we created confidence and in an entire people's ability to create the future.

The UFW's survival—its existence—was not in doubt in my mind when the time began to come—after the union became visible—when Chicanos started entering college in greater numbers, when Hispanics began running for public office in greater numbers, when our people started asserting their rights on a broad range of issues and in many communities across the country.

The union's survival—its very existence—sent out a signal to all Hispanics:

That we were fighting for our dignity,

That we were challenging and overcoming injustice,

That we were empowering the least educated among us, the poorest among us.

The message was clear: If it could happen in the fields, it could happen anywhere—in the cities, in the courts, in the city councils, in the state legislatures.

I didn't really appreciate it at the time, but the coming of our union signaled the start of great changes among Hispanics that are only now beginning to be seen.

I've traveled to every part of this nation. I have met and spoken with thousands of Hispanics from every walk of life from every social and economic class.

One thing I hear most often from Hispanics, regardless of age or position—and from many non-Hispanics as well—is that the farm workers gave them hope that they could succeed and the inspiration to work for change.

From time to time you will hear our opponents declare that the union is weak, that the union has no support, that the union has not grown fast enough. Our obituary has been written many times. How ironic it is that the same forces which argue so passionately that the union is not influential are the same forces that continue to fight us so hard.

The union's power in agriculture has nothing to do with the number of farm workers under union contract.

It has nothing to do with the farm workers' ability to contribute to Democratic politicians.

It doesn't even have much to do with our ability to conduct successful boycotts.

The very fact of our existence forces an entire industry—unionized and nonunionized—to spend millions of dollars year after year on improved wages, on improved working conditions, on benefits for workers. If we're so weak and unsuccessful, why do the growers continue to fight us with such passion? Because so long as we continue to exist, farm workers will benefit from our existence even if they don't work under union contract.

It doesn't really matter whether we have a hundred thousand

members or five hundred thousand members. In truth, hundreds of thousands of farm workers in California—and in other states—are better off today because of our work. And Hispanics across California and the nation, who don't work in agriculture, are better off today because of what the farm workers taught people—about organization, about pride and strength, about seizing control over their own lives.

Tens of thousands of the children and grandchildren of farm workers—and the children and grandchildren of poor Hispanics—are moving out of the fields and out of the barrios and into the professions and into business and into politics. And that movement cannot be reversed!

Our union will forever exist as an empowering force among Chicanos in the Southwest. And that means our power and our influence will grow and not diminish.

Two major trends give us hope and encouragement:

First, our union has returned to a tried and tested weapon in the farm workers' nonviolent arsenal—the boycott! After the Agricultural Labor Relations Act became law in California in 1975, we dismantled our boycott to work with the law.

During the early and mid-seventies, millions of Americans supported our boycotts. After 1975, we redirected our efforts from the boycott to organizing and winning elections under the law. The law helped farm workers make progress in overcoming poverty and injustice.

At companies where farm workers are protected by union contracts, we have made progress in overcoming child labor, in overcoming miserable wages and working conditions, in overcoming sexual harassment of women workers, in overcoming dangerous pesticides which poison our people and poison the food we all eat. Where we have organized, these injustices soon pass into history.

But under Republican Governor George Deukmejian, the law that guarantees our right to organize no longer protects farm workers—it doesn't work anymore!

In 1982 corporate growers gave Deukmejian one million dollars to run for governor of California. Since he took office, Deukmejian has paid back his debt to the growers with the blood and sweat of California farm workers. Instead of enforcing the law as it was written against those who break it, Deukmejian invites growers who break the law to seek relief from the governor's appointees.

The Louis Harris poll revealed that 17 million American adults boycotted grapes. We are convinced that those people and that good will have not disappeared.

That segment of the population which makes our boycotts work are the Hispanics, the Blacks, the other minorities, and our allies in labor and the church. But it is also an entire generation of young Americans who matured politically and socially in the 1960s and '70s—millions of people for whom boycotting grapes and other products became a socially accepted pattern of behavior. If you were young, Anglo, and on or near campus during the late '60s and early '70s, chances are you supported farm workers.

Fifteen years later the men and women of that generation are alive and well. They are in their mid-thirties and forties. They are pursuing professional careers. Their disposable income is relatively high. But they are still inclined to respond to an appeal from farm workers. The union's mission still has meaning for them.

Only we must translate the importance of a union for farm workers into the language of the 1980s. Instead of talking about the right to organize, we must talk about protection against sexual harassment in the fields. We must speak about the right to quality food—and food that is safe to eat.

I can tell you that the new language is working; the 17 million are still there. They are responding—not to picket lines and leafletting alone, but to the high-tech boycott of today, a boycott that uses computers and direct mail and advertising techniques which have revolutionized business and politics in recent years. We have achieved more success with the boycott in the first eleven months of 1984 than we achieved in the fourteen years since 1970.

The other trend that gives us hope is the monumental growth of Hispanic influence in this country—and what that means in increased population, increased social and economic clout, and increased political influence.

South of the Sacramento River in California, Hispanics now make up more than 25 percent of the population.

That figure will top 30 percent by the year 2000.

There are 1.1 million Spanish-surnamed registered voters in

California; 85 percent are Democrats; only 13 percent are Republicans.

In 1975, there were two hundred Hispanic elected officials at all levels of government. In 1984, there are over four hundred elected judges, city council members, mayors, and legislators. In light of these trends it is absurd to believe or suggest that we are going to go back in time as a union or as a people!

The growers often try to blame the union for their problems, to lay their sins off on us, sins for which they only have themselves to blame. The growers only have themselves to blame as they begin to reap the harvest from decades of environmental damage they have brought upon the land—

The pesticides, the herbicides, the soil fumigants, the fertilizers, the salt deposits from thoughtless irrigation.

The ravages from years of unrestrained poisoning of our soil and water.

Thousands of acres of land in California have already been irrevocably damaged by this wanton abuse of nature.

Thousands more will be lost unless growers understand that dumping more poisons on the soil won't solve their problems—on the short term or the long term. Health authorities in many San Joaquin Valley towns already warn young children and pregnant women not to drink the water because of nitrates from fertilizers which have contaminated the groundwater.

The growers only have themselves to blame for an increasing demand by consumers for higher quality food—food that isn't tainted by toxins, food that doesn't result from plant mutations or chemicals which produce red, luscious-looking tomatoes that taste like alfalfa.

The growers are making the same mistake American automakers made in the '60s and '70s when they refused to produce small, economical cars and opened the door to increased foreign competition.

Growers only have themselves to blame for increasing attacks on their publicly financed handouts and government welfare: water subsidies, mechanization research, huge subsidies for not growing crops. These special privileges came into being before the Supreme Court's one-person, one-vote decision at a time when rural lawmakers dominated the legislature and the Congress.

Soon, those handouts could be in jeopardy—as government searches for more revenue and as urban taxpayers take a closer look at farm programs and whom they benefit. The growers only have themselves to blame for the humiliation they have brought upon succeeding waves of immigrant groups which have sweated and sacrificed for a hundred years to make this industry rich. For generations, they have subjugated entire races of dark-skinned farm workers. These are the sins of the growers—not the farm workers:

We didn't poison the land.

We didn't open the door to imported produce.

We didn't covet billions of dollars in government handouts.

We didn't abuse and exploit the people who work the land.

Today, the growers are like a punch-drunk old boxer who doesn't know he's past his prime. The times are changing. The political and social environment has changed. The chickens are coming home to roost and the time to account for past sins is approaching.

I am told, these days, why farm workers should be discouraged and pessimistic: The Republicans control the governor's office and the White House. They say there is a conservative trend in the nation.

Yet we are filled with hope and encouragement. We have looked into the future and the future is ours!

History and inevitability are on our side. The farm workers and their children—and the Hispanics and their children—are the future in California. And corporate growers are the past!

Those politicians who ally themselves with the corporate growers and against the farm workers and the Hispanics are in for a big surprise.

They want to make their careers in politics. They want to hold power twenty and thirty years from now.

But twenty and thirty years from now—in Modesto, in Salinas, in Fresno, in Bakersfield, in the Imperial Valley, and in many of the great cities of California—those communities will be dominated by farm workers and not by growers, by the children and grandchildren of farm workers and not by the children and grandchildren of growers.

These trends are part of the forces of history which cannot be stopped! No person and no organization can resist them for very long. They are inevitable! Once social change begins, it cannot be reversed.

You cannot uneducate the person who has learned to read. You cannot humiliate the person who feels pride. You cannot oppress the people who are not afraid anymore.

Our opponents must understand that it's not just a union we have built. Unions, like other institutions, can come and go. But we're more than an institution! For nearly twenty years our union has been on the cutting edge of a people's cause. And you cannot do away with an entire people. You cannot stamp out a people's cause.

Regardless of what the future holds for the union—regardless of what the future holds for farm workers—our accomplishments cannot be undone! "La Causa"—our cause—doesn't have to be experienced twice. The consciousness and pride that were raised by our union are alive and thriving inside millions of young Hispanics who will never work on a farm!

Like the other immigrant groups, the day will come when we win the economic and political rewards which are in keeping with our numbers in society. The day will come when the politicians do the right thing by our people out of political necessity and not out of charity or idealism.

That day may not come this year.

That day may not come during this decade.

But it will come, someday!

And when that day comes, we shall see the fulfillment of that passage from the Book of Matthew in the New Testament, "The last shall be first and the first shall be last." And on that day, our nation shall fulfill its creed and that fulfillment shall enrich us all.

Wrath of Grapes

Delivered in 1986. As part of the boycott of table grapes, Chavez publicized the horrific effects of pesticides used in growing these grapes. His purpose was not just to alert the public to the dangers posed to farmworkers, but to the dangers posed to anyone who ate the fruit.

I am speaking to you about our Wrath of Grapes Boycott because I believe our greatest court, the court of last resort, is the American people. And I believe that once you have taken a few moments to hear this message you will concur in this verdict along with a million other North Americans who are already committed to the largest grape boycott in history. The worth of humans is involved here.

I see us as one family. We cannot turn our backs on each other and our future. We farm workers are closest to food production. We were the first to recognize the serious health hazards of agriculture pesticides to both consumers and ourselves.

Twenty years ago over 17 million Americans united in a grape boycott campaign that transformed the simple act of refusing to buy grapes into a powerful and effective force against poverty and injustice. Through the combined strengths of a national boycott, California farm workers won many of the same rights as other workers—the right to organize and negotiate with growers.

But we also won a critical battle for all Americans. Our first contracts banned the use of DDT, DDE, Dieldrin on crops, years before the federal government acted.

Twenty years later our contracts still seek to limit the spread of poison in our food and fields, but we need your help once again if we are to succeed.

A powerful self-serving alliance between the California governor and the $4 billion agricultural industry has resulted in a systematic and reckless poisoning of not only California farm workers but of grape consumers throughout our nation and Canada.

The hard-won law enacted in 1975 has been trampled beneath the feet of self-interest. Blatant violations of California labor laws are constantly ignored. And worst of all, the indiscriminate and even illegal use of dangerous pesticides has radically increased in the last decade causing illness, permanent disability, and even death.

We must not allow the governor of California and the selfish interests of California grape growers to threaten lives throughout North America.

We have known for many years that pesticides used in agriculture pollute the air, earth, and water, contaminate animals and humans, and are found in the tissue of newborn infants and mothers' milk. This March, the *New York Times* reported that the Environmental Protection Agency finally considers pesticide pollution its most urgent problem, noting virtually everyone is exposed to pesticides.

The Environmental Protection Agency experts have warned that

1. Pesticide residue is being found in a growing number of food products.
2. Some poisons registered for use in the last thirty years cause cancer, mutations, and birth defects.
3. Most chemicals on the market have insufficient and sometimes fraudulent test results.
4. Underground water supplies of twenty-three states are already tainted, and farm workers suffer some pesticide-induced illness in alarming numbers.

Consumers must be alerted now that no one can actually define or measure so-called safe exposure to residual poison that accumulates in the human body, as environments differ and each person's tolerance is unique. What might be safe statistically for the average healthy forty-year-old male might irreparably harm an elderly consumer, a child, or the baby of a pregnant mother.

What we do know absolutely is that human lives are worth more than grapes and that innocent-looking grapes on the table may disguise poisonous residues hidden deep inside where washing cannot reach.

Let me share the frightening facts with you. Last July the *New York Times* and national television reported that nearly one thousand California, Pacific Northwest, Alaskan, and Canadian consumers became ill as the result of eating watermelons tainted with the powerful insecticide Aldicarb, labeled the most acutely toxic pesticide registered in the United States. Yet Aldicarb cannot be legally used on watermelons.

In June local agriculture officials quarantined fields in Delano, California, grape ranches because residues of the pesticide Orthene were found in the vineyards; yet Orthene cannot be legally used on table grapes.

And a new study shows pesticides used in growing may be responsible for the illness of over three hundred thousand of the nation's 4 million farm workers.

But of the twenty-seven legally restricted toxic poisons currently used on grapes, at least five are potentially as dangerous or more hazardous to consumers and grape workers than deadly Aldicarb and Orthene.

Here are five major threats to your health that cling to California table grapes:

• Parathion and Phosdrin are highly poisonous insecticides, similar to nerve gas, and are responsible for the majority of deaths and serious poisoning of farm workers. They cause birth defects and are carcinogens.
• Captan, a proven cancer-causing and birth-defect-producing agent known as fungicide.
• Dinoseb, a highly toxic herbicide that has caused worker deaths.
• Methyl bromide, a more potent mutagen (an agent affecting genetic material) than mustard gas and is a highly poisonous and proven carcinogen.

Statistics and news articles do not relate the real cost, the human anguish that originates from poisons on our food. They do not tell the tragedies I personally learn of daily.

How can I explain these chemicals to three-year-old Amalia Larios, who will never walk, born with a spinal defect due to pesticide exposure of her mother.

What statistics are important to Adrián Espinoza, seven years old and dying of cancer with eight other children, whose only source of water was polluted with pesticides.

What headlines can justify the loss of irrigator Manuel Anaya's right hand, amputated due to recurrent infection from powerful herbicides added to the water he worked with in the fields.

How do we comfort the mother of maimed and stillborn infants, the parents who watch their teenage children sicken or die.

What report can be cited at the hospital beds I visit, at growing numbers of wakes I attend.

What court will hear the case of thirty-two-year-old Juan Chaboya, murdered by deadly chemicals in the freshly sprayed fields outside San Diego, his dead body dumped by the growers forty-five miles away at a Tijuana clinic. What excuse for justice will we offer his four children and his widow if we do nothing.

Now is the time for all of us to stand as a family and demand a response in the name of decency. Too much is at stake. This is a battle that none of us can afford to lose because it is a fight for the future of America. It is a fight we can win, and it is a fight that everyone can join.

Add your voice to our demands of decency as we call for

1. A ban on the five most dangerous pesticides used in grape production—Parathion, Phosdrin, Dinoseb, methyl bromide, and Captan.
2. A joint UFW/grower testing program for poisonous residues on grapes sold in stores with the results made public.
3. Free and fair elections for farm workers to decide whether to organize and negotiate contracts limiting the use of dangerous poisons in the fields.
4. Good faith bargaining.

Until these demands of decency are met, we will carry the message of the Wrath of Grapes Boycott from state to state. Ten years ago, 12 percent of the country boycotted grapes and the growers were forced to accountability. California Governor Deukmejian and agribusiness cannot withstand the judgment of outraged consumers who refused to purchase their tainted products. Every month over 1 million grape consumers like yourselves receive our message across North America. State and federal law makers, mayors and city councils, religious and labor leaders, students and senior citizens, mothers and fathers, rich and poor, concerned individuals in every walk of life have endorsed the Wrath of Grapes Boycott. With their commitment and their donations, they in turn have reached out to their friends and relatives to help bind the foundation of a growing coalition of decency.

Now I am reaching out to you for help because consumers and farm workers must stand together as one family if we are to be heard. I am not asking you to give up wine or raisins. I am asking you to give us your commitment and valuable support.

I am asking you to join us now and be counted to join the growing family of individuals who will boycott grapes until the demands of decency have been met.

And hard as it is for me to ask for money, I am asking you to contribute to the cause, $100, $50, $15, whatever you can afford, whatever you would have spent on grapes this year. Insure that every week 1 million more consumers will know the truth.

You have my personal pledge that every cent of your contributions will be spent on the Wrath of Grapes Campaign bringing this message into every home in America because this message is the source of our combined strength.

My friends, the wrath of grapes is a plague born of selfish men that is indiscriminately and undeniably poisoning us all. Our only protection is to boycott the grapes, and our only weapon is the truth. If we unite we can only triumph for ourselves, for our children, and for their children. We look forward to hearing from you soon.

At Pacific Lutheran University

Using the tragic stories of children with cancer and genetic deformities caused by pesticides in the fields of Delano, California, Chavez spoke in March 1989 of the humanitarian struggles of farmworkers and the reasons why the public should be concerned about the growers' abuses.

What is the worth of a man or a woman? What is the worth of a farm worker? How do you measure the value of a life?

Ask the parents of Johnnie Rodríguez.

Johnnie Rodríguez was not even a man; Johnnie was a five-year-old boy when he died after a painful two-year battle against cancer.

His parents, Juan and Elia, are farm workers. Like all grape workers, they are exposed to pesticides and other agricultural chemicals.

Elia worked in the table grapes around Delano, California, until she was eight months pregnant with Johnnie.

Juan and Elia cannot say for certain if pesticides caused their son's cancer. But neuroblastoma is one of the cancers found in McFarland, a small farm town only a few miles from Delano, where the Rodríguezes live.

"Pesticides are always in the fields and around the towns," Johnnie's father told us. "The children get them when they play, outside, drink the water or hug you after you come home from working in fields that are sprayed."

"Once your son has cancer you hope it's a mistake, you pray," Juan says. "He was a real nice boy. He took it strong and lived as long as he could."

I keep a picture of Johnnie Rodríguez. He is sitting on his bed, hugging his teddy bears. His sad eyes and cherubic face stare out at you. The photo was taken four days before he died.

Johnnie Rodríguez was one of thirteen McFarland children diagnosed with cancer in recent years; and one of six who have died from the disease. With only 6,000 residents, the rate of cancer in McFarland is 400 percent above normal.

In McFarland and in Fowler, childhood cancer cases are being reported in excess of expected rates. In Delano and other farming towns, questions are also being raised.

The chief source of carcinogens in these communities are pesticides from vineyards and fields that encircle them. Health experts think the high rate of cancer in McFarland is from pesticides and nitrate-containing fertilizers leaching into the water system from surrounding fields.

Last year California's Republican Governor, George Deukmejian, killed a modest study to find out why so many children are dying of cancer in McFarland. "Fiscal integrity" was the reason he gave for his veto of the $125,000 program, which could have helped eighty-four other rural communities with drinking water problems.

Last year, as support for our cause grew, Governor Deukmejian used a statewide radio broadcast to attack the grape boycott.

There is no evidence to prove that pesticides on grapes and other produce endanger farm workers or consumers, Deukmejian claimed.

Ask the family of Felipe Franco.

Felipe is a bright seven-year-old.

Like other children, Felipe will someday need to be independent. But Felipe is not like other children: he was born without arms and legs.

Felipe's mother, Ramona, worked in the grapes near Delano until she was in her eighth month of pregnancy. She was exposed to Captan, known to cause birth defects and one of the pesticides our grape boycott seeks to ban.

"Every morning when I began working I could smell and see pesticides on the grape leaves," Ramona said.

Like many farm workers, she was assured by growers and their foremen how the pesticides that surrounded her were safe, that they were harmless "medicine" for the plants.

Only after Ramona took her son to specialists in Los Angeles was she told that the pesticides she was exposed to in the vineyards caused Felipe's deformity. The deep sadness she feels has subsided, but not the anger.

Felipe feels neither anger nor sadness. He dreams of what only a child can hope for: Felipe wants to grow arms and legs. "He believes he will have his limbs someday," his mother says. "His great dream is to be able to move around, to walk, to take care of himself."

Our critics sometimes ask, "Why should the United Farm Workers worry about pesticides when farm workers have so many other more obvious problems?"

The wealth and plenty of California agribusiness are built atop the suffering of generations of California farm workers. Farm labor history across America is one shameful tale after another of hardship and exploitation.

Malnutrition among migrant children. Tuberculosis, pneumonia, and respiratory infections. Short life expectancy.

Savage living conditions. Miserable wages and working conditions. Sexual harassment of women workers. Widespread child labor. Inferior schools or no school at all.

When farm workers organize against these injustices they are met with brutality and coercion—and death.

Under Governor Deukmejian, California's pioneering law guaranteeing farm workers the right to organize and vote in secret ballot union elections is now just one more tool growers use to oppress our people.

Thousands who thought the law protected them were threatened and fired and beaten by the growers; two were shot to death by gunmen their employers had hired.

For one hundred years succeeding waves of immigrants have sweated and sacrificed to make this industry rich. And for their sweat and for their sacrifice, farm workers have been repaid with humiliation and contempt.

With all these problems, why, then, do we dwell so on the perils of pesticides?

Because there is something even more important to farm workers than the benefits unionization brings.

There is something more important to the farm workers' union than winning better wages and working conditions.

That is protecting farm workers—and consumers—from systematic poisoning through the reckless use of agricultural toxics.

There is nothing we care more about than the lives and safety of our families. There is nothing we share more deeply in common with the consumers of North America than the safety of the food all of us reply upon.

What good does it do to achieve the blessings of collective bargaining and make economic progress for people when their health is destroyed in the process?

If we ignored pesticide poisoning, then all the other injustices our people face would be compounded by an even more deadly tyranny. But ignore that final injustice is what our opponents would have us do.

"Don't worry," the growers say.

"The UFW misleads the public about the dangers of pesticides," the Table Grape Commission says. "Governor Deukmejian's pesticide safety system protects workers," the Farm Bureau proclaims.

Ask the family of Juan Chabolla. Juan Chabolla collapsed after working in a field sprayed only an hour before with Monitor, a deadly pesticide.

But instead of rushing Juan to a nearby hospital, the grower drove him forty-five miles across the U.S.-Mexico border and left him in a Tijuana clinic. He was dead on arrival.

Juan, 32, left his wife and four young children in their impoverished clapboard shack in Maneadero, Mexico.

Just after Juan died, Governor Deukmejian vetoed a modest bill, strongly opposed by agribusiness, that would have required growers to post warning signs in fields where dangerous pesticides are applied.

Two hundred and fifty million pounds of pesticides are applied each year to crops in California; in 1986, 10 million pounds went on grapes.

Grapes is the largest fruit crop in California. It receives more restricted use of pesticides than any fresh food crop.

About one-third of grape pesticides are known carcinogens—like the chemicals that may have afflicted Johnnie Rodríguez; others are teratogens—birth-defect-producing pesticides—that doctors think deformed Felipe Franco.

Pesticides cause acute poisoning—of the kind that killed Juan Chabolla—and chronic, long-term effects such as we're seeing in communities like McFarland.

More than half of all acute pesticide-related illnesses reported in California involve grape production.

In 1987 and '88, entire crews of grape workers—hundreds of people—were poisoned after entering vineyards containing toxic residues.

In all those episodes, the grapes had been sprayed weeks before. All the *legal* requirements were followed.

But farm workers were still poisoned.

Illegal use of pesticides is also commonplace.

Grape growers have been illegally using Fixx, a growth enhancer, for twenty years. Another illegal pesticide, Acephate, which causes tumors, has also been used on grapes.

Over 2,000 consumers were poisoned in 1984 after eating watermelons illegally sprayed with Aldicarb.

And these are only cases where growers were caught applying illegal chemicals.

Farm workers and their families are exposed to pesticides from the crops they work. The soil the crops are grown in. Drift from sprays applied to adjoining fields—and often to the very field where they are working.

The fields that surround their homes are heavily and repeatedly sprayed. Pesticides pollute irrigation water and groundwater.

Children are still a big part of the labor force. Or they are taken to the fields by their parents because there is no childcare.

Pregnant women labor in the fields to help support their families. Toxic exposure begins at a very young age—often in the womb.

What does acute pesticide poisoning produce?

Eye and respiratory irritations. Skin rashes. Systemic poisoning. Death.

What are the chronic effects of pesticide poisoning on people, according to scientific studies? Birth defects. Sterility. Stillbirths. Miscarriages. Neurological and neuropsychological effects. Effects on child growth and development.

Cancer.

Use of pesticides are governed by strict laws, agribusiness says. Growers argue reported poisonings involved only 1 percent of California farm workers in 1986.

But experts estimate that only 1 percent of California pesticide illness or injury is reported. The underreporting of pesticide poisoning is flagrant and it is epidemic.

A World Resources Institute study says 300,000 farm workers are poisoned each year by pesticides in the United States.

Even the state Department of Food and Agriculture reported total pesticide poisoning of farm workers rose by 41 percent in 1987.

Yet the Farm Workers aren't sincere when we raise the pesticide issue, grape growers complain.

They won't admit that the first ban on DDT, Aldrin, and Dieldrin in the United States was not by the Environmental Protection Agency in 1972, but in a United Farm Workers contract with a *grape grower* in 1967.

Who will protect farm workers from poisoning if it isn't the farm workers' union?

The Environmental Protection Agency won't do it.

They're in bed with the same agricultural and chemical interests they are supposed to regulate.

It was an accident of history that EPA got stuck with regulating pesticides. It happened after the federal Occupational Safety and Health Administration—which is supposed to safeguard all American working people—refused to protect farm workers.

The law won't do it.

Agribusinesses lobbied mightily to exclude farm workers from federal job safety and health laws. And they won.

You think the National Rifle Association wields a powerful lobby? They're pussycats compared to organizations that lobby for agribusiness.

Too many people still think of small family farmers—an image corporate agribusiness likes to promote. The American Medical Association tries to do the same thing, except most people don't believe doctors still make house calls. But we all know what farming is today in states like California: a $14 billion a year industry dominated by huge corporations—the state's richest industry.

There has never been a law at the state or national levels that has ever been enforced for farm workers and against growers: child labor, minimum wage and hour, occupational health and safety, agricultural labor relations.

Now will agribusiness protect farm workers from pesticides?

The agrichemical industry won't do it.

It's out to maximize profits. Using smaller amounts of safer chemicals more wisely is not in the interest of chemical companies and agribusiness groups like the Farm Bureau that have heavy financial stakes in maintaining pesticide use.

There is nothing wrong with pesticides, they claim; the blame rests with abuse and misuse of pesticides.

It's like the NRA saying, "Guns don't kill people, people kill people."

Universities won't do it. America's colleges and universities are the best research facilities in the world. But farm workers are of the wrong color; they don't speak the right language; and they're poor.

The University of California and other land grant colleges spend millions of dollars developing agricultural mechanization and farm chemicals. Although we're all affected in the end, researchers won't deal with the inherent toxicity or chronic effects of their creations.

Protecting farm workers and consumers is not their concern.

Doctors won't do it. Most physicians farm workers see won't even admit their patients' problems are caused by pesticides. They usually blame symptoms on skin rashes and heat stroke. Doctors don't know much about pesticides; the signs and symptoms of acute pesticide poisoning are similar to other illnesses. Those who work for growers and most rural physicians won't take a stand.

Two years ago in Tulare County, 120 orange grove workers at LaBue Ranch suffered the largest skin poisoning ever reported. The grower altered a pesticide, Omite CR, to make it stick to the leaves better. It did.

It also stuck better to the workers. Later they discovered the delay before reentering the field had to be extended from seven to forty-two days.

After the poisoning, the company doctor said workers should just change clothes and return to work. When we demanded the workers be removed from exposure, the doctor replied, "Do you know how much that would cost?"

Workers endure skin irritations and rashes that none of us would tolerate. They continue to work because they desperately need the money. They don't complain out of fear of losing their jobs.

Farm workers aren't told when pesticides are used. They have no health insurance. They are cheated out of workers compensation benefits by disappearing labor contractors or foremen who intimidate people into not filing claims.

In the old days, miners would carry birds with them to warn against poison gas. Hopefully, the birds would die before the miners.

Farm workers are society's canaries.

Farm workers—and their children—demonstrate the effects of pesticide poisoning before anyone else.

But the unrestrained use of agricultural chemicals is like playing Russian Roulette with the health of both farm workers and consumers.

So much of so many pesticides are used and so little is known about them.

Hundreds of farm pesticides leave residues on food; most can't be detected by commonly used tests—many can't be detected by any test at all.

Forty-four percent of the pesticides applied on grapes that can't be detected by tests used to check for toxic residues pose potential health hazards for humans.

Many pesticides used on food—that have government tolerance levels—can cause cancer in human beings.

Almost all of those tolerance levels were set by the federal government without adequate testing for potential harmful health effects on consumers.

Some safety studies on these pesticides were conducted by an Illinois lab that was closed after it was found to be reporting fraudulent data to the EPA Two toxicologists were jailed.

The U.S. General Accounting Office estimates that it will take EPA until well into the twenty-first century to ensure all pesticides now on the market meet current health and safety standards.

Most pesticides were approved by the U.S. Department of Agriculture in the 1940s and '50s. Little or no testing for chronic health effects was required.

Not long ago the Delaney Amendment, passed by Congress, banned any food additive known to cause cancer in animals or humans. That ban applies to everything—except farm pesticides.

The agrichemical industry convinced Congress that pesticides which cause cancer are not really food additives since they are added to food before it is harvested.

In 1978, EPA allowed new chemicals to be registered conditionally without complete testing for chronic health effects. Testing on half of all new pesticides registered between 1978 and 1984 did not meet current health and safety testing standards.

All this means that we do not know if pesticide residues on the food you buy in supermarkets cause cancer, birth defects, and other tragedies.

And EPA has made no effort to encourage the use of safer alternatives to toxic pesticides.

The chemical companies have convinced the growers—and they want you to believe—that if it wasn't for them, the whole world would succumb to malaria and starvation.

But, brothers and sisters, pesticides haven't worked. Crop loss to pests is as great or greater than it was forty years ago. The pesticides haven't changed anything.

Because Darwinian evolution has favored pests of all kinds with this enormous ability to resist and survive.

It's why antibiotics stop working after awhile. If you don't kill everything, the organisms that survive are tougher and more resistant; and they're the ones that breed.

There are mosquitoes that can survive any combination of pesticides delivered in any dose. There is a startling resurgence of malaria around the world. And it's much worse now because forty years ago we relied entirely on a chemical solution.

So we ignored alternatives: draining ponds, dredging ditches, observing sound crop practices, encouraging use of natural predators.

In the long run, more lives will be lost because for thirty years we also stopped developing malaria vaccines. You can't fool Mother Nature. In time, insects can outfox anything we throw at them. People thought pesticides were the cure-all—the key to an abundance of food. They thought pesticides were the solution; but they were the problem.

The problem is this mammoth agribusiness system. The problem is the huge farms. The problem is the pressure on the land from developers. The problem is not allowing the land to lay fallow and rest. The problem is the abandonment of cultural practices that have stood the test of centuries: crop rotation, diversification of crops.

The problem is monoculture—growing acres and acres of the

same crop; disrupting the natural order of things; letting insects feast on acres and acres of a harem of delight . . . and using pesticides that kill off their natural predators.

Meantime, these greedy chemical companies, multinational corporations, try to sanctify their poisons. They would have us believe they are the health givers—that because of them people are not dying of malaria and starvation.

When all the time, they just want to defend their investments. They just want to protect their profits. They don't want anything to change.

The chemical companies believe in the Domino Theory: all chemicals are threatened if any chemical is questioned. No matter how dangerous it may be.

It's a lot like that saying from the Vietnam War: we had to destroy the village in order to save it.

They have to poison us in order to save us. But at what cost? The lives of farm workers and their children who are suffering? The lives of consumers who could reap the harvest of pesticides ten, twenty years from now? The contamination of our ground water? The loss of our reverence for the soil? The raping of the land?

We see these insane practices reflected in the buy-outs and takeovers on Wall Street. It's the same thing: exchanging long-term security for short-term gain.

You sacrifice a company for the immediate rewards. But you destroy what produces jobs and livelihoods and economic health.

If you eat the seed corn, you won't have a crop to plant.

Oscar Wilde once said, "A cynic is someone who knows the price of everything and the value of nothing."

We look at the price, but we don't look at the value. Economics and profit drive everything. People forget that the soil is our sustenance. It is a sacred trust. It is what has worked for us for centuries. It is what we pass on to future generations. If we continue in this thoughtless submission to pesticides—if we ruin the topsoil—then there will not be an abundance of food to bequeath [to] our children.

Farm workers and consumers cannot get pesticide regulation because those who make the rules are captives of these bankrupt forty- and fifty-year old policies that have been shown not to work.

So they don't ban the worst of these poisons because some farm worker might give birth to a deformed child.

So they don't imperil millions of dollars in profits today because, someday, some consumers *might* get cancer.

So they allow all of us, who place our faith in the safety of the food supply, to consume grapes and other produce which contain residues from pesticides that cause cancer and birth defects.

So we accept decades of environmental damage these poisons have brought upon the land.

The growers, the chemical companies and the bureaucrats say, "These are acceptable levels of exposure."

Acceptable to whom?

Acceptable to Johnnie Rodríguez's parents?

Acceptable to Felipe Franco?

Acceptable to the widow of Juan Chabolla and her children?

Acceptable to all farm workers who have known tragedy from pesticides?

There is no acceptable level of exposure to any chemical that causes cancer. There can be no toleration of any toxic that causes miscarriages, stillbirths, and deformed babies.

Risk is associated with any level of exposure. And any level of exposure is too much.

Isn't that the standard of protection you would ask for your family and your children? Isn't that the standard of protection you would demand for yourself?

Then why do we allow farm workers to carry the burden of pesticides on their shoulders?

Do we carry in our hearts the sufferings of farm workers and their children?

Do we feel deeply enough the pain of those who must work in the fields every day with these poisons? Or the anguish of the families that have lost loved ones to cancer? Or the heartache of the parents who fear for the lives of their children? Who are raising children with deformities? Who agonize the outcome of their pregnancies?

Who ask in fear, "Where will this deadly plague strike next?"

Do we feel their pain deeply enough?

I didn't. And I was ashamed.

I studied this wanton abuse of nature. I read the literature, heard from the experts about what pesticides do.

I talked with farm workers, listened to their families, and shared their anguish and their fears. I spoke out against the cycle of death.

But sometimes words come too cheaply. And their meaning is lost in the clutter that so often fills our lives.

That is why, in July and August of last year, I embarked on a thirty-six-day unconditional, water-only fast.

The fast was first and foremost directed at myself—to purify my own body, mind, and soul.

The fast was an act of penance for our own members who, out of ignorance or need, cooperate with those who grow and sell food treated with toxics.

The fast was also for those who know what is right and just. It pains me that we continue to shop without protest at stores that offer grapes; that we eat in restaurants that display them; that we are too patient and understanding with those who serve them to us.

The fast, then, was for those who know that they could or should do more—for those who, by not acting, become bystanders in the poisoning of our food and the people who produce it.

The fast was, finally, a declaration of noncooperation with supermarkets that promote, sell, and profit from California table grapes. They are as culpable as those who manufacture the poisons and those who use them.

It is my hope that our friends everywhere will resist in many nonviolent ways the presence of grapes in the stores where they shop.

So I ask of you, take the pledge: boycott grapes. Join the many hundreds who have taken up where my fast ended—by sharing the suffering of the farm workers—by going without food for a day or two days or three.

The misery that pesticides bring farm workers—and the dangers they pose to all consumers—will not be ended with more hearings or studies. The solution is not to be had from those in power because it is they who have allowed this deadly crisis to grow.

The times we face truly call for all of us to do more to stop this evil in our midst.

The answer lies with you and me. It is with all men and women who share the suffering and yearn with us for a better world.

Our cause goes on in hundreds of distant places. It multiplies among thousands and then millions of caring people who heed through a multitude of simple deeds the commandment set out in the book of the Prophet Micah, in the Old Testament: "What does the Lord require of you, but to do justice, to love kindness, and to walk humbly with your God."

Thank you. And boycott grapes.

On Public Schools

Delivered in Sacramento, on April 3, 1991. In an effort to fight against the persistence of inequalities through future generations, Chavez spoke out in support of public schools. His union not only worked for farmworkers, but for their children.

Some people may ask, "Why should the farm workers be concerned about the condition of public schools in California?"

Let me answer them: Who do you think are in the public schools today in California?

Public schools serve more farm workers than any other publicly financed social institution in society.

Public schools provide the greatest opportunity for upward mobility to Hispanics and to all ethnic minorities in this state.

Yet today, it is a Republican governor and his allies in the legislature who are less concerned than we are about preserving public schools. That is ironic because it was not always the case.

In the 1960s and early seventies, another Republican governor—Ronald Reagan—was leading the fight for more support of public education. But there was a big difference. Back then, the majority of public school children were white, and they were from middle- or upper-middle-income families.

Today, the majority of children in our public schools are minority—African American, Hispanic, Asian—and they are from poor and working-class families.

Back then, under Ronald Reagan, Californians spent five cents out of every dollar of personal income on public schools. Today, under Pete Wilson, Californians spend a little over three cents out of every dollar on education. And if he has his way, it will go down even more.

There is another institution in society that is funded by the state and that is dominated by minorities: the state prisons—and they have fared very well.

Over the last nine years—under Governor Deukmejian and now

Governor Wilson—California has carried out a policy of dramatically expanding state prisons while it starves public schools.

What message do those priorities send? Does this mean that the only way our sons and daughters can get recognition from the state of California is by using drugs and committing crimes?

We have looked into the future and the future is ours! Asians and Hispanics and African Americans are the future in California. That trend cannot be stopped. It is inevitable.

Then why do they want to cut funds for schools and other vital services—now? Why do Governor Wilson and his allies seek to reduce the commitment to public education—now? If the majority of children in school were white and if they lived in affluent suburban communities, we wouldn't even be debating how much money to spend on public education.

But it is *our* children—the children of farm workers and Hispanics and other minorities—who are seeking a better life. It is for them, for their future—and for the future of California—that we must say "no" to suspending Proposition 98.

We must say "no" to cutting essential services for the needy instead of tax loopholes for the wealthy.

We must say "no" to making *our* children and *their* teachers scapegoats for the budget crisis.

Sal Si Puedes

This speech was delivered before the Building Industry Association of Northern California, in San Jose, California, on November 21, 1991. By juxtaposing the personal and the political, it's the best summary and update of Chavez's vision before his death.

I always feel like I'm coming home when I visit San Jose. My family often called this place home when we became migrants after the bank foreclosed on my father's small Arizona farm during the late 1930s.

After World War II we returned to San Jose, to a little house on Sharf Avenue in the tough eastside barrio they nicknamed Sal Si Puedes—which for those of you who are culturally deprived translates "get out if you can."

The nickname came about because it seemed as though the only way young men left Sal Si Puedes was to go off to jail, the military, or the cemetery. A lot of people who lived in Sal Si Puedes were farm workers who scratched out a living in the orchards and vineyards that used to flourish on the outskirts of town.

I was one of them, working in the apricots in 1952, when I began my organizing career by starting up the first local chapter of the Community Service Organization (CSO), a civil rights–civic action group among the Hispanics that grew into the most militant and effective organization of its kind in the country.

Throughout California we registered people to vote and turned them out at the polls. We fought segregation. We battled police brutality—the roughing up of young guys and the breaking and entering without warrants. We opposed the forced removal of Hispanics to make way for urban renewal projects. We fought to improve the poor conditions that were so common in Sal Si Puedes and in other minority neighborhoods, the mean streets and walkways, the lack of street lights and traffic signals, the polluted creeks and horse pastures where kids played, the poor drainage, the overflowing cesspools, the amoebic dysentery.

Some things change and some things never do.

I understand San Jose recently named its first Hispanic Chief of Police—Luis Covarrubias, a twenty-six-year veteran of the force. And Hispanics have been elected to the City Council and the Board of Supervisors.

My mother still lives on Sharf Avenue. But most of Sal Si Puedes is gone; it was taken years ago when they put in the freeway.

That neighborhood and many of those conditions may no longer exist in San Jose. But as we meet here this evening—only a short drive from this place—farm workers are living in caves and crude shacks, under trees and bridges, and in wretched farm labor camps.

In the Almaden Valley, right here in Santa Clara County, massive sanitation and safety violations were documented at two labor camps, including raw sewage on the ground.

Some workers in labor camps, who can't find space in crowded barracks, sleep out in the open, while farm labor contractors deduct money from their paychecks for *utility* expenses.

Many are without plumbing or electricity. They bathe in irrigation water that is laden with pesticides.

Entire migrant families are homeless—people living out of their cars near fields and vineyards or under stands of trees.

In Santa Clara and Monterey and San Benito counties—in the Central Valley and throughout California—these savage conditions are often the rule and not the exception.

Farm labor in this state and nation is one shameful tale after another of hardship and exploitation. The wealth and plenty of California agribusiness has been built atop the suffering of these men, women, and children. It was true when my family and I were migrants in the thirties and forties. It is true even more so today.

We created the United Farm Workers to battle these injustices; it's what we've done with our lives for the last twenty-nine years. It's why we have conducted strikes and marches and fasts and demonstrations. It's why we are once again asking the public to boycott California table grapes.

But we also recognize that many of the social problems plaguing farm workers stem from the denial of housing that is decent and affordable.

The fastest-growing population in California are the Hispanics.

The neediest segment of the Hispanic population are the farm workers.

What better place to go if you really want to build affordable, entry-level housing for the people who need it the most?

We have. And let me tell you—it *can* be done. Those who work to develop housing for migrant farm workers often meet stiff resistance from local established residents. Some people believe their property values will be affected if farm workers move in nearby.

Through a nonprofit, tax-exempt organization—the National Farm Workers Service Center—we've begun an aggressive program to build single-family and rental housing in rural California for low-income farm workers, Hispanics, other minorities, and Anglo families.

Just because it's housing for farm workers and other low-income rural residents doesn't mean it has to be shabby or second-rate. All projects developed by the Service Center come with amenities not generally found in farmworker housing: wall-to-wall carpeting, central heat and air, two-car garages, large lots, tile roofs, bay windows, garbage disposals, and dishwashers.

We insist on those amenities for the same reason you and other home builders do: so the houses we build will appreciate at the same rate as other houses in the community.

Sometimes we've been frustrated by federal restrictions that place limits on these amenities. We're not interested in building projects that become instant ghettos. We don't accept federal bureaucrats who want to tell us that our houses have to be inferior to the houses offered to more affluent home buyers—just because our homes are for farm workers and other low-income families.

Almost all of our projects seek out available state or local financial assistance. Our staff work with local redevelopment agencies to obtain help for land acquisition and infrastructure. We help families qualify for modest grants that they often need to get into a home.

Sale prices at our seventy-one-lot subdivision in Parlier, near Fresno, start at $49,500—for four models of three- and four-bedroom homes. At this project, for the first time, low-income families could personalize their homes—for example, by deciding on colors for carpets and paint.

We helped low-income home buyers in Parlier obtain below-market interest rates to lower monthly mortgage payments. In addition, we helped these families qualify for government grants to write down the costs of loans.

Under the state's Farm Worker Grant Program, low-income people who work in agriculture and need money for down payments can qualify for up to $15,000 in grants. With a $15,000 grant, a family that purchased a Service Center home for $49,500 would only need to qualify for a $34,000 mortgage. This state grant program was discontinued, although there is talk about reinstating it for next year.

We built the first single-family subdivision in twenty years in the West Fresno County town of Firebaugh—a 104-lot single family subdivision—with four floor plans and home buyer financial assistance. Most home buyers were local residents. But we also sold to some families from as far away as Oakland and Richmond that were willing to make the daily commute to their jobs.

Our forty-five-lot subdivision for low-income buyers in Avenal even includes front-yard landscaping.

Our 81-unit apartment complex in Parlier, our 106-unit complex in Fresno, and our 56-unit complex in Tehachapi all serve very low to low-income families, many of them farm workers. In Fresno 90 percent of our tenants earn far below the median income. Rents are also considerably below average. Yet the amenities, especially in Fresno, are on a par with higher-rent apartments. There are no vacancies.

The Padilla family is a typical example of what the Service Center has been able to achieve. Steve Padilla works in the area's grape and citrus fields. He, his wife, and three children used to live in a small, rat- and cockroach-infested two-bedroom apartment. It had no carpeting or central heat and air.

His new residence is an apartment at the Service Center's La Paz Villa Apartments in Parlier. The Padillas live in a three-bedroom apartment with wall-to-wall carpeting, central heat and air, dishwasher, and garbage disposal. The rent they pay at La Paz Villa is 30 percent less than what they paid for their previous apartment.

Many of the tenants in our apartment projects used to live in garages, labor camps, and other substandard housing. A lot of them were affected by last December's freeze. Lack of jobs and a steady income are constant problems.

The Service Center works with its tenants, helping them stay in their housing—even when that means making arrangements for late rent payments.

The labor movement is working to create some innovative programs to help working people own their own homes. Under a first-of-its-kind contract negotiated by the Boston Hotel and Restaurant Employees Union, employers are paying five cents an hour into a joint trust fund. The fund will help hotel workers with new home purchases. Money from the fund will go to help make down payments, cover closing expenses or bank costs, or secure more favorable interest rates.

Before the housing trust fund could be set up, Congress had to amend the Taft-Hartley Act of 1947 so that employers could write off their contributions to the fund as tax deductions.

The national AFL-CIO created the Union Member Mortgage program, which just began operating earlier this year. During the program's first six months, more than twelve hundred union members have obtained over $100 million in home mortgage financing commitments. More than seventy thousand union members have phoned Union Member Mortgage's toll-free numbers for more information.

The program is funding refinancing of high-interest mortgages on present homes, purchases of new homes by union members who are "buying up," and new home purchases by first-time home buyers. It offers down payments as low as 5 percent, competitive interest rates, and financing through a wholly union-owned bank in New York. It helps first-time buyers by reducing the up-front cash needed to purchase a home.

Housing is not the National Farm Workers Service Center's sole activity. The Service Center has sponsored economic development programs to help rural agricultural-based farm worker communities diversify and expand their tax bases. That, in turn, produces improvements in basic municipal services—such as fire and police protection—as well as new employment opportunities for local residents.

The first and most challenging economic development project was a ten-thousand-square-foot commercial center in Parlier.

Most of the existing retail in Parlier used to consist of bars and pool halls. There was no place to buy clothes, no neighborhood family oriented shopping center in town. The commercial project developed by the Service Center features a number of small retailers, including a meat market, clothing store, and sit-down restaurant.

The Service Center is developing another, slightly larger commercial center. It is bringing in a flower shop, pizza parlor, auto parts store, and sit-down cafe.

Parlier is finally being promoted as a place where families can live and prosper. These economic development projects are changing the reputation of the town; other developers are bringing their own projects on line—they're coming to see Parlier as a place where they can build and be successful.

New housing and commercial projects are planned for farm worker areas in other parts of the state.

We're now working in Hollister with city officials and a nonprofit group representing more than five hundred low-income families to develop a ten-lot single-family housing project in that San Benito County community.

A major obstacle to developing affordable housing in the Hollister area is the high cost of land. Land costs in the San Joaquin Valley are around $25,000 per acre. In Hollister, the average cost of land reaches $1—, 000 an acre.

One of the reasons land costs are being driven up is the high demand for housing created by out-of-town families—especially from Santa Clara and Monterey counties—that are seeking more affordable housing.

Added to the high cost of land are city and school fees, which exceed $14,000 for a twelve-hundred-square-foot house.

These predevelopment costs make the construction of affordable housing for low-income families unprofitable for traditional home builders and very difficult even for the nonprofit National Farm Workers Service Center.

Still, we're trying hard to come up with an innovative plan that will produce a 105-unit subdivision for farm workers and other low-income people in Hollister.

The BIA has often made the point—quite correctly—that owning your own home is a dream that is being denied to more and more people in California. Across the country, 64 percent of Americans are homeowners. If things continue as they are, the percentage of homeowners in the Bay Area may soon fall below 50 percent.

In today's housing market, only about 10 percent of Bay Area residents can afford the median price of a home—tagged at $268,000. That means households earning more than $70,000 a year can't afford to buy homes.

Those statistics also mean that low- and moderate-income working-class people in urban communities were long ago frozen out of the home market. Most farm workers and other low-income residents in rural areas don't even have a chance to attain home ownership.

Home ownership has been the path to security and prosperity for tens of millions of people in this country. It is the way working men and women have built up wealth for themselves and their children. It is often what people have to show for years of sweat and sacrifice.

Should owning a home of your own be the dream all Americans can work toward—*except* farm workers and Hispanics and other working families, rural or urban?

Should home ownership be *everyone's* right—except farm workers and Hispanics and other working families?

Should *all* people be able to work for the day when they can purchase a home—unless their skin is brown or black, or they work on a farm or in a factory?

When I got out of the navy at the end of World War II, home builders were universally respected because of the opportunities they helped bring to a whole generation of Americans. My family, and many others, never achieved home ownership because we were farm workers.

I want future generations of farm workers—the people of the land—to have what too many of us were denied: the right to own a decent home, a home of our own. We're working toward that goal. I ask you to join us in that effort.

Juana Estrada Chavez

In a poignant eulogy for his mother, delivered on December 18,
1991, Chavez's words outline the generous spirit of giving that
shaped his commitment to social justice. His religious faith was al-
ways a prominent part of his life, and his homage to his mother
shows the influence of that faith over his actions.

Thanks be to God that our mother's family—those she loved so much—were able to be at her bedside during the final hours. Our mother left us a beautiful heritage of courage and faith, a heritage that, please God, will sustain us come what may.

In a passage from the Book of Proverbs, King Solomon offers his description of a good woman:

> Strength and honour are her clothing; and she shall rejoice in time to come. She openeth her mouth with wisdom; and in her tongue is the law of kindness. She looketh well to the ways of her household, and eateth not the bread of idleness. Her children arise up and call her blessed; her husband also, and he praiseth her. Favour is deceitful, and beauty is vain; but a woman that feareth the Lord, she shall be praised. Give her of the fruit of her hands; and let her own works praise her in the gates.

Juana Estrada Chavez does not need for any of us to speak well of her this day. The simple deeds of a lifetime speak far more eloquently than any words of ours about this remarkable woman and the legacy of hope and strength that she leaves behind.

Rather than bore you by talking about how good she was, let us share some of the events we witnessed and some of the lessons we learned growing up as the children of Juana Chavez.

It was the Depression years of the late 1930s and early forties. But as poor as we were and with what little we had, Mamá would send my brother Richard and me out to railroad yards and other places for "hobos" we could invite to our tent to share a meal.

In those days the highways were littered with families whose cars or pickup trucks had broken down—with no place to go and no way to get there. When we were on the road, no matter how badly off we were, our mother would never let us pass a family in trouble.

She brought in a whole assortment of homeless families who didn't have a place to stay. We didn't either. But she'd bring them into our tent and make room for them in what little space we had.

Our mother would tell us, "You always have to help the needy, and God will help you."

Lifelong friendships were born that way. Some of the people she befriended more than fifty years ago are here today.

It was the rainy winter of 1939. We were living in a farm labor camp for cotton pickers outside the small farm town of Mendota in West Fresno County. The camp was unpaved. It was pouring rain. The mud was so bad that cars couldn't get in or out. A young girl was giving birth to her first baby. There was no way to take her to the doctor. So my mother rolled up her sleeves and delivered the baby. And it wasn't the last time it happened.

In those days few people had money for doctors. Many hadn't even set foot in a doctor's office. A lot of the farm workers also didn't speak the language. Many didn't believe in doctors.

Our mother was a folk healer. Besides delivering babies and curing common colds and headaches, she cured children of *sustos, empacho, mollera, pujón y ojo.*

Her favorite herbs were yerba buena, yposote, yerba del pasmo, sauco—and she really believed in manzanilla.

I'd go to her and say, "Mamá, I have a headache." She'd say, "manzanilla." "Mamá, I have a stomachache." "Manzanilla." "Mamá, I feel depressed." "Manzanilla." So much so that my nickname came to be Manzi.

It was also that year when Dad was hurt in an auto accident and couldn't work—for a *whole* year.

Our mother and the oldest sister, Rita, supported the family tying carrots in the Imperial Valley. But they didn't know how to do the work. They were farm workers, but they were fresh from a little farm in Arizona and had never done that kind of work before.

So they'd leave home at 3:30 in the morning. And they didn't get back until 7:00 in the evening. They earned $3 a week. But they kept us together until Dad was able to work again.

One January or February we were driving to the Imperial Valley from that labor camp in Mendota when we ran out of money in Los Angeles. Mamá quickly sold two beautiful quilts she had crocheted. And we had money to buy gas and continue on our journey.

It was 1941 and there was very little work. We were lucky to find jobs picking cotton in the San Joaquin Valley. When our big, heavy sacks were full, we'd line up and wait to have the sacks weighed by hanging them on a hook at the truck of the labor contractor. You'd get 3/4 cent per pound of cotton.

But sometimes the contractor would cheat the workers by putting his knee under the sack so it'd weigh less. Instead of getting credited for a hundred pound sack, the worker would get marked down for only eighty pounds. All this would happen pretty fast, and the victim's view was usually blocked.

Well, Mamá was pretty sharp. She saw the contractor cheating a worker who was in line in front of her—and she called him on it. The contractor was furious. The entire Chavez family got fired. It didn't bother her. Our mother used to say there is a difference between being of service and being a servant.

We were living in Delano during the early forties when I started driving. All of us—especially Rita and I—became a traveling service center. Our mother would have us do all kinds of errands, often driving people to Bakersfield, thirty miles away, to see the doctor or police or district attorney or welfare office.

We drove many a girl having a baby to the General Hospital. One baby was born in the back seat of our car.

After going to work in the fields early in the morning, by 10:00 A.M. we'd have to change out of our work clothes, jump in the car to Bakersfield, return home, change back into our work clothes, and try to get some more work done.

Mamá never let us charge a penny for our troubles, not even for gas.

When she wasn't helping people or getting us fired for challenging labor contractors, we were the strikingest family in all of farm labor. Whenever we were working where there was a strike or when the workers got fed up and walked off the job, she'd be the first one to back up our dad's decision to join the strike.

Our mother taught us not to be afraid to fight—to stand up for our rights. But she also taught us not to be violent.

We didn't even know enough at the time to call it nonviolence. But from an early age, through her *dichos* and little lessons, she would always talk to us about not fighting, not responding in kind.

She taught her children to reject that part of a culture which too often tells its young men that you're not a man if you don't fight back.

She would say, "No, it's best to turn the other cheek. God gave you senses like eyes and mind and tongue, and you can get out of anything. It takes two to fight, and one can't do it alone."

This is a day of sadness for Rita and Richard and Eduwiges and Librado and me, for all the grandchildren and great-grandchildren and great-great-grandchildren who are here today. But the services this morning are not an occasion for sadness, much less for despair. Rather, this is a time to celebrate, in the spirit of Christian joy, our mother's life and the goodness and mercy of God. Her ninety-nine years are a story of triumph over cruelty and prejudice and injustice. She was a wise woman who fulfilled God's Commandments by loving and serving her neighbors—even to the point of sacrifice. Our mother's good deeds—good deeds above all of charity and compassion and kindness—are known to many of you.

All who knew our mother as a personal friend or more immediately as a member of the family can vouch for the fact that she had understanding. By this I mean that she had the gift of faith—that gift of knowing what is truly important in life.

We are here today to say that true wealth is not measured in money or status or power. It is measured in the legacy we leave behind for those we love and those we inspire. We are here today because our lives were touched and moved by her spirit of love and service. That spirit is more powerful than any force on earth. It cannot be stopped.

Death comes to us all and we do not get to choose the time or the circumstances of our dying. The hardest thing of all is to die rightly. Juana Chavez died rightly. She served her God and her neighbor.

Now it is for you and me to finish the work Juana Chavez has begun among us in her quiet and simple ways, until we too can say that we have obeyed the commandment set out in the Book of the Prophet Micah in the Old Testament: "What does the Lord require of you, but to do justice, to love kindness, and to walk humbly with your God.

"Happy are those who died in the Lord; let them rest from their labor for their good deeds go with them."

Amen.

Fred Ross

Written in San Francisco, on October 17, 1992. As community or-ganizers, Fred Ross and Chavez formed a bond rooted in their commitment to serving the underserved and fighting for basic hu-man rights. Both gave up a great deal to help others, bringing them closer through their suffering as part of the farmworkers' commu-nity. Chavez's eulogy for Ross shows his deep respect and admira-tion for the man who allowed him to live his own organizer's tale.

The first time I met Fred Ross, he was about the last person I wanted to see. Fred had come to San Jose in the spring of 1952 to organize a chapter of the Community Service Organization—the CSO. I was working in apricot orchards outside of town and living with Helen and our then four kids in a rough barrio on the east-side of San Jose that they nicknamed Sal Si Puedes (Get Out If You Can).

In those days, it seemed as if the Anglos who came to Sal Si Puedes were college students down from Berkeley or Stanford who were writing their theses on the barrio and asking insulting ques-tions like, "How come Mexican Americans have so many kids?"

I thought Fred was one of them—only I wasn't quite sure be-cause he was this lanky guy who drove a beat-up old car and wore wrinkled clothes.

I finally agreed to have a "housemeeting" so Fred could talk about CSO with a group of friends we invited to our home. But I hatched a plan with some of my young Pachuco buddies to scare him away. At a prearranged signal from me, they'd start insulting him; that way, we thought, Fred would leave and we would get "even."

Fred found a cold reception from the people packed into our liv-ing room. Then he started talking—and changed my life.

After a while my Pachuco buddies, waiting for my signal, were getting restless. One of them interrupted Fred. I told him in *caló*, Pachuco talk, to shut up or get out; he shut up.

What followed was a frenetic forty days and nights as we registered four thousand new voters—the first such drive in Sal Si Puedes.

Together, Fred and I organized twenty-two CSO chapters across California in the 1950s; he began eight chapters on his own.

CSO turned people who were compliant and submissive into courageous champions of their families and communities. Some five hundred thousand Hispanics were registered to vote; fifty thousand Mexican immigrants obtained citizenship and old-age pensions. We won paved streets and sidewalks, traffic signals, recreational facilities and clinics. CSO curbed police brutality and resisted "urban removal" of Hispanics from redevelopment projects.

Fred used to say that "you can't take shortcuts, because you'll pay for it later." He believed society could be transformed from within by mobilizing individuals and communities. But you have to convert one person at a time, time after time. Progress only comes when people just plow ahead and do it. It takes lots of patience. The concept is so simple that most people miss it.

Fred applied those principles during an organizing career that spanned six decades.

I tagged along to every one of Fred's house meetings during that first campaign in San Jose, sometimes two a night. Studied every word he spoke, every move he made. Questioned him repeatedly, having him explain how in hell the house meetings would turn people out to the general organizing meeting.

The organizing meeting at Mayfair School in East San Jose was a huge success. But there were some folks standing around outside. I told Fred they didn't want to come in. "It's OK," he replied, "*Menos burros, más elotes*" [fewer donkeys, more corn]. I went outside anyway to ask them to come inside and happened to overhear some established Chicano leaders finding every excuse why all these people shouldn't be at this meeting, saying things like, "There aren't any leaders in that crowd; they're old people."

At home that night I told Helen how what had happened at the meeting was pure magic—and I was going to learn it. Come what may, I wouldn't stop until I learned how to organize.

For a long time, I'd call him Mr. Ross, and he'd say, "Just Fred." It took me a long time to call him Fred. I'd go to work in the fields daydreaming about the house meeting to be held that evening.

I would find any excuse to be with Fred. I even started trying to imitate him. Fred noticed. One day he said, "Cesar, you don't have to parrot me to learn to organize. Just be yourself, follow the procedures, and you'll be OK."

The thing I liked most about Fred was there was no bullshit, no pretensions, no ego gimmicks; just plain hard work—at times grinding work.

Fred's accomplishments were even more amazing when you consider that he had a lot to overcome. At times there was much reverse discrimination. Fred was Anglo. He was Protestant. He was middle class.

I watched him at first very closely for the signs of paternalism and superiority. Never, ever did I see any of those signs in Fred. He never looked down on us. But he also never pitied us. He was a tough, unrelenting taskmaster.

One evening after an executive board meeting of the San Jose CSO chapter at José and Blanca Alvarado's house, Fred talked to us about old-age pensions for noncitizens. He said it would be a great issue, help a lot of old timers who had no money or pensions—and relieve a lot of pressure on their kids. But he warned us that it would be a lot of work setting up the campaign to enact the state old-age pension law. It would take a long time.

We would get impatient. Fred would say, "*Calma*," have patience. It'll come. It was eight years before the law was passed, but it was a super victory. And I learned once again about Fred's gift of faith and stick-to-it-ness. Those lessons came in handy years later with the boycott and other union efforts.

Then one day in mid-1952, kind of suddenly, Fred wanted to know if it was OK to ask Saul Alinsky to put me on the payroll. My heart sank to my knees. What followed were many occasions for self-doubt and a lot of Fred's time spent holding my hand and reassuring me that I could do it.

In Oakland, organizing the first CSO chapter on my own, I'd call Fred every day to make sure I was on track. After the first community-wide organizing meeting was over, I called to give him my report: "Fred, counting all the priests at St. Mary's school, the janitor and myself, we had 327 people."

He said, "I knew it. I knew it. I knew you could do it." I was looking for my pat on the back, and I found it.

After organizing the CSO chapter in Madera in 1954, the whole local leadership was turned against me after a Red-baiting campaign from the Immigration authorities, the district attorney, and some immigration coyotes. I was dumbfounded.

Poor Fred had to leave his job and come hold my hand once more. He said, "Cesar, listen, you're stirring a hornet's nest—and some of 'em will come after you. *No hay mal que por bien no venga.* (Literally translated it means there is no bad thing that will not be followed by a good thing—or every negative has its positive.)

The company and Teamsters were united against us during our campaign at DiGiorgio Fruit Corporation in 1966. Many of Fred's organizers were volunteers who were also against the Vietnam War. Many trade unionists also helping us were for the war. Fred had to keep peace among them—and fight the war against the Teamsters and DiGiorgio.

The night before the election I got home late, turned on the TV news and bigger than life there was this story from Las Vegas, where they set the odds six to ten against us. I called Fred. He said, "We'll win, don't worry. Get some rest. You'll need it for tomorrow's celebration." We hung up. A moment later he called back: "Cesar, remember this is only a battle, and maybe a very small battle, in the history of this union. The war is yet to be decided." With that, I went soundly to sleep.

It was 1967. The grape boycott was having severe problems because boycotted grape growers were switching labels with growers who weren't being boycotted. I was caught in a strange moral dilemma. Somehow, I couldn't get myself to boycott growers we weren't striking—even though some of them were giving their labels to the struck growers.

Fred and Dolores [Huerta], in New York on the boycott, argued that it could be done—it had to be a generic boycott of all grapes. They made me see the light. And the boycott turned around pretty quickly.

Fred died of natural causes on September 27. He was eighty-two. His deeds live on in the hundreds of organizers he trained and inspired. Not the least of them is his son, Fred Jr., who made his father proud.

I have been thinking through how best to memorialize Fred's contribution to society and have come to the conclusion that it would be most fitting to focus it around what I believe is his greatest contribution: developing the organizing of people for action into an art form.

That art form must now be preserved in aphorisms, so that future organizers can learn and be trained from the lessons Fred taught. While guarding this inheritance, we must take pains to keep it clean and pure—God forbid that it be corrupted by some PhD's analysis and interpretations.

At one point Dolores Huerta, David Martínez, and Artie Rodríguez and I got together and decided that we should mount a campaign to have Fred awarded the Nobel Peace Prize—and win it for him with the kind of campaign he taught us to run. We organized support from a number of U.S. senators and congressmen, bishops, and others.

I had to take it to Fred—and I knew it would be a hard sell. I came to see him, but when I talked to him about it, he furrowed his brow and said, "Cesar, there's a lot of good work you can do instead of this nonsense."

Fred Ross gave me and so many others a chance. And that led to a lot of things. But he did more than discover and train me.

The other day, preparing for this memorial, I was reading though correspondence between Fred and myself from the early 1960s that I hadn't seen in thirty years.

We saw each other then infrequently. But we wrote as often as we could—often long letters—and Fred would usually include a modest contribution to help tide us over. Listen to just a few excerpts from some of our letters.

May 2, 1962. "Dear Fred: Sure happy to receive your letter this morning. Cheque or no cheque, your letters will give me that which I need so badly right now.

"Dolores was here. I filled her in on all of the plans and asked her to join the parade. As you know, she is all for it and will begin soon. . . . [W]e did some work on the list of towns to work throughout the Valley. Helen, [Dolores] and I decide[d] on the name of the group. 'Farm Workers Ass[ociation].'

"I have in fact done some work in the fields. Driving Grape Stakes, Chopping Cotton and Suckering Vines. After about two hours out there I felt about 80 years old. Like Los Viejitos that come to the CSO for Pensions.

"Will be moving to another house, lower rent, on the 15th of May. . . . But for the time being, keep your letters coming to this address.

"Am very sorry to hear about the ulcer. If I'm going to follow in your footsteps, I guess I'll have to get one myself, if I don't already have one and more. Seriously, I hope it isn't too bad.

"Am expecting the Income Tax Return [check] any day now, I hope. Also received the shirts [you sent]. Muchas gracias. [D]on't have a telephone. [P]robably won't get one just now.

"Please write whenever you can. As ever, Cesar.

"P.S. Birdie-boy says hello to Fed Oss." (Birdie or Anthony, our youngest son, was then two years old. He couldn't pronounce the "Rs.")

June 4, 1962. (From Fred to me.) "Hola! Mi General: This'll be a short one because I've seen you so recently and . . . I want to get the little propina [Spanish for gratuity or contribution] in the mail. This time it'll have to be a bill because Frances went off with the cheque-book. Should have sent it yesterday, but got so busy putting the bite on others—forget to bite myself.

"When I get to Stockton [I'll] try to get a few of them to maybe start a 'Buck a Week' Club and assign one of them to collect the money and send it to you. OK?

"Well, you're the one with the news that soothes. So shoot some my way, eh? Warmest & best, Fred."

July 9, 1962. "Dear Cesar: Well, I'm enclosing the usual & hope I hear from you soon with some more marvelous stories."

June 5, 1962. (Me to Fred.) "Estimado Jefe (Dear chief): Gracias muchas por su bondadosa oferta. [Many thanks for your generous donation.]

"I have so many things to tell you that I hardly know where to start."

August 7, 1962. (Me to Fred.) "Hola Jefe: Well, I'm up in Merced County now and things have been going my way. After that Mendota failure, guess I got scared and really did some work. My meetings haven't missed and my pitch [message] has finally developed so that I don't have to be changing around every time I give it.

"On the Peace Corps matter, I called Rockefeller. He says that they are having their difficulties in getting good people for community development. Want[s] me to send him names of people whom I feel are qualified for this work. Do you know anybody we don't particularly want around California for at least two years? Maybe we can outdo Saul [Alinsky] on this.

"Gracias mil por la contribución. [A thousand thanks for the contribution.] Su amigo Cesar."

October 3, 1962. "Dear Cesar: Well, viejo [old one], you've really done a [great] job! I know there's a long way to go, but with that miraculous mana of yours and judging by the glory I saw pouring from the eyes of the farm workers sitting around that table all afternoon, and with luck, you'll make it. I'm absolutely sure of it. Meantime, keep the old dream coming true and drop me a bit of news . . . Fred."

January 7, 1963. "Dear Fred: Sure enough I had your letter upon my return. I don't know whether I mentioned that both Corcoran and Hanford are go go go. Your latest silent contribution is being applied to the materials for Laton.

"Will see what happens as the drive progresses. Personally, I think it will get better as time passes.

"Mejor deseo vero que escribirle. [I prefer seeing you than writing to you.] Como siempre, Cesar. Viva La Causa."

January 10, 1963. "Dear Cesar: I hope you'll forgive me for letting you down this once. I didn't prepare the introduction to the petitions. . . . On the roses, a couple of Pearl Scarlets would be nice, if you can get them (for me). Am sending along 20 maracas más [20 dollars and more]. Best and warmest to you, Elena y los esquinlis [Helen and the kids], Fred."

March 11, 1963. "Dear Fred: Am terribly sorry for not writing. I've been chasing the rat for the past two weeks, not that I have accomplished very much. But nevertheless, have had to devote every bit of time to it. Before I forget, doesn't our bird [the union's Aztec-eagle symbol] resemble the N.R.A. (New Deal) bird of yesteryear?

"Financially we are still in the dust—but hope to get up and out gradually within the coming months. I think that if we can keep our present membership we can pay ourselves about $50.00 per week and pay for the gas expense. The great if, of course.

"Thank you very much for the contribution. . . . Hope this is the last one we have to burden you with. Regards to all, Cesar."

May 14, 1963. "Dear Cesar: Knowing how well things are going for you has both bucked me up & turned me a screaming shad of envidioso verde [envious green]. Mientras, aquí va un cuero de iguana. [In the meantime, I am sending an iguana skin—a $20 bill.] Como siempre, Fred."

January 3, 1964. (From Fred.) "Dear campañero de la pluma [Dear friend of the pen]: It's a good thing our pal-ship doesn't depend on la pluma or it would long since have withered away. And I certainly can't excuse the lapse by telling you how awfully busy and productive I've been, because, as you know so well, these holidays shoot hell out of everything in our line [of work].

"There's little likelihood I'll be down in the Valley in the near future, and I don't suppose you'll be coming up to San Jose. But if you do, let me know and we'll have one at the 'Hole in the Wall' for the sake of auld lang syne. Warmest regards, Fred." (The Hole in the Wall was a coffee shop in San Jose where we hung out 40 years ago.)

After hearing that Fred was ill, David Martínez and I drove up to see him at the community where he was living in Mill Valley. I'm very grateful that we had a chance to spend time with Fred about a week before he died.

Fred Jr. had warned me that his dad might not recognize us. He was sitting on a chair in the hall when we arrived. He looked at me the way he did forty years ago, eyes and arms open in a big smile, and said, "Oh, Cesar."

We spent three hours walking around the grounds. We did a lot of reminiscing, spoke about his book, *Conquering Goliath*, spoke about the union and the boycott.

I told him how grateful we were for everything he had done for us. Fred, always humble and with no trace of ego, said, "Come on, I didn't do anything for you. You guys did it all."

"No," I replied. "We'll never forget the lessons you taught us. Every time we take a shortcut, we get in trouble. There are no shortcuts in organizing, remember?"

We talked about the organizing techniques I first learned from him so many years ago. I wanted to keep them in my head. Fred was sharp as a tack. He remembered a lot of stuff. We talked about how it is that people understand the difficult things very quickly. It's the simple things that take a long time for people to understand.

Fred was lucid and animated. He was not one to complain about his health or much else. So on that day last month in Mill Valley it didn't occur to me that he would die soon.

And I didn't have a chance to tell him that in addition to training me and inspiring me and being my hero, over forty years he also became my best friend.

I shall miss him very much.

Aphorisms

Popular lore records scores of aphorisms by Cesar Chavez. The following selection is culled from his speeches, correspondence, and interviews:

"Being of service is not enough. You must become a servant of the people."

"When any person suffers for someone in greater need, that person is human."

"We draw our strength from despair."

"History will judge societies and their institutions . . . by how effectively they respond to the needs of the poor and the helpless."

"The rich have money—and the poor have time."

"We must understand that the highest form of freedom carries with it the greatest measure of discipline."

"Love is the most important ingredient in nonviolent work."

"We don't ask for more cathedrals. We don't ask for bigger churches or fine gifts. . . . We ask for the Church to sacrifice with the people for social change, for justice, and for the love of brother."

"The picket line is a beautiful thing because it makes a man more human."

"The people who give you their food give you their heart."

"In this world it's possible to achieve great material wealth, to live an opulent life. But a life built upon those things alone leaves a shallow legacy."

"It's how we use our lives that determines the kind of men we are."

"You are never strong enough that you don't need help."

"Preservation of one's own culture does not require contempt or disrespect for other cultures."

"It's ironic that those who till the soil, cultivate and harvest the fruits, vegetables, and other foods that fill your tables with abundance, have nothing left for themselves."

"God writes in exceedingly crooked lines."

"We are confident, since we have ourselves."

"The first principle of nonviolent action is that of noncooperation with everything humiliating."

"The challenge before us is plain: to carry on the struggle to build one national union that will unite all farm workers regardless of race, sex, creed, or nationality."

"There is no such thing as a defeat in nonviolence."

"It's not enough to change a person. You've got to change his environment."

"Democracy is expensive."

"Nonviolence means people in action. It's not discussion. It's not for the timid or the weak. Nonviolence is hard work. It's the willingness to sacrifice. It's the patience to win."

"Talk is cheap. It's the way we organize and use our lives every day that tells what we believe in."

"We can't be free ourselves if we don't free our women."

"We seek our basic, God-given rights as human beings. Because we have suffered, and aren't afraid to suffer in order to survive, we're ready to give up everything—even our lives—in our struggle for social justice."

"We are suffering. We have suffered. And we aren't afraid to suffer to win our cause."

"We are above all, human beings, no better and no worse than any other cross-sections of human society; we are not saints because we are poor, but by the same measure neither are we immoral."

"In giving of yourself, you will discover a whole new life full of meaning and love."

"We must never forget that the human element is the most important thing we have—if we get away from this, we are certain to fail."

"One brotherhood, one people, one union."

"By remaining nonviolent in the face of violence we win them to our side, and that's what makes strength."

"It's not so much the money, it's the whole principle of being cheated out of something you had to sweat so hard to earn."

"Leadership is only a mental condition."

"Community organizing is very difficult. You can't put it in the freezer for a couple of years and then thaw it out and you're in business again."

"Violence only seems necessary when people are desperate; frustration often leads to violence."

"The truest act of courage, the strongest act of manliness, is to sacrifice ourselves for others, in a totally nonviolence struggle for justice. To be a man is to suffer for others."

THE STORY OF PENGUIN CLASSICS

Before 1946 . . . "Classics" are mainly the domain of academics and students; readable editions for everyone else are almost unheard of. This all changes when a little-known classicist, E. V. Rieu, presents Penguin founder Allen Lane with the translation of Homer's *Odyssey* that he has been working on in his spare time.

1946 Penguin Classics debuts with *The Odyssey*, which promptly sells three million copies. Suddenly, classics are no longer for the privileged few.

1950s Rieu, now series editor, turns to professional writers for the best modern, readable translations, including Dorothy L. Sayers's *Inferno* and Robert Grave's unexpurgated *Twelve Caesars*.

1960s The Classics are given the distinctive black covers that have remained a constant throughout the life of the series. Rieu retires in 1964, hailing the Penguin Classics list as "the greatest educative force of the twentieth century."

1970s A new generation of translators swells the Penguin Classics ranks, introducing readers of English to classics of world literature from more than twenty languages. The list grows to encompass more history, philosophy, science, religion, and politics.

1980s The Penguin American Library launches with titles such as *Uncle Tom's Cabin* and joins forces with Penguin Classics to provide the most comprehensive library of world literature available from any paperback publisher.

1990s The launch of Penguin Audiobooks brings the classics to a listening audience for the first time, and in 1999 the worldwide launch of the Penguin Classics Web site extends their reach to the global online community.

The 21st Century Penguin Classics are completely redesigned for the first time in nearly twenty years. This world-famous series now consists of more than 1,300 titles, making the widest range of the best books ever written available to millions—and constantly redefining what makes a "classic."

The Odyssey continues . . .

The best books ever written

PENGUIN ((🐧)) CLASSICS

SINCE 1946

Find out more at www.penguinclassics.com

Visit www.vpbookclub.com

CLICK ON A CLASSIC
www.penguinclassics.com

The world's greatest literature at your fingertips

Constantly updated information on more than a thousand titles,
from Icelandic sagas to ancient Indian epics, Russian drama to
Italian romance, American greats to African masterpieces

•

The latest news on recent additions to the list, updated
editions, and specially commissioned translations

•

Original essays by leading writers

•

A wealth of background material, including biographies
of every classic author from Aristotle to Zamyatin, plot
synopses, readers' and teachers' guides, useful Web links

•

Online desk and examination copy assistance for academics

•

Trivia quizzes, competitions, giveaways, news on
forthcoming screen adaptations